DILEMMAS FACING THE NATION

DILEMMAS
FACING THE
NATION

EDITED BY

HERBERT V. PROCHNOW

HARPER & ROW, PUBLISHERS

NEW YORK, HAGERSTOWN, SAN FRANCISCO, LONDON

FIRST EDITION

Designed by Stephanie Winkler

Library of Congress Cataloging in Publication Data

Main entry under title:
    Dilemmas facing the nation.
    1. United States—Economic conditions—1971–
—Addresses, essays, lectures. 2. Laissez-faire—Addresses, essays, lectures. I. Prochnow, Herbert Victor,
1897–
HC106.7.D54 1979   330.9′73′092   78–2157
ISBN 0–06–013448–8

79 80 81 82 10 9 8 7 6 5 4 3 2 1

Contents

Contributing Authors

A. W. Clausen
  President and Chief Executive Officer, BankAmerica Corporation and Bank of America N.T. & S.A., San Francisco, California

David P. Eastburn
  President, Federal Reserve Bank of Philadelphia, Philadelphia, Pennsylvania

Irving S. Friedman
  Senior Vice President and Senior Adviser for International Operations, Citibank, New York, New York

Carter H. Golembe
  Chairman and Chief Executive Officer, Golembe Associates, Inc., Washington, D.C.

Robert C. Hill
  Former U.S. Ambassador to Costa Rica, El Salvador, Mexico, Spain, and Argentina

James Day Hodgson
  Former U.S. Secretary of Labor and U.S. Ambassador to Japan

John Addison Howard
  Director, Rockford College Institute, Rockford, Illinois

Philip M. Klutznick

Chairman, Executive Committee, Urban Investment and Development Corporation, Chicago, Illinois; Past U.S. Commissioner Federal Public Housing Authority

Paul W. McCracken

Edmund Ezra Day University Professor of Business Administration, University of Michigan, Ann Arbor, Michigan; Past Chairman of the President's Council of Economic Advisers

George Meany

President, American Federation of Labor and Congress of Industrial Organizations, Washington, D.C.

Thomas A. Murphy

Chairman and Chief Executive Officer, General Motors Corporation, Detroit, Michigan

Don Paarlberg

Former Assistant to the President of the United States and Assistant Secretary of Agriculture

George Romney

Former U.S. Secretary of Housing and Urban Development and Governor of Michigan

William E. Simon

Former U.S. Secretary of the Treasury

Robert Strausz-Hupé

Former U.S. Ambassador to Ceylon (Sri Lanka), Belgium, and Sweden and U.S. Permanent Representative at the North Atlantic Council

John E. Swearingen

Chairman of the Board, Standard Oil Company (Indiana), Chicago, Illinois

Murray L. Weidenbaum

Director, Center for the Study of American Business, and Mallinckrodt Distinguished University Professor, Washington University, St. Louis, Missouri

Acknowledgement

I should like to acknowledge my indebtedness to Herbert V. Prochnow, Jr., for his invaluable assistance in preparing and editing this book from its inception to its completion.

Introduction

The United States is today the most powerful nation in the world. And yet, as we stand at the peak of our power, we are faced with some of the most difficult problems in our history.

How will we meet the problem of providing the energy essential to the life of an industrial nation? How will we solve the problem of the extraordinary deficits in our federal budget and in our international trade? How will we stop the erosion of many of our metropolitan centers? Will we accept the discipline and take the necessary steps to reduce substantially the rate of inflation? Will we do anything about a vastly expanded bureaucracy and an incredible growth of government regulations? These are only a few of the problems that confront us as we seek to retain our leadership and discharge our responsibilities as the world's major power. Will we solve our problems or will we fail? Other nations in history have attained world power and then have declined.

It would be easy to utter some threadbare and comforting platitudes about the problems that confront us. But the truth is that the problems are perplexing and difficult. We can solve them and continue our record of great national achievement if the American people and their political leaders demonstrate those qualities which brought this nation to world leadership.

The contributing authors of this book have distinguished themselves in many of the most important areas of the nation's life. They present here their thoughtful analyses of the complex problems which now confront us. They bring to their discussions not only the distinction of unusual personal accomplishment, but also many years of practical experience in dealing with major problems. Each author is responsible only for the views expressed in his presentation.

In his *Hamlet*, Shakespeare said, "We know what we are, but know not what we may be." Perhaps this statement has its greatest significance in relation to nations.

One night I stood on the top of the Mount of Olives with one of the world's great scholars who was in Jerusalem translating the Dead Sea Scrolls of the Old Testament. Only a short distance away was the little village of Bethany and on beyond in the distance was the City of Jericho, the oldest city known to man. To the right was the Dead Sea, and the soft light of an October moon was falling gently across its calm waters.

We turned and looked in the other direction down the barren, rocky slope of the Mount of Olives over the dark, gnarled, old olive trees where the Garden of Gethsemane had been. Just across a little valley a few blocks in width was Jerusalem on the opposite hill. In that historic spot that evening it seemed to me I could look down through the centuries. There was the place where Solomon—who "exceeded all the kings of the earth in riches and in wisdom"—had built his temple. There was the place where many of the heroic figures of Jewish and Christian history—Abraham and Isaac and David and Peter and John and Matthew—had walked.

There was the birthplace of both the Jewish and Christian religions. There was the place where many of the ideals of Western civilization had been cradled. There the authorities of the great Roman government had once ruled in all their majesty, when the Roman empire had flung its legions to those remote frontiers. It had the greatest armies and the most powerful fortifications in its history. With their skill in law and government, with their distinguished jurists and generals, the citizens of Rome could say with pride, "We know what we are—the greatest nation of our time." But they did not know that the Roman empire would gradually disintegrate and fall.

As I looked down the centuries that night I also saw Egypt, once the mother of the arts and sciences, but now with her people in poverty. I saw Athens, where Plato taught and Pericles gave his nation the Golden Age. Athens knew what she was as she beheld her greatness. In her pride, Athens may well have believed that her culture would mold the future of architecture, science, mathematics, and medicine for centuries, and it did. But Athens did not know that she would fall and never again regain her former power. In these great centers of civilization there was wisdom. There was genius. There was power. They knew what they were, but they did not know what they were to be.

That evening I saw other great empires through the centuries—Great Britain, Spain, Portugal, France, Austria-Hungary, Germany, Belgium, Turkey, the Netherlands. They knew what they were—powerful empires of their time. But they did not know that one night in August 1914, the somber shadow of war would fall across the world, only to be followed by a second world war, engulfing almost all of mankind and ending only when the terrifying clouds had left behind their dead at Hiroshima. These great empires did not know that the winds of political freedom would pull down the pillars of reverence and loyalty from under empires and ruling groups that had provided the world for years with some stability.

In 1783, thirteen colonies had won a revolutionary war. Men had sacrificed eight years out of their lives to face a seemingly hopeless future. There was no unity. European nations did not know whether they were dealing with one nation or thirteen. The country was impoverished and saddled with a great war debt. Soldiers were clamoring for their pay. The government had no power to enforce its acts. A band of soldiers marched upon the government at Philadelphia, demanding their pay at the bayonet's point, and Congress fled to Princeton, New Jersey. Riots broke out. The country was flooded with paper money that was rapidly to become practically worthless. But out of that chaos came the Constitutional Convention and a Constitution which was to assure independence, freedom, and equality to all men. In that convention, old Benjamin Franklin quietly placed all the weight of his wisdom and experience at the service of the nation he was founding. Robert Morris, financier of the Revolution, was there to add his judgment. Hamilton swayed the assembly with his eloquence. Madison wrote with a clarity that had in it no slick political subterfuge. Then with George Washington as President, Thomas Jefferson as Secretary of State, and Alexander Hamilton as Secretary of the Treasury, a new nation opened for business. These men could say, "We know who we are—landowners,

surveyors, printers, businessmen." But they did not know that they
were to be the founders of what was to become the most powerful
nation in all history. We have become, beyond the fondest dreams of
the nation's founders, the best example in history of how a people
enrich life and raise their whole level of economic well-being when
they are given justice, liberty, and incentive.

As we look back over the centuries it is clear that nations know
what they are but they do not know what they may be. By the
decisions of their people and their governments they gradually
determine, year after year, their ultimate destiny. They determine
whether the nations will meet the problems of national existence and
leadership, however difficult, with wisdom and courage, or whether
they will fail to deal with them and decline in power and prestige. In
the life of the United States there have been booms and depressions,
crop failures and monetary crises, triumphs and the tragedy of a
Civil War. But once the people understood an issue they chose
wisely the course they would follow.

There were the fabulous years from 1870 to 1914 when, despite
the crises of 1873 and 1893, the American people chose the course
of dynamic economic expansion. They chose the course of risk-
taking with losses for failure and rewards for successful business
venture. They spanned a continent with covered wagons and railroads. By 1880, the value of manufactured products and the capital
invested in manufacturing industries had each increased to over five
times the level of 1850, only thirty years earlier. In this period of
enormous expansion, human nature was swinging the pendulum
high. There was speculation. There were economic excesses and
unfair business and labor practices, but each time the people
departed from sound principles, they returned to them. They eliminated those abuses. They paid off their losses from speculative
ventures and got back on solid ground. The thrifty, those who work,
those who save, and those who accumulate new capital for financing
the economy soundly, have always finally swayed the issue.

In the years from 1914 to the present, we have had one of the
most amazing chapters in our history. We are now the most
powerful nation in history. In the development of this nation the
American people chose a government and a constitution that gave
them religious and political freedom and encouraged initiative,

private enterprise, responsibility, industry, thrift, and inventive genius.

No other nation can approach in magnitude the industrial power of the United States and its capacity to improve the economic welfare of the people of this nation and of the world. The gross national product of the United States is far larger than that of its nearest rival, Soviet Russia, and also far larger than that of Japan or West Germany. We have witnessed in this nation the social ministry of a machine civilization under a system of private enterprise and free labor which has made increasingly available to the American people the comforts, conveniences, and cultural advantages that once were the privilege of the few.

If one measures the American economy by its gross national product, personal income, wage scales, insurance, savings, travel, education, health, recreation, transportation, communication, highways, housing, food, clothing, the whole standard of living, history reveals no comparable record where so many have fared so well.

And yet, as this nation stands at the peak of its power, it is faced with extraordinarily difficult problems. We stand in the conduct of our national affairs at one of those decisive moments in history. In the processes of history, nations as well as men are finally judged. Nations succeed and nations fail.

Consider briefly only one or two of the problems that now confront us. Many of them are discussed more fully by the contributing authors to this book. For years we have believed that it may be appropriate for the federal government to have a deficit in its budget when the economy needs to be stimulated. But we have also believed that the government must show at least a balanced budget in times of business prosperity. This has been our economic gospel for many years. But the hard realities are that we do not believe it, or we lack the self-discipline to practice what we profess. We are unwilling to pay for our spending even when we are prosperous. This has been true for many years. We show no willingness to bring government spending into line with government income. To paraphrase a distinguished American journalist, "Sometimes a nation's character needs to assert itself. Sometimes a nation needs to say that it is willing to pay for what it is willing to spend."

If the American people really believe that the budgets of federal, state, and local governments must be balanced over time, they will be balanced.

The present inflationary trends, which are largely due to government spending, are resulting in hardships to millions of thrifty persons who have no adequate means of protecting themselves against the erosion of their purchasing power and the value of their life savings. Moreover, inflation destroys the incentive to save the funds necessary to keep our productive facilities efficient and adequate to meet the demands made upon them in a highly competitive world. If the American people really believe that inflation is bad because it erodes the value of bonds, pensions, insurance policies, and savings deposits, and destroys the incentive to save upon which the economic growth and integrity of the nation depend, then they will adopt policies that end the danger of inflation.

There are other matters on which we also need to decide where we stand. As our economy has become more complex, the role of government has increased. Are we expanding the functions of government faster than necessary as we seek more rapid economic growth and still higher standards of living? With government as the regulator now of countless segments of our economic life, with government by far the largest purchaser of goods and services, and with government security and welfare programs constantly expanding, are we moving into far more centralized control with the gradual loss of many individual freedoms? In the years ahead will we retain the freedom of individual choice that has helped American business and labor to build an economic security and richness of life never before attained by any people?

One evening late in the summer of a national election year, and at the height of the presidential campaign, some of us visited on a university campus with one of the most respected and experienced members of the Senate of the United States. He said regretfully that it was no longer possible to be elected and to ask anything of the American people. One could only promise them benefits without sacrifices. This was not the comment of a cynic. It was the thoughtful judgment of a public servant who served his country for many years with distinction. If a nation ultimately is only as strong, and only as great, as the character, integrity, ideals, and vision of its people, then this statement constitutes a serious indictment. But is it true? Is there a widespread intellectual and social disintegration, or is there rather a failure to understand clearly that continued sacrifices are essential if a nation is to remain free? Have we offered this alternative, or have we offered people merely the deceptive lure of benefits without sacrifices? We may well be at a critical turning point in our history when a courageous decision to put our affairs in order would meet the overwhelming approval of the American people.

The government has now become a vital factor in most of the nation's major economic decisions, whether they involve business, agriculture, or labor. Furthermore, there seems to be a widespread willingness to have government assume this role. While we advocate a free market economy, we contribute our time and money to an infinite number of organizations which seek to get something from the government or urge the government to expand its activities. There is little point in blaming Washington. We are responsible. To paraphrase Shakespeare, "The fault, dear Brutus, is not in our stars, but in ourselves" that government grows bigger and bigger.

We protest the increasing role of government over the world, but we encourage it here. With one hand we work to reduce the role of government in our economic life. With the other hand we work even harder to increase it. We ask for a reduction in government expenditures, but not where it would affect us. We demand that government expenses be cut, but not for the federal projects in our own communities. On one day, we write our Congressmen to reduce government expenses and taxes. The next day we write urging them to bring home the federal bacon to our communities.

We need to recognize that in the highly competitive economic struggle in which we are engaged with other major industrial nations we shall not reach our objectives of better economic standards by striving constantly for more leisure and less work. The economic well-being of a people and the economic survival of any society depend upon work, thrift, and personal sacrifice and not upon leisure, extravagance, and personal indulgence. We need all the economic strength we can command by hard work, thrift, and energy in the struggle to improve the well-being of all.

In the years immediately ahead, will government perform essentially those functions which private individuals cannot perform as well—or will we as a people gradually become less self-reliant, less willing to assume the often difficult responsibilities which freedom requires of individuals, and seek increasingly the delusive shelter and deceptive security of government, until finally we will have lost our priceless heritage of individual liberty?

We have moved steadily away from the sedative hum of the hand spinning wheel and the village feed mill to huge gray factories silhouetted against the urban skyline. Great power-driven factories, great organizations of labor, and great markets make highly improbable any broad return of government to the Arcadian simplicity of colonial days.

As President Eisenhower stated, "The demands of modern life and the unsettled status of the world require a more important role for government than it played in earlier and quieter times."

But this does not mean that we should now thoughtlessly turn over the management of the economy to an all-powerful state. It means that we need more than ever critically to examine the role of government.

Perhaps we need to recognize that the issue which confronts us today is whether a free society can survive when people are faced with the necessity of self-restraint in every area, including fiscal policy, the use of energy, and the demands on government.

We know what we are—a nation at the peak of its greatest prosperity, and yet unwilling to balance its budget, and this has been true for many years. A nation with great industries and a highly skilled labor force, but with a large deficit in its international trade. A nation whose people have one of the highest standards of living in history, but whose great cities need a major development of educational facilities, housing, and transportation. A nation with a serious problem of providing the energy essential to the continued growth of its economy. We know how great our achievements have been, but have we the wisdom and courage now to meet the hard problems confronting us and determine what we are to be in the years ahead?

In the chapters which follow, a number of the nation's leaders discuss our achievements and our problems.

—HERBERT V. PROCHNOW

CHAPTER 1

------------◄∞►------------

The Crucial Issue
Is Freedom

Contrary to the popular assumption that governments can somehow identify, solve, and pay for all of our national problems, their real role is to create a supportive environment that will contribute to orderly and sustained economic growth using fiscal, monetary, and regulatory policies. Each policy decision should be compared with this general guideline to minimize expedient actions that create unwanted inflation, unemployment, and widespread uncertainty that restricts consumption and investment. Such long-term perspectives are difficult to maintain, however, in an economy dominated by changing conditions and diverse interests. Basic political, social, technological, and international developments further complicate difficult economic policy decisions, creating widespread demand for achievement of narrow goals using simplistic solutions. Nor does the ineffectiveness of this approach seem to diminish the pressures.

It is obvious that most Americans support the same basic goals of sustaining the current output and employment gains, of moderating the still unsatisfactory rate of inflation, of reducing the unacceptable rate of unemployment, and of correcting the monetary, trade, and investment problems which have periodically disrupted the international economic system. But there can be disagreement about what trade-offs will be required to achieve simultaneous progress toward all of these goals, about the best mix and timing of fiscal and

monetary actions, and about the proper time horizon for planning
current policies.

DIVERSITY OF ECONOMIC GOALS

The economic policy debate has intensified since the mid-1960s as
the American people have recognized the major impact of these
issues on their daily lives. While the real standard of living has
continued to increase, several disappointing experiences have dominated the performance of our national economy: repetitions of the
boom-and-recession cycle; chronic inflation at historically high
levels; debilitating unemployment that wastes resources and creates
severe social problems; uncertainties about the adequacy of raw
materials and productive capacity; and development of a massive
trade deficit with related pressures on the international value of the
dollar. In focusing on these *specific* problems there is an unfortunate
tendency to forget that national economic policies must concentrate
on the *general* welfare of the American people. It is ironic that so
many major economic problems have occurred during a peacetime
era when maximum progress in improving the overall standard of
living should be occurring. The reality, of course, is that current
events in the economy, including budget deficits, energy problems,
welfare reform, tax policies, foreign trade issues, etc., are the result
of the cumulative policy decisions of the past.

The gross national product is usually used to evaluate the pace
and balance of economic activity. While this single statistic is not a
comprehensive measure of the overall quality of life it does indicate
that America will produce over $2 trillion worth of goods and
services in 1978. The basic goals of striving: "to promote maximum
employment, production, and purchasing power" in a manner "calculated to foster and promote free competitive enterprise and the
general welfare," as described in the famous Employment Act of
1946, provide a general policy framework, but they are not specific
enough to give direction to the thousands of decisions made each
day throughout the government. Individuals and families must focus
their attention on wages, prices, and specific regulations that determine their personal economic status. The costs of energy; the
efficiency of the education, transportation, and communication

systems; the quality of the environment; the availability of imported products; and, most of all, personal employment opportunities and current inflation pressures represent the economic issues Americans are most concerned about. Inflation and unemployment are the dual pressures confronting most nations today.

Throughout most of the postwar era prices increased slowly and improved productivity created additional purchasing power for most Americans. The acceleration of inflation in the mid-1960s was disturbing, but few of us were prepared for the sharp increase in prices beginning in 1973 and peaking at double-digit rates in 1974. By way of comparison, the Consumer Price Index increased at an average annual rate of 1.8 percent from 1956 through 1966; from 1966 through 1976 this inflation measure increased at an annual rate of 5.8 percent. Since 1974 there has been some progress in reducing the pace of price increases but the Consumer Price Index still rose 6.7 percent from December 1976 through December 1977. Furthermore, most public and private forecasts expect prices to continue to rise at least 6 percent in 1979. The swing from relative price stability to rapid inflation beginning in the mid-1960s has created severe distortions throughout the economy which have disrupted consumption, business spending, and government budgets. Inflation, particularly the volatile kind of the last decade, is difficult for Americans to cope with when they do not have the political clout and economic power to increase their incomes at a comparable pace. This disadvantaged group includes low-income families, the elderly trying to survive by relying on accumulated financial assets and pension funds established prior to the surge of inflation, and those employees who have not been able effectively to maintain their incomes by demanding an adjustment for inflation. If the goal of national economic policies is to promote the *real* standard of living of Americans—and other nations—the results since the mid-1960s are clearly disappointing in terms of inflation.

Employment opportunities are equally important as a measure of economic performance and personal welfare. Since the current economic expansion began in March of 1975 employment has increased rapidly and there now are over 8.5 million additional jobholders. This is an impressive accomplishment. The unemployment rate, however, remains unacceptably high, at over 6 percent, as we enter the fourth year of strong economic growth. There are

also many unresolved structural problems involving specific types of
workers, certain geographical areas, and individual industries. It is
true that the composition of the labor force has changed dramatically in recent years, as large numbers of women and teenagers have
entered the job markets, and that extended social programs designed
to transfer public services and income to unemployed workers have
eased the transition problem. Nevertheless, these actions cannot
overcome the tragic personal frustration of being unable to find a
job or effectively neutralize the strong political and social pressures
caused by rising unemployment.

Continuation of the levels of inflation and unemployment experienced since the mid-1960s will lead to escalating pressures to turn to
simplistic policy actions, such as wage and price controls and capital
allocation schemes, that have failed in the past and most certainly
would create more problems than solutions if implemented in the
future. There is, however, an unfortunate tendency to concentrate
on only one problem at a time rather than recognizing that progress
must be made against both inflation and unemployment or else
there will be a joint failure. Inflation creates serious housing
construction problems, erodes the purchasing power of consumers,
and discourages business capital investment, causing economic recessions and related unemployment. In a comparable way the loss of
output and productivity caused by unemployment contributes to
rising price pressures. There may be temporary periods when one
specific problem dominates national concerns, but over time a
reasonable balance must be developed to sustain economic progress.
Intense political and social pressures develop to force public officials
to concentrate on either inflation or unemployment but experience
clearly demonstrates that joint efforts are required or else both
problems deteriorate. The failure to recognize this basic point underlies much of the disappointing fine-tuning experiments of the last
fifteen years which have created economic instability and a serious
erosion of confidence among consumers and business leaders.

BALANCE OF NATIONAL ECONOMIC POLICIES

Recognizing the diversity and interdependence of national economic problems, it follows naturally that a broad mix of public

policies must be used. Excessive reliance on only one policy tool creates the same distorting imbalances as concentrating on specific rather than comprehensive public goals. Ideally, a balanced package of fiscal, monetary, and regulatory policies which reinforce and complement each other should be adopted. Major problems develop when policy actions become contradictory or when extreme emphasis is required on one of the tools. Once again, it may be necessary to make short-term adjustments but over time fiscal, monetary, and regulatory policies should all be contributing to achieving the same general goals.

Fiscal policies refer to the spending and tax actions of the government. Since the mid-1960s fiscal policies have often been used to stimulate the entire economy, which has created considerable momentum in the pace of federal spending and recurring tax cuts. For example, the federal budget increased from $135 billion in fiscal year 1966 to $402 billion in fiscal year 1977. As a result, federal budget deficits have been reported in eleven of the last twelve years along with considerable net borrowing necessary to finance a number of federal credit programs which are not included in the unified budget figures. In fiscal year 1978 federal outlays are expected to rise to about $460 billion and in 1979 to approximately $500 billion. Large deficits are expected to continue for the foreseeable future even though we are now entering the fourth year of economic expansion. The actual amounts of spending and deficits will, of course, depend upon the actions of Congress and overall economic conditions, but it is obvious that federal policy decisions on fiscal issues will be a major factor in the future growth and stability of the entire national economy.

Monetary policies focus on the availability and cost of money and credit. Management authority is vested in the Federal Reserve System, which is independent "within" the government and functions as both a controller of monetary policy and as an important part of the financial institution regulatory system. The Federal Reserve System provides necessary flexibility by influencing the growth of the various monetary aggregates and financial market conditions including interest rates, savings flows, and overall liquidity. A variety of tools—ranging from broad adjustments in the supply of reserves to specific guidelines concerning borrowing from the Federal Reserve Banks and the level of legal reserves required for outstanding deposits—are used to achieve the policy goals developed by the Federal Reserve System. The key point is that monetary policies are fundamental in shaping the overall economic environment, but they do not independently control the course of events. The basic challenge is to have monetary policies that will contribute to the reduction of inflation while sustaining real output gains necessary to increase employment and further reduce unemployment.

A third sphere of government policies, which is growing rapidly, concerns the role of hundreds of regulatory agencies and administrative departments. Crucial policy issues involving energy, welfare, transportation, environmental standards, housing, agriculture, labor standards, antitrust issues, foreign trade and investment, and thousands of other economic concerns are considered by the operating departments within the Executive Office and the numerous regulatory agencies. The decisions of each of these groups typically do not have the same pervasive impact as general fiscal and monetary actions, but they do directly influence the types and costs of economic activity. In fact, the major impact of the government on the economy increasingly occurs through these thousands of policy decisions made by the many regulatory agencies and the various departments of the Executive Office. The amazing detail and broad scope of their power accounts for much of the concern and confusion that many businessmen and private individuals feel about the increasing intervention of government controls.

The meaning of this discussion is that economic policies should be concerned more about the lasting impact of government decisions on the American people and other nations. Despite the attractive rhetoric of specific-interest groups there are no single goals or simplistic solutions. The reality is that many specific decisions must be coordinated within a general framework of policies that need to be sustained over time. Contrary to the claims of some analysts, these basic goals are mutually consistent and interdependent. Balanced progress on all of them is required to sustain improvement on each specific objective. Inflation and unemployment are not a simple trade-off but actually represent part of the same distortions caused by a poorly functioning national economy. This general approach is easier to describe than it is to operate effectively because of the complexity of the national problems considered, the diversity of interest groups, the continuous debate over short-term versus long-term needs, the political pressures created by recurring elections at least every two years, and the growing impact of international economic events on domestic policies. Nevertheless, the coordination of national economic policies is fundamentally and critically important.

THE FUTURE AGENDA FOR FISCAL POLICIES

As the nation turns its attention to the future it will again confront the persistent problems that have plagued policy makers for almost two decades. The claims and promises made by most political candidates will be tested against the harsh realities of the real world and the expectations of the people will be matched against the basic capacity of the system to deliver even more goods and services. During the last fifteen years real output of goods and services has almost doubled and the real income of the average American has risen rapidly. But despite these remarkable gains the American people are increasingly dissatisfied with the national state of affairs and their personal status. Part of this frustration is a healthy refusal to tolerate many real problems that exist. The American drive to improve, to help those less fortunate, to seek ever higher personal standards of living is commendable when it leads to a more creative and productive system and increased concern for the needs of others. But there is also an unhealthy aspect in much of the cynicism and negativism that we find in America today. I believe this more ugly mood is the result of the demonstrated failure of collectivist big-government approaches to national problems that promised so much but delivered so little. In the process, a mood of dependence on government has increased which feeds upon itself, creating still more demands for benefits without recognizing that the bills must be paid—either directly in current taxes or indirectly through accelerating inflation and economic disruption.

The accumulation of economic distortions must now be faced. The longer we delay the hard adjustment decisions the more difficult and costly the needed solutions will become. And if we delay too long the opportunities to restore stable economic progress may be lost.

The future agenda for America, then, is basically a consideration of the multitude of conflicting claims to arrive at the greatest long-term benefit for all of our people. In that process the most important factor to be considered is the freedom and dignitiy of the individual. No matter what material progress occurs the loss of personal freedom and dignity is too great a price. In short, we must decide what kind of economic and political systems will best serve the real long-term interests of the American people.

In looking to the future the American people should ask this basic question each time the government comes up with a new economic policy initiative: will this action contribute to sustained and orderly economic growth, or will it merely perpetuate the familiar stop-and-go patterns of the past involving increased government spending without regard for the chronic deficits and economic and financial disruption created, excessive expansion of the money supply, even more governmental controls over the private economy, and increased intervention in private wage and price decisions? The disappointing performance of the U.S. economy during much of the last decade emphasizes the basic need for more stable policies. In the mid-1960s the United States began an unfortunate series of exaggerated booms and recessions: serious overheating of the economy created severe price pressures; accelerating inflation caused recessions by restricting housing construction, personal spending, and business investment; the recessions created unwanted unemployment which wasted resources and caused personal suffering; rising unemployment too often triggered poorly planned and ill-timed government fiscal and monetary policies, setting off another round of excessive stimulus leading again to overheating—inflation—recession—unemployment—and more government intervention.

In general there must be more widespread recognition of the fundamental importance of stable economic growth in the future as the only true foundation for maximum employment opportunities and lower unemployment rates, for more moderate rates of inflation which will protect the purchasing power of all Americans and encourage more capital investment that will provide the permanent and productive jobs that people desire, for more efficient use of human and material resources and protection of our environment, and for fulfillment of our international responsibilities in monetary, trade, and investment policies. Naturally, there are disagreements about how best to achieve these basic goals, but I am convinced that a longer-term time horizon must be used.

First, the diversity of problems must be recognized to avoid concentrating on a single issue. Inflation, unemployment, declining output, the availability of productive resources, international trade and investment all must be considered simultaneously to create a balanced program for stable economic growth. The beginning point for sustaining economic growth without the boom and recession distortions of the past is to avoid a return of destructive inflation pressures. From 1890 to 1970 prices in the United States increased at an annual rate of 1.8 percent. From December 1973 to December 1974 they jumped 12.2 percent. That horrendous development was finally controlled by effective leadership and the restoration of large output gains as the economy began its relatively strong and well-balanced expansion in early 1975. From December 1975 through December 1976 the pace of consumer price increases was cut to 4.8 percent. Prices again accelerated in 1977, however, and at the present time there is justifiable concern that existing inflation trends may disrupt the entire economy once again. In fact, over the last decade, consumer prices have increased at an annual rate of about 6 percent. It seems so obvious that any long-term solution to our economic problems requires better control of inflation, which has distorted the spending and savings decisions of all Americans. Inflation must be clearly recognized for what it is: the greatest threat to the sustained progress of our economy and the personal standard of living of most Americans, as well as the survival of a free society.

From these experiences there is one basic conclusion: our desire for economic progress, through improved living standards and employment opportunities, will be frustrated unless we better control the insidious inflation which has destroyed economic stability and today threatens not only our goal of sustained growth but the ultimate survival of all of our institutions. When inflation distorts the economic system and destroys the incentives for real improvement, the people will no longer support that system and creative and productive society will also collapse if we permit inflation to dominate economic affairs. There is no trade-off between the goals of price stability and low unemployment, as some critics have erroneously claimed. To the contrary, the achievement of one goal depends on achievement of the other. If we are to increase the output of goods and services and reduce unemployment, we must make further progress in reducing inflation.

The intensity of my feelings about inflation has resulted in some critics labeling me as obsessed. However, I am not so much obsessed as I am downright antagonistic toward those who consistently vote for inflation through rapid increases in government spending and chronic budget deficits. We must always remember that it is inflation that causes the recessions that so cruelly waste our human and material resources and the tragic unemployment that leaves serious economic and psychological scars long after economic recovery occurs. It is inflation that destroys the purchasing power of our people as they strive—too often in a losing struggle—to provide the necessities of food, housing, clothing, transportation, and medical attention and the desired necessities of education, recreation, and cultural opportunities. Inflation is not now, nor has it ever been, the grease that enables the economic machine to progress. Instead, it is the monkey wrench which disrupts the efficient functioning of the system. Inflation should be identified for what it is—the most vicious hoax ever perpetrated for the expedient purposes of a few at the cost of many. And there should be no uncertainty about its devastating impact, particularly for low-income families, the elderly dependent upon accumulated financial resources, and the majority of working people who do not have the political or economic leverage to beat the system by keeping their incomes rising even more rapidly than inflation. When inflation takes over an economy the people suffer, and it is time that this basic point is emphasized by every responsible citizen and the full brunt is brought to bear on their elected officials.

Second, government policies must solve more problems than they create. During a period of difficulty it is expedient to respond to strident calls to "do something—anything to demonstrate political leadership." But this naïvely activist approach is too often the basic source of problems rather than the solution. Courage and wisdom are always required to avoid actions offering the illusion of short-term benefits in exchange for further erosion of the free enterprise system that has served this nation so well in creating the premier economy of the world and providing the greatest degree of personal opportunities. The conventional wisdom that a few billion dollars of additional government spending somehow makes the difference between success or failure of the entire U.S. economy—which has now expanded to an annual level of output of goods and services of $2 trillion—has always amazed me. There is an important role for governments in protecting certain basic public interests, but the claim that governments can or should control the economy is totally false. We would all be better off if government officials would recognize that the real creativity and productivity of America depend upon the private sector.

The third basic requirement is to lengthen the time horizon of policy planning. There is a natural tendency to concentrate too much on short-run needs without adequate consideration of the cumulative impact of decisions into the future. This point is particularly important at this time because of the short-term benefits claimed for rapidly stimulating the economy with the slack that still remains at this stage of the economic expansion. Because of the painful inflation recently experienced, however, there must be greater concern about the reactions in the private sector to actual and potential government policies. Employees are anxious to restore their real wage gains, and business wants to restore profit margins which have been eroded by inflation. If the real growth in the economy is stimulated too rapidly, both real and perceived inflation pressures will quickly escalate because of concerns about the future. Another repetition of inflation and recession would result in even more unemployment and lost output. Lower rates of unemployment and inflation are obviously the desired goal, but we must consider the prospects over the next few years, not the next few months. A mix of policies designed to provide temporary relief at the expense of higher rates of inflation and unemployment in future years is inappropriate.

It is particularly important to consider the longer-run government spending trends. The amount of adjustment in any specific federal budget may appear to be relatively limited because of the legislative decisions of the past. However, decisions better to control federal spending today will have major significance on the levels of outlays in 1979, and beyond as existing programs continue to expand. It will never be easy to make these fundamental shifts, and there is a tendency to wait for a more "convenient" time to begin the painful process of regaining fiscal control, but I am convinced that the longer we permit the existing trends to continue the more difficult, perhaps impossible, the ultimate correction process will be. To come to grips with this issue we must follow a responsible mix of economic policies that will bring about durable, lasting economic prosperity which will benefit our nation with sustainable and increasing employment.

Fourth, and most important of all, there must be a proper balance in the shared responsibilities of the private and public sectors. This is a difficult assignment because of the confusion and pessimistic appraisals of the future caused by the political and economic shocks that have occurred. Maintaining and improving the creativity and productivity of the U.S. economic system against the attacks of critics who favor a big-government solution for the problems of society has become a major challenge. The simplistic cure of having government spend ever increasing amounts of borrowed money has not only not solved many of our problems, but it has created serious economic distortions that will continue long into the future. We now have a federal government that is trying to do more than its resources will permit, to do many things that it cannot do very well, to do some things that it should never do at all, and to do all of these things at the same time. As a result, we now have more government than we want, more than we need, and more than we can afford. Nevertheless, much of the current political rhetoric continues to claim that we aren't spending enough, aren't creating enough new government programs, and aren't pushing enough panic buttons. Despite the unmatched accomplishments of the U.S. economy these critics attack the free enterprise system and demand comprehensive governmental control over economic planning for the allocation of our national resources—the rationing of capital to selected industries—guaranteed government jobs for all who want them—increased control over private economic activities—even a return to the counterproductive wage and price controls that have always failed. Although the American free enterprise system feeds, clothes, and houses our people more effectively than any other system in the world, provides the real basis for all of our public services, and most importantly is fundamental to our individual freedoms, it is increasingly subject to criticism from those who seem to favor turning to less efficient approaches which would waste our human and material resources and eventually erode our economic progress and political freedoms.

Part of the problem is a matter of image. Those who support

increased government spending and pervasive controls over our daily lives are often perceived as being more concerned and socially progressive. Those who allegedly "care more" are given considerable attention when they call for more spending to solve the unmet needs of society even though the growth of big government has become a large part of the problem and not the solution it is alleged to be. At the same time, those who favor the free enterprise system too often converse in simplistic slogans that lack humane appeal. Worst of all, many businessmen who travel to Washington seem to want to surrender their existing freedoms in exchange for protection from the competition that has made our system so dynamic.

It is now time—in fact the need is long overdue—for those who believe in the free enterprise system to promote more effectively its basic values. America has become the world's premier economy because it provides basic incentives to its people to work hard and to be creative. For the individual family this approach leads to a higher standard of living. For the business firm it means increased markets and larger profits. For our government it means increased effectiveness and public support.

In short, too many Americans—especially those who have known only the affluent society—are unaware of the real source of economic growth in our country. The material abundance, the freedoms of choice, the opportunities for meaningful work are all largely the result of the creativity and productivity of our free and competitive economic system. This is the crucial theme that must be communicated to all Americans until they understand it. The American economy is the wellspring of our nation's basic strength in every sphere—political, social, military, and economic. It is the source of our present abundance and the basis of our hopes for a better future. We can solve our recognized problems best by preserving and strengthening, rather than weakening, our uniquely productive system. And in doing this we will preserve our other freedoms that have made America so great.

NATIONAL ECONOMIC PRIORITIES

The American people need to understand better the competing demands in making priority decisions as well as the remarkable creativity and productivity of the U.S. economic system when it is allowed to function properly. We must recognize that government decisions should emphasize economic goals that stretch beyond the next scheduled election; that our future productivity and employment opportunities require increased rates of capital investment; and that vigorous competition within the framework of a free enterprise economy is still the best approach to maintaining the strength and creativity of the United States.

We still have the premier economy of the world, and rapid, though somewhat erratic, economic growth continues to occur. But Americans increasingly realize that output gains and high per-capita incomes do not instantaneously solve all of our national problems. When we apply too much pressure on our system to produce goods and services, the inevitable result is inflation and shortages. If increased government spending exceeds the resources available and the monetary system finances the resulting deficits, the economy eventually becomes overheated. The underlying growth trends of the U.S. economy will provide sustained progress, but we cannot realistically expect to satisfy every new claim.

While the need for responsible demand management is generally accepted, each special-interest group assumes that its claim is unique and deserves satisfaction. Unfortunately, we have clearly forced the level of government spending beyond the willingness of society to pay for the programs provided. At the conclusion of the fiscal year of 1978 we recorded our seventeenth federal budget deficit in the last eighteen years. This was the fortieth deficit in the past forty-eight years (see Table 1). And the budget outlook over the next few years is clearly a matter of great concern. In trying to respond to so many diverse interest groups the federal government has frequently distorted the efficiency and stability of the entire economic system and has created an accelerating momentum of outlays which has eroded our fiscal flexibility in responding to changing priorities and current problems.

The most disappointing result of the loss of fiscal control in the mid-1960s is the uncontrollable momentum of the federal budget, which is now estimated to be approximately three-fourths "fixed" obligations. In theory, there should be no uncontrollable budget categories since Congress appropriates the funds each year, but existing contracts, interest on the national debt, and the eligibility standards of existing programs effectively obligate the federal

Table 1

CHANGES IN FEDERAL BUDGET UNIFIED BUDGET OUTLAYS
BY FISCAL YEAR, 1960–1979
(dollars in billions)

Fiscal Year	Federal Outlays	Dollar Increase	Percentage Increase	Surplus or Deficit
1961	$ 97.8	$ 5.6	6.1	$ −3.4
1962	106.8	9.0	9.2	−7.1
1963	111.3	4.5	4.2	−4.8
1964	118.6	7.3	6.6	−5.9
1965	118.4	−0.2	−0.1	−1.6
1966	134.7	16.3	13.8	−3.8
1967	158.3	23.6	17.5	−8.7
1968	178.8	20.5	13.0	−25.2
1969	184.5	5.7	3.2	+3.2
1970	196.6	12.1	6.6	−2.8
1971	211.4	14.8	7.5	−23.0
1972	232.0	20.6	9.7	−23.4
1973	247.1	15.1	6.5	−14.8
1974	269.6	22.5	9.1	−4.7
1975	326.1	56.5	20.9	−45.1
1976	365.6	39.5	12.1	−66.4
Transition quarter	94.7	—	—	−13.0
1977	401.9	36.3	9.9	−45.0
1978[e]	462.2	60.3	15.0	−61.8
1979[e]	500.2	38.0	8.2	−60.6

e = estimated
Source: The Budget of the United States Government, FY 1979, January 1978.
NOTE: Under provisions of the Congressional Budget Act of 1974, the fiscal year for the federal government shifted beginning with FY 1977. Through 1976, the fiscal year ran from July 1 through June 30; starting in October 1976 (FY 77), the fiscal year runs from October 1 through September 30. The 3-month period from July 1, 1976 through September 30, 1976 is a separate fiscal period known as the transition quarter.

government to make the majority of outlays based on the decisions of the past. When economic recessions occur, the combination of declining tax revenues and relatively fixed spending commitments creates large deficits, particularly in recent years. The government also reacts to economic difficulties by adding "emergency" counter-cyclical spending programs to offset the loss of private consumption and investment. After the real or "emergency" problems end, the new spending programs remain, creating a significantly increased base level of outlays. The results are that government officials rarely have an opportunity to shape the long-term trends of the budget and their responsiveness to current problems is limited because the bulk of the federal budget is locked into the priorities of the past.

The basic problem is that federal budget decisions reflect the momentum created by past decisions. It is usually impossible to predict the future outlays associated with each new legislative initiative when it is initially approved, and there is a tendency for certain categories, particularly social programs involving the transfer of income, to accelerate rapidly. Officials did not anticipate the growth of federal spending in the mid-1960s or the massive deficits that have accumulated. For example, federal outlays in fiscal year 1966 were $135 billion; ten years later they had increased to $365 billion, an increase of $230 billion, or 170 percent. By way of comparison, the gross national product rose from $753 billion in calendar year 1966 to $1,706 billion in 1976, a gain of 127 percent. The acceleration of government spending—at the federal, state, and local levels—explains the prevailing upward trend of the government sector in the total economy. In the 1930s government spending as a share of the gross national product averaged about 10 percent; in the 1950s the figure was about 20 percent; and during the 1970s the government share has increased to almost 40 percent. There is no definitive target that specifies that 40 percent is wrong and 20 percent is correct, but the trend is clearly a cause for concern for those who believe in the superiority of market economies. Economists at the Organization for Economic Cooperation and Development (OECD) recently published a comprehensive study that demonstrates that there is a negative correlation between the growth rate of real output in each country and the proportion of the gross national product committed to government spending. Once again, governments rarely make explicit decisions to increase the government sector by transferring responsibilities and resources away from the private sector. The actual results simply reflect the cumulative effects of hundreds of specific legislative and administrative decisions over the years. These "good intentions" of government officials largely explain the extraordinary acceleration of federal government spending from the mid-1960s to date. Furthermore, the cumulative impact of these many decisions appears to be increasing. For example, from fiscal year 1974 to fiscal year 1978 federal outlays jumped from $270 billion to an expected level of approximately $462 billion, an increase of $193 billion in just four years and a percentage gain of 71 percent.[1] From fiscal year 1976 to fiscal year 1978 federal spending is expected to increase almost $97 billion, or 26 percent in just two years. In fiscal year 1978 federal spending is expected to be near the one-half-trillion-dollar benchmark. The strong upward momentum and largely uncontrollable nature of the federal budget represents a very serious policy problem that tends to swamp short-term fiscal and monetary decisions, leading to economic uncertainty and instability. The "go-and-stop" pattern of the U.S. economy since the mid-1960s reflects the distortions caused by volatile economic policies.

The federal government obviously has a fundamental role in decisions about the uses of the national output. Unfortunately, it is widely believed that the government's role is limited simply to balancing the federal budget over time. In reality, federal decisions influence the entire economy through direct purchases, taxes, transfer payments, and a variety of research and grant programs which serve as seed capital for determining private sector activities. Total government spending now comprises over one-third of the total economy, and the upward trend may accelerate if the current growth of transfer payments continues to increase rapidly. In describing the pervasive influence of federal decisions in allocating available resources among competing claims I am not suggesting that we should have a controlled economic system. To the contrary, I am strongly committed to the private sector as the superior source of economic progress, and my experiences in government have reinforced those beliefs. But we must recognize the major impact of government decisions on every sector of our ecomony.

Unfortunately, debates about setting national economic policies are too often limited to arguments about the allocation of functions between the public and private sectors. In considering national economic priorities a much broader perspective is required. The total productive capability of the entire *economy* must be first identified before attempting to rank and select specific claims against that potential output. Estimating the *total* economic capac-

1. This period includes the transition quarter described in Table 1.

ity of the system avoids the simplistic arguments that additional government programs can be continuously created to meet every claim by simply shifting resources from the private to the public sector. Adding new government commitments is not feasible if the total production capacity of the economy is exceeded. This guideline has been frequently violated as total demand has increased too rapidly for the economic system to absorb. When this happens the economy begins a boom-and-bust sequence with severe inflation, and unemployment distortions, such as occurred in the late 1960s and throughout much of the 1970s. The inflation and unemployment caused by these wide swings disrupt the entire U.S. economy and international stability. Unfortunately, the overheating process has often been caused by excessive rates of increase in government spending. The results of such excesses persist long after economic conditions change because spending programs are rarely eliminated.

A study of total capacity was prepared in 1969 by the Council of Economic Advisers and published in the *Economic Report of the President* for 1970. The pattern of real increases in gross national product was projected for 1976 using trend estimates of the growth of the labor force, national productivity gains, expected unemployment, and the annual average number of hours worked per person. The existing claims against the projected GNP were then identified, including personal consumption, business investment, housing, and government spending. All of these claims were adjusted to reflect demographic and economic assumptions. Federal spending was projected to include only existing programs plus new proposals for revenue sharing, welfare reform, and pollution abatement outlays. As summarized in Table 2, the fulfillment of the total claims already identified in 1969 required a relatively rapid expansion of output to keep pace:

> . . . the existing, visible, and strongly supported claims already exhaust the national output for some years ahead. This is not to say that no other claims will be satisfied, or that claims included in these calculations should have preference over claims not recognized here. The basic point is that if other claims are to be satisfied some of those recognized here will have to be sacrificed.[2]

2. *Economic Report of the President,* 1970, p. 80.

Table 2

REAL GROSS NATIONAL PRODUCT, 1955, 1966, AND 1969—PROJECTIONS FOR 1975–76

| | 1955 | Actuals | | Projections | |
		1966	1969	1975	1976
		Billions of dollars, 1969 prices			
Gross national product available	569.0	845.5	931.4	1,199	1,251
Claims on available GNP	569.0	845.5	931.4	1,188	1,232
Federal Government purchases	69.8	88.3	101.3	83	83
State and local government purchases	53.8	94.4	110.8	140	144
Personal consumption expenditures	344.3	519.2	577.5	788	802
Gross private domestic investment	96.9	137.5	139.8	192	198
Business fixed investment	55.1	92.0	99.3	128	134
Residential structures	34.5	29.4	32.0	52	52
Change in business inventories	7.3	16.1	8.5	12	13
Net exports of goods and services	4.2	6.1	1.9	5	5
Unallocated resources	.0	.0	.0	11	19
Addendum: Federal surplus or deficit (−), national income accounts basis	5.6	−.2	9.3	25	32
Per capita personal consumption expenditures	2,083	2,637	2,842	3,529	3,641

Table 2 (continued)

REAL GROSS NATIONAL PRODUCT, 1955, 1966, AND 1969—PROJECTIONS FOR 1975–76

| | 1955 | Actuals | | Projections | |
		1966	1969	1975	1976
		Percent of total GNP available			
Gross national product available	100.0	100.0	100.0	100	100
Claims on available GNP	100.0	100.0	100.0	99	99
Federal Government purchases	12.3	10.4	10.9	7	7
State and local government purchases	9.5	11.2	11.9	12	12
Personal consumption expenditures	60.5	61.4	62.0	34	64
Gross private domestic investment	17.0	16.3	15.0	16	16
Business fixed investment	9.7	10.9	10.7	11	11
Residential structures	6.1	3.5	3.4	4	4
Change in business inventories	1.3	1.9	.9	1	1
Net exports of goods and services	.8	.7	.2	¹	¹
Unallocated resources	.0	.0	.0	1	2
Addendum: Federal surplus or deficit (−) national income accounts basis	1.0	.0	1.0	2	3

¹Less than 0.5 percent. Note: Projections are based on projected Federal expenditures and their influence on various components of GNP.
Source: Council of Economic Advisers, *Economic Report of the President*, January 1971, p. 95.

The projections in the Council of Economic Advisers analysis were hypothetical estimates based on somewhat arbitrary assumptions, and actual results have varied during the intervening years since the study was completed. Nevertheless, a crucial point is evident: decisions on national economic priorities must reflect total output potential and all existing claims rather than focusing only on federal budget outlays. Whenever resources are limited recommendations to add new government programs must consider the prospective impact on the private sector. In short, the creation of new priorities, or expansion of existing commitments at an accelerated rate, will require giving up or curtailing some existing claim. Once it is recognized that the potential GNP has already been committed to existing claims, the consideration of new outlay requests should become more realistic. Spending decisions should then concentrate on realigning claims rather than merely adding additional commitments to satisfy diverse interest groups. This point is particularly important in considering the massive amounts of private capital investments required to meet future capacity and employment needs. Instead of reducing capital investment to release resources for government social programs, the amount of private outlays must be accelerated. This basic requirement means that government spending and tax policies should be directed toward creating a more balanced budget over extended periods of time so that the future flow of savings is not diverted away from private investment into the financing of large government deficits.

The traditional view of the government's role has been that a balanced budget is a symbol of fiscal responsibility. Accordingly, when deficits occurred, the government was expected to restrict outlays and/or increase taxes. However, it is obvious that as a result of economic fluctuations the surplus or deficit for any specific year will inevitably be different from the arbitrary target. The "annual balance" rule eventually was replaced by the concept that balance should occur over the course of the business cycle so that fiscal policies could be used to stimulate the economy despite any resulting deficits. The relatively unknown corollary of this "pump-priming" policy, of course, is that budget surpluses should occur during periods of above-average economic activity to create the desired balance over time. Unfortunately, the actual pattern has been completely asymmetrical, with deficits occurring almost every year (see Table 1). While some economists and politicians have tried to justify this pattern, I believe that by concentrating on short-term economic stabilization goals rather than long-term allocation of resources our fiscal policies have become a disruptive force. Too often fiscal policies have lagged economic developments so that the desired stimulus or restraint typically arrives long after the business cycle changes. Thus the "emergency" spending programs created to pull the economy out of a recession often add to the subsequent overheating of the economy and create additional commitments that last far into the future. A corresponding reduction of these programs during periods of economic expansion is unusual. The result is an escalating pattern of government programs which are oriented toward the problems of the past and restrict the government's ability to respond to new national priorities or current problems. Finally, the "full employment" budget was introduced to correct the asymmetrical pattern of deficits, but this tool has not provided the necessary discipline. All of these approaches have failed because the executive branch and Congress have been unwilling to shift their attention to longer-term goals or to face up to the agonizing experience of saying no.

These concerns raise fundamental questions about the proper allocation of resources and decision making between the public and private sectors. The key, of course, is what is the appropriate balance. If the balance is almost entirely in the private sector, the public's interest may not be properly safeguarded. There would be little or no national defense, national parks, or other public goods of this sort, and we would still have the difficult challenge of providing a basic level of income and services for those Americans who are currently not able to pay for their basic needs. Clearly, there is an important role for government.

However, when resource allocation and other economic decisions become dominated by a government bureaucracy, innovation and productivity are too often restricted. Moreover, the individual finds he has less freedom of economic choice as greater portions of his paycheck go to support growing government outlays at all levels, as prices rise, and as the total economy becomes less productive. As an economy becomes increasingly dominated by the government, individual initiatives fade away. The potential entrepreneur considering a new business because he has an idea he thinks is really good finds himself stymied at almost every turn. The danger of all of this is that in many cases he concludes that the risks and inconvenience far outweigh the potential rewards and he drops the idea. At the extreme, economic decision making by people in the market is supplanted by people in government, individual incentives evaporate, and the economy deteriorates into conditions of "stagflation."

Reasonable people will agree that we do not want either extreme. Too little government results in an absence of public goods and safeguards of the public interest. Too much government, on the other hand, stymies the workings of efficient and competitive markets and reduces the individual's freedom of economic choice. We obviously must have a balance. But what is the appropriate mix of public and private decision making? There is no precise answer to this question, but I do believe that we can make a reasoned assessment.

We must redress this imbalance and restore to the American people greater discretion over personal spending decisions. They are usually able to decide what is best for them and, within limits, competitive markets are able to respond to these desires in the most efficient and responsive manner. I am not talking about a reduction in the absolute level of government expenditures. What I am advocating is a slowdown in the upward momentum of government spending that began to accelerate in the mid-1960s so that the relative portion of resource allocation decisions made by the private sector increases. In this way, the overall efficiency of our economic system can increase and we can bring about higher economic growth.

I believe that the balance has tipped too far in the direction of bigger and bigger government at the relative expense of the private sector. The American people are beginning to resent this growth, for many of them know that ultimately it must be paid for directly with their taxes and/or indirectly by accelerating inflation.

It cannot be emphasized often enough that the true wealth of a nation is in its ability to produce goods and services.[3] Improvements in this ability come mainly from the private sector. We can debate how the total pie should be divided, but we should not lose sight of

3. It must also be emphasized that government doesn't produce our wealth; the people do.

the fact that we are no better off as a nation unless the pie continues to increase in real terms. To do so and realize a durable prosperity, we should restore incentives to the private sector by tipping the scales toward greater relative growth of the private sector.

IMPACT OF FISCAL POLICIES ON ECONOMIC STABILITY

Turning next to the question of economic stabilization, there is certainly an important role to be played by fiscal and monetary policies in evening out extreme moves in the economy. There have unquestionably been times, however, when such moves and policies have been counterproductive. For example, additional government stimulus frequently takes effect at times when the total productive capacity of the economy cannot absorb the increased demand for goods and services. The result is inflation, dislocations in the economy, and eventually, unemployment. Increased government spending programs have proven to be a cumbersome tool for short-term economic stabilization purposes. There usually is a considerable lag between the time a need is identified, or a claim is made by a special-interest group, and the time there is a specific response by Congress to the proposal. Then there is another time lag before the expenditures actually occur and begin to spread throughout the economic system. At the time a proposal was initially considered there may have been underutilization of resources in the economy, but by the time the program actually comes on stream resources are often fully employed so that the additional government spending leads to greater inflation.

If there were some way that old programs could be phased down or eliminated during a period of rapid economic expansion, fiscal policy might be more effective as a tool for stabilization purposes. However, experience has shown that this is not the case and that programs initiated in a period of economic slack tend to become a permanent part of the budget. It is extremely difficult to reduce or eliminate even the obviously ineffective or obsolete programs; to scale down existing programs for countercyclical purposes has been, for all practical purposes, impossible. This is particularly true when the sizable outlays of the many state and local governments are added to the total.

This implies that we must avoid abrupt and excessive changes in government expenditures. No matter how well intentioned, such sharp swings in spending tend to accentuate rather than stabilize the business cycle and serve to increase the uncertainty of developing policies to meet future needs. In turn, this uncertainty is felt in the consumer markets, in the markets for capital goods, and in financial markets.

The actual pattern of federal budget surpluses and deficits has not followed the balanced pattern suggested. As summarized in Table 1, budget deficits prevail, and their size has increased sharply in recent years. It is particularly significant that after three years of relatively strong and balanced economic growth beginning in early 1975 large budget deficits will definitely occur in fiscal year 1978 and again in fiscal year 1979. The theoretical goal of running surpluses during extended periods of strong economic performance has not been met. In addition, there are over one hundred other "off-budget" spending programs and federal credit programs for housing, agriculture, students, veterans, exporters, etc. During the latest fiscal decade, from fiscal year 1968 through fiscal year 1977, the cumulative federal budget deficits totaled $260 billion, and "net" borrowing for the "off-budget" and credit programs added up to another $230 billion. This means that the federal government extracted approximately one half of a trillion dollars from the capital markets in a single ten-year period that was an era marked by historically high interest rates and recurring "credit crunches" with severe repercussions for the housing and business capital investment sectors. It is interesting to speculate on what might happen to the supply and cost of capital needed for housing and business investment—as well as personal consumption—if the federal government fiscal policy would balance the budget over time and accumulate surpluses during periods of strong economic growth. The reality, of course, is that the deficits are chronic and unusually large. In fact, the national debt has increased from $344 billion in fiscal year 1968 to an estimated $700 billion at the end of fiscal year 1977, and the Administration has recently requested a new debt ceiling authority for fiscal year 1979 of $870 billion. Interest on this enormous public debt totaled $42 billion in fiscal year 1977, and will be approximately close to $50 billion in 1978. Interest payments are now the third largest item in the federal budget, after social program transfer payments and defense. The rapid growth of this "uncontrollable" outlay puts additional pressure on the total budget, which means that other programs must be restricted or tax reductions foregone.

The chronic federal budget deficits place the U.S. Treasury in a difficult position of competing with private demands for funds. The recent avalanche of Treasury securities has created distortions in the traditional patterns of funds being raised by various sectors in the capital markets as well as in the sheer magnitude of total funds raised. In my judgment, this has contributed to making our financial markets less efficient in recent years in channeling the savings of society to investment opportunities. As a result, capital formation is impeded.

The problem becomes far more critical as the overall economic expansion progresses and the financing needs of the private sector intensify. If deficits remain large, the Treasury, by being first in the credit line, will always get its needs financed but in so doing will make it difficult for companies with less than prime financial ratings to obtain the financial resources they need at acceptable interest rates.

This problem of "crowding out" does not imply a dollar-for-dollar displacement of Treasury for private borrowing, but rather describes strains in the financial markets. These strains result in certain private borrowers not being satisfied and in the financial markets as a whole being less efficient in their function of channeling savings in our society to investment opportunities.

The size of the deficit also affects the rate of capital formation in the private sector, and this is a matter of great concern. As the recovery progresses, private capital investment must rise to sustain the recovery. In the longer run, the need for increased capital formation has been carefully documented by the Treasury, by numerous outside studies, and in Chapter 1 of the *Economic Report of the President* published in February 1976. If we are to meet our goals for increased employment and productivity in a noninflationary environment as well as our environmental, safety, and energy goals, we must have an increase in the rate of national savings and private direct investment relative to the total GNP. More specifically, we must increase the percentage of business fixed investment from the average figure of 10.4 percent of our gross national product the last decade to approximately 11½ percent over the next decade. In another sense, total investment, including residential construction, must increase from approximately 14½ percent to 16 percent.

Consumption is important—it represents two-thirds of the total GNP and tends to drive the economy. But inadequate investment has very high costs: inflation, unemployment, inadequate productivity, production bottlenecks, and erosion of competitiveness in world markets. This was the underlying argument in many of the testimonies I presented as Secretary of the Treasury advocating a slight tilt in the allocation of resources from consumption to savings and investment.

The achievement of our capital formation goals depends on the necessary expenditures being financed in the private sector. In turn, the adequacy of capital flows depends on the savings of society being less and less used to finance federal expenditures and more and more focused on capital formation. This is the only way we can sustain a durable recovery over the long run and bring down the level of inflation. If the private sector is unable to finance capital formation because of the huge demands on savings by the federal government and because of the resulting inefficiencies introduced in financial markets, the boom-and-recession sequence of the last decade will be repeated. Therefore, it is imperative that we reduce the federal deficit and work toward a budget surplus during periods of economic expansion.

THE CRUCIAL ISSUE IS STILL FREEDOM

The United States now faces a basic choice. Yet we hear misleading political rhetoric that we can achieve our basic economic goals without making the necessary sacrifices required to produce and pay for the desired goods and services. Our magnificent country is capable of achieving any worthy goal it identifies but we must face up to many economic realities, particularly the obvious point that goods and services cannot be distributed to the consuming public unless they are first produced. We have the human and material resources necessary to operate our open and competitive economic system to achieve our goals if we will create the proper environment. How well we make these basic decisions will ultimately determine what future historians will write about America.

To find the answers we must begin with the correct questions. What has made this a great nation? What has made people throughout the world talk about the American Dream?

Has it been the land and our natural resources? We have certainly been blessed with an abundance of resources. But in the Soviet Union we see a land mass that is much larger than our own which is equally well endowed. Yet, the Soviet system provides much less for the people. They must turn to the United States for the grain they need to feed their own people and for our technology and capital.

Does our strength depend only on the qualities of our people? We are clearly blessed with one of the largest and most talented populations that the world has ever known. But in China today we see a population that is four times as large as our own, whose civilization at one time was developed far in advance of the rest of the world. Yet their present material standard of living and personal freedoms are most disappointing.

So while our land, resources, and people have been essential parts of the American story, there is another factor that is too often missing in other countries that has contributed to America's progress. That crucial factor has been our national commitment to liberty and individual dignity.

For two hundred years people have streamed to our shores in search of various freedoms—freedom of religion, freedom of speech, freedom of the press, freedom of assembly, and freedom to seek their fortunes without fear or favor of the government. All of these freedoms are planted firmly in our Constitution. But they have become such a familiar part of our lives that I wonder whether we now take them too much for granted.

There is nothing artificial about freedom, nor is there any guarantee of its permanency. As Dwight Eisenhower once said, "Freedom has its life in the hearts, the actions, and the spirits of men, and so it must be daily earned and refreshed—else like a flower cut from its life-giving roots, it will wither and die."

There are many ways this can happen, some of them very slow and subtle. For example, there has been an accelerating trend toward collectivist policies in the United States as people have been persuaded that the problems of our society have become so large that individuals can no longer cope with them. Many Americans now expect the government to assume responsibility for solving their problems and to do things for them that they once did for themselves. Government has been gradually cast into the role of trying to solve all the difficult challenges of modern life.

That trend began to accelerate in the 1960s as governments promised the rapid solution of complex political, economic, and social problems and the end of economic cycles based on the clever manipulation of government policies. We failed to note that resources are always limited, even in a nation as affluent as ours. Unfortunately, the inflated expectations and broken promises of the past have left a residue of disillusionment. Many young people are skeptical about our basic institutions, and I can't say that I blame them.

International problems, the energy crisis, disappointing harvests, excessive government regulations, wage and price controls, and thousands of other specific problems have contributed significantly to the unsatisfactory levels of inflation and unemployment. But the underlying momentum has been basically caused by the government's irresponsible fiscal and monetary policies and the excessive economic stimulus it has provided for almost two decades.

The greatest irony of these misguided policies is that they were based on the mistaken notion that they would specifically help the poor, the elderly, the sick, and the disadvantaged. Yet when these stop-and-go government policies trigger inflation and unemployment, who gets hurt the most? The very same people the politicians claimed they were trying to help—the poor, the elderly, the sick, and the disadvantaged.

Even more fundamentally, there has been a trend toward big government and the diminishing of economic and personal freedoms in the United States. The federal government has now become the dominant force in our society. It is the biggest single employer, the biggest consumer, and the biggest borrower. Fifty years ago, total government spending comprised approximately 10 percent of the gross national product; by 1976 that figure exceeded 35 percent. If the government spending trends of the last two decades continue, the total government share of economic activity in the United States will be approaching 60 percent by the year 2000. If the government exercises such a dominating influence in the economy, it will also control many of the personal decisions of its citizens. History shows that when economic freedom disappears personal and political freedoms also disappear. The inextricable relationship between economic freedom and personal freedom is sometimes overlooked by those who constantly seek to expand the powers of government, but it is plain to see in many countries around the world where these freedoms have been lost.

Unfortunately, there is no convenient scapegoat to blame our problems on. As modern governments have usurped the power increasingly to control our daily lives they have done so with good intent, thinking that they are the proper authority to determine and then implement the ideals of society. In the process, governments have sacrificed individual freedoms for a collective system of rules needed to impose their view of what is best for each of us. But this behavior is merely a reflection of what they believe the people want. It is not "the government" that we should blame—that is a simplistic excuse—but most of the institutions of society that have created an environment in which equality of status is mistaken for equality of opportunity, and security, albeit a false sense of well-being, is exchanged for personal freedom. As a result there is an increasing mood of frustration as public skepticism increases about our ability to handle the problems of the future. If this trend continues, most of the freedoms that we cherish will not survive, for personal, political, and economic freedoms are all intertwined and cannot exist alone. The great historian Gibbon noted this tendency in writing an evaluation of ancient Greece:

> In the end, more than they wanted freedom, they wanted security. They wanted a comfortable life and they lost it all—security, comfort, and freedom. When the Athenians finally wanted not to give to society but for society to give to them, when the freedom they wished for most was freedom from responsibility, then Athens ceased to be free.

Our basic challenge, then, is to determine how much personal freedom, if any, we are willing to give up in seeking collective security. It is certainly not easy to live with the uncertainties that exist in a free society, but the real personal benefits created are far superior to those of any other system. It is this heritage of personal freedom that has made America a land blessed above all others. To protect this remarkable privilege is a goal worthy of our greatest personal and institutional commitment.

CONCLUSION

My experiences in government service convince me that we must become much more rigorous in evaluating new claims against our future national output. The economy will continue to grow and meet many of our needs, but we cannot realistically expect to satisfy every competing claim. Some will have to be eliminated or restrained. Accordingly, in assessing the growth of federal spending, we must recognize the realistic growth capabilities of the total economy. For many years, we have lacked the discipline to maintain the necessary balance as the functions and powers of government have increased. Some would welcome this acceleration of federal spending because they favor a different approach to allocating functions between the private and public sectors. I strongly disagree because I believe the private enterprise system is the world's most efficient approach to increasing output and preserving personal freedoms. But whichever course our mixed economy takes in the coming years, the need for a more rigorous consideration of national economic priorities is necessary.

Twenty years ago it was apparent in this country that we were heading for an energy crisis. One report after another confirmed it, but instead of providing wisely for the future, we insisted upon living foolishly for the moment. Now we are beginning to pay the price, and we will go on paying for some time to come.

In the same way, we have seriously abused the private enterprise system and have so encouraged the enormous growth of government that we are heading toward another serious crisis. The United States is rapidly coming to a crossroads where we must decide what type of economic system and consequently what kind of society we wish. I fervently hope that we will continue to emphasize the free enterprise system in America and roll back the forces of restrictive government. The choice is one that our generation is called upon to make. However, unless we act soon, the decision will be made for us by default.

—WILLIAM E. SIMON

CHAPTER 2

---◦◦◦◦---

The Future of Our
Freedom-Based Economy

The American people, since the very beginnings of this nation, have understood clearly that there is a price for individual political freedoms, and that this price is, in Jefferson's resounding phrase, "eternal vigilance." We have been steadfastly alert to recognize and repel even the most subtle attempts at infringement.

In ironic contrast, we have shown little constancy and less conviction in encouraging a like vigilance to safeguard our economic freedoms—the freedoms of personal economic choice, enterprise, and opportunity in the private sector which have impelled the United States to its present unrivaled level of affluence.

As the United States progresses into its third century, the blurring of valid private and public functions and the increasingly lopsided emphasis given political over economic priorities combine to create an issue of more than academic significance. Put simply, that issue is how to restore a balanced interaction between the government sector and the private sector.

Fortunately, most of the challenges we face are still at a point where reasonable people can aspire to deal with them constructively if we confront this supra-issue forthrightly.

The commentaries that Herbert Prochnow brings together in this book, varied as they are in subject and outlook, suggest there is reason to believe that the American people at this juncture have arrived at an appreciation of the fundamental interdependence of our economic capabilities and our social and political objectives.

Individuals of widely differing background and interests, both inside and outside the business community, now openly acknowledge that profits and social goals are merely two sides of the same coin. This growing acceptance of the premise that we can't have social gains without economic gains, and vice versa, is of far-reaching importance. Properly tended and encouraged, it holds out the prospect of a broad consensus of national purpose that has been lacking, or at least obscured, in our debates about business and society over the past generation.

The dialogue continues to turn on our collective assessment of who is the best guardian of national progress—the individual or the state, or a prudent balance of both. The theme will be recognized as a recurring one in human history. None has stated it more cogently than that most articulate of eighteenth-century British parliamentarians, Edmund Burke, who observed that "one of the finest problems in legislation (is) to determine what the state ought to take upon itself to direct by the public wisdom and what it ought to leave, with as little interference as possible, to individual exertion." This is as basic in our day as it was in Burke's.

I shall develop my own thoughts around six related points:

First, the economic accomplishments of the U.S. private enterprise system are real, despite critics of the extreme right and left.

Second, within the United States and probably within most of the world's other market economies, the corporate enterprise is emerging as the most important social institution of our time.

Third, what we have described so often as the free enterprise system has undergone a gradual transfiguration over time, and those of us who believe in its original values and utility must recognize this change without self-deception.

Fourth, the agenda of unfinished national and global issues suggests that government needs the resources and skills that abound in business, but by the same token, the business community needs affirmative assistance of government.

Fifth, the disproportionate growth of government relative to available private sector resources has itself compounded three of today's dominant economic problems—inflation, unemployment, and investment disincentives—and this must be redressed.

And sixth, the rewards of success in making both economic and social gains are so great that we can and should be willing to put up with temporary inconvenience in working together toward their accomplishment. The price of failure almost certainly would be the disappearance of both the political and economic freedoms that we've come to cherish.

It seems fitting to begin with the incontrovertible economic accomplishments made possible by our profit-motivated competitive private enterprise system. In terms of future policy making and, indeed, personal daily outlook, we will slight ourselves and the future if we underestimate the vast progress already achieved.

Of the numerous possible yardsticks of this progress, I shall choose just two: the awesome rise in real per-capita income and the related creation of jobs in the United States. They stand as an immense escarpment on the plain of human history.

In 1978 the population of the United States numbered more than 218 million human beings, nearly triple our population in 1900. In this time, real personal income has risen nearly twelvefold, so real per-capita income is up fourfold.

Closely related to this is the steady rise in jobs. In 1900 some 27 million Americans were employed. By 1978 the count exceeded 94 million, and nearly 40 million of these jobs have come into existence in the past quarter century.

These two sets of facts underscore the remarkable thrust and vitality of the American economic system. In citing them, I don't mean to imply we have eliminated privation or overcome imbalances within some segments of our country. Perfection continues to elude us.

In selecting real per-capita income and employment growth, my point is to document the broadest measures of national affluence. The opportunity to do creative and productive work and to increase our financial rewards in return for this work seems to me to provide just such measures. Without them, the other economic needs would be difficult if not impossible to satisfy. It is also relevant that the overwhelming proportion of jobs created are direct results of the private economy and the capacity of the private marketplace to spur investment in the plants and equipment that add to total jobs available.

The domestic successes of the United States have a significance that transcends our own borders. These successes have had immense symbolic importance to other nations, even those ideologically committed to nonmarket economies. More tangibly, the financial strength, productive capacity, and technological experience of this country's private sector made it possible to extend reconstruction assistance to other nations in the aftermath of World War II. This assistance in no small way created the foundation for the greatest boom in the world economy in all history. From 1948 to 1973, the world's real gross domestic product grew by more than three and a half times, a world rate exceeding 5 percent a year. As Daniel Bell, the Harvard sociologist, has noted, "This real per capita growth was shared almost equally by about half the world (the middle-income countries—e.g., Brazil and Mexico—being slightly the largest gainers)," and he noted further that "the very poor countries grew at an annual rate of 1.8 percent, small in comparison with the others, respectable on the basis of their own past."

By the standards of history, life in New York, London, Djakarta, Rio, Lagos, and Vladivostok today has more in common than it has in difference. By the standards of history, the quality of life is gaining. I don't think it's jingoistic to suggest that the success of the U.S. economic system made recent advances happen sooner and faster than if it didn't exist.

Not everyone may agree, at initial encounter, with my second point—that the profit-motivated private corporation is the most important social institution of our time. Yet I believe the concept is true on two counts.

For one thing, running a business in an efficient manner to sustain and create jobs, generate a profit for shareholders, and provide a needed product or service in itself is a socially valuable contribution.

The income and savings of the individuals participating in private enterprise, after all, form the underpinning of wealth from which government derives its revenue.

Government, by contrast, can expropriate real wealth but it cannot of itself create it. This is implicit in Edmund Burke's reference to "individual exertion."

There is a second attribute that gives the private corporation special importance in today's society. In the aggregate, our private business organizations and institutions exist as a countervailing force to offset the power of government. It has become an unforeseen but nonetheless useful addition to our historic system of checks and balances, comparable to the two-party political system or the separation of powers among executive, legislative, and judicial branches of government.

The emergence of what amounts to a de facto balance of power leads to my third major point—that the free enterprise system in the United States over time has experienced a transfiguration. The bare-knuckled, secretive, often exploitive attitude of business adventurers who stalk the pages of nineteenth- and early-twentieth-century history is no longer tenable in today's world. Unfortunately, their actions and schemes are in no small part the source of much public suspicion of business to this day.

The very term "free enterprise system" is reminiscent of Alexander Woollcott's comment that the Holy Roman Empire was neither holy, Roman, nor an empire. Certainly the composite U.S. business community is not free, if by that word we mean to convey unrestricted. The range within which its enterprise can be exerted today is increasingly circumscribed. And anyone who thinks it approaches the coherence of a system will find it instructive to attend the national convention of almost any trade group that comes to mind.

What we do have is a functioning open market system. We do have a market of private choice that's the envy of the world. And we do still have a profit-motivated community of business firms with remarkable capability to organize the work of private individuals to move toward specific productive goals that remains less onerous than the organization of an authoritarian state.

The evolution of the corporation in the twentieth century has moved with a perceivable acceleration in the past generation. Let me explain that by recalling a little of where we were—in attitude particularly—in 1968. I pick that year more as a matter of convenience than as any particular benchmark in corporate social awareness. Certainly by then we found ourselves, along with government leaders, inundated with an onrush of social demands, each charged with a sense of urgency and all thrust pell-mell upon us, without the least concern for the economic feasibility or adverse consequences of attempting instant solutions.

Many of us in business, I'm sure, can recall going to meetings with advocates of one special cause or another, and as often as not we went in a spirit of defensiveness, looking more for ways to insulate ourselves from trouble than seeking to participate in solving a problem.

More than a few business executives were talking about profit maximization as the only road to social prosperity. Well, this isn't the case today, and the change is profoundly important in moving toward a national consensus for action.

Today, profits and social goals are almost always spoken of in the same breath. The health of our communities is recognized as directly related to business success. Executives don't relegate it to separate, occasional study sessions. We live and work with the questions of environment, minorities, affordable health care, vocational opportunities, community safety, day in and day out, because they are part and parcel of making intelligent and effective business decisions.

What's more, we've learned a few things we really didn't understand or appreciate before.

We've learned what we should have known all along—that American women can be valuable additions to the labor force and to management. We've learned that our many minorities have useful and important contributions to make to our total production system as workers and as managers—and we discovered that, often unwittingly, we have neglected or wasted this human resource.

We've learned that our natural resources—indeed, the physical resources of the whole earth—are not unlimited but finite, and that, as with some of our human resources, we are squandering them. We've learned that expending funds on school facilities, without due respect for the quality of school faculties, does not automatically guarantee informed, skilled, or enlightened citizens.

We've learned also that government action alone does not resolve our social problems or achieve our social goals. And we've learned, or relearned, that neglect of the incentives of the marketplace can cripple even an economy as vigorous as our own.

In the process of change, we have learned—I think for the betterment of all. Parenthetically, those of us in the corporate world should not be discouraged if our efforts are not immediately recognized. We will continue to have critics, and it's the nature of most criticism to emphasize shortcomings at the expense of accomplishments. We cannot permit the absence of applause to slow our momentum or beguile us into the nostalgic belief that we can stop by the wayside.

It is the critical diehard who is outside the mainstream of American life, not the other way around. I detect no change in this nation's historic preference for avoiding extremes.

This brings me to my fourth point: the need for the constructive support of government. The major economic issues and the multiplying social needs of our nation are neither simple nor small in dimension. To cope with them, we will need the collaboration of all sectors of this country.

To cope with—and I don't think I'm excessively optimistic in saying, to settle and solve—them without paying a political price that is utterly intolerable, we must develop a much more intensive, open, and consistent collaboration between government and the private sector than we have managed to date. If the evidence of the recent past means anything at all, we must conclude that such collaboration does not require further proliferation of regulation and restraint, nor new penalties on an individual's financial success.

In passing, I must observe that the typical governmental response to a public problem is often as not in the form of the negative. We need some affirmatives for the private business sector—not subsidies, not protective fences to shield us from competition, but incentives that will encourage innovation and investment for the long haul.

In any workable collaboration between the private sector and government, we reasonably can expect regulatory agencies to base their actions on five criteria. These guidelines aren't mine, by the way. They were included in a recent analysis from the Council on Wage and Price Stability. They are:

- Make regulatory decisions on the basis of sufficient information, which means seeking expert inputs from the sector of industry to be regulated.
- Make sure the costs of regulation don't outweigh its potential public benefit.
- Consider the cost-effectiveness of individual segments of the regulation proposed.

- Consider alternative approaches.
- Consider the impact on the total economy as well as the single sector or industry for which the agency has jurisdiction.

This is a good list of checkpoints. The Council's study indicates they are areas where regulatory agencies consistently fall short.

Point Five in the development of my theme involves the major economic issues that amount to national policy imperatives between now and the close of the century. It's unnecessary to discuss them at length. They are more than familiar to all of us: the incubus of inflation, the continuing proportion of Americans in the civilian labor force who don't have jobs, and the faltering pace of investment in new productive capacity and efficiency.

I mention them not to appraise the business climate but rather to emphasize that these three economic issues are more than economic in portent. They have profound impact on the noneconomic issues of our world, and ultimately on global tranquility and our own political destiny.

Each of these economic issues affects both our profit system and our national social goals.

The profit element is only one part of the total equation, but it remains a pivotal one if our economic system is to provide the new jobs we'll need between now and the close of this century, if we are to develop new plants and equipment that will permit us to utilize fully our human resources, and if we are to find new efficiencies that will permit us to lower the costs that contribute to some of today's inflation.

We can surmount these problems because each is finite and can be dealt with through the application of productivity and new technology. We can—if we have the will, the mind, the courage, and the patience to allow ourselves the time.

In the past ten years, we have moved in a hopeful direction. Time is the additional dimension we now must grapple with. And it is in terms of time that I make my sixth and final point—our solutions must be held within the context of the democratic rather than the totalitarian approach. This is perhaps the most important imperative of all. Solutions without adequate respect for private freedoms will ultimately solve nothing.

The challenge of matching national social goals with national economic wherewithal is not a recent American phenomenon. As a nation we have taken pride in our sense of idealism literally since our founding. Our forefathers came and settled this great land for reasons of spiritual and political freedom at least as frequently as they came for economic opportunity. In cherishing each, they achieved all.

For three hundred years, we have been engaged on this continent in the building of a good, fair, prosperous, and equitable society. We owe a moral debt to those who came before us and a moral obligation to those who will come after us to continue the work of building this society. This debt, this obligation cannot in any meaningful way be separated from our business enterprise.

Conversely, we cannot encumber, deplete, or leave unmaintained that economic system because to do so will deprive us and our children of the means to meet our finest expectations.

—A. W. Clausen

CHAPTER 3

Our Vanishing Golden Age?*

One of my most memorable experiences was a visit some time ago to Greece, where I had the opportunity to examine the remains of classical Greek civilization. Much of what I saw was the product of a relatively brief frenzy of activity around 450 B.C. when Pericles was in power. This was a golden age for Greece, remarkable in its time, but it has passed.

A number of analysts of our current civilization are saying that we have seen a golden age in the past thirty-odd years and that this, too, is vanishing. I want to examine the idea, what's behind it, and what it implies for the future.

THE GOLDEN GENERATION

A generation is roughly thirty years. Individuals born at least thirty years ago—about half of the population—have lived through a truly remarkable era. Let me review a few facts.

First off, there has been a substantial change in how much we earn. A family now has about twice the purchasing power—even after allowing for inflation—of a family at the end of World War II. A typical worker in 1947 had to work almost nine months to earn

*I am indebted to Lee Hoskins for help in preparing this article. The views expressed, however, are mine and do not necessarily reflect those of my colleagues in the Federal Reserve System.

42 David P. Eastburn

enough for a car; today, he can earn enough in less than five months. And because of these rising incomes, total real wealth per person has quadrupled.

Along with the growth in wealth, we have made progress against poverty and appear to have reduced disparities among the incomes of Americans. A rough measure of the degree of poverty is the number of families officially classified as poor. Government analysts calculate what they consider a family's minimum needs for housing, food, and medical care, then estimate the cost of this package, and finally adjust for inflation. Families earning less than this cost figure are classified as poor. In 1959, about one out of five Americans fell below the line. But by 1976, only one out of eight could be officially classified as poor. Moreover, progress against poverty is greater than these numbers indicate, for they do not take account of the impact of government in-kind transfers such as food stamps, rent supplements, and Medicaid.

In addition to reducing the number of poor people, the last three decades seem to have brought a trend toward more equality. This trend does not show up in money income figures, but when money income is adjusted for in-kind transfers and other items, there is a noticeable trend toward equality over the last three decades. One study indicates that the share of adjusted incomes for the poorest fifth of U.S. families increased from 7.8 percent in 1952 to 12.6 percent in 1972, while the top fifth decreased from 35.3 percent to 31.9 percent during the same period. Experts disagree over the adjustments made to money income, but an increasing number of them conclude that there has been a trend toward more equality.

The leap in health, education, and housing has been tremendous. We now can transplant organs as complicated as the heart, kidney, and parts of the eye. A shattered knee can be replaced with an artificial joint, and the threat of polio has been all but eliminated. A child born today can expect to live about 15 percent longer than his counterpart of thirty years ago, and his chances of surviving the ordeal of birth are about 50 percent greater.

We are better educated. The proportion of the population over twenty-five years old with four or more years of college has jumped by 50 percent, and the typical American now has better than twelve years of schooling compared to nine years three decades ago.

What we live in has also changed dramatically. Nearly half the population lived in dilapidated or substandard housing at the end of

World War II. Today, only 7 percent of the population lives in such a fashion. Two-thirds of us now own our homes; thirty years ago the majority rented. And our homes are filled with TV sets, air conditioners, and dishwashers that were rare or nonexistent a few decades back.

But perhaps the most striking and far-reaching developments have occurred in technology, science, and information. We have the computer. Today, business simply could not function without the computer. It has allowed us to analyze the burgeoning information flow with a speed and accuracy unimaginable a generation ago. It played a major role in putting men on the moon and is crucial in our satellite communications network. In short, it has greatly accelerated the spread and implementation of new technology.

We take jet travel, atomic and nuclear energy, television satellite communication, and space shots for granted, yet none of these was a part of the world thirty years ago. Moreover, the rate at which new technology is being implemented is estimated to be some 70–80 percent faster than it was prior to World War II.

So we have become healthier and wealthier, if not wiser, at an astounding rate during the past three decades. This explosion of technology and material well-being seems to outstrip by far that of any other period. Many students of progress do label it a golden age.

This is not to say that the past thirty years have been all sweetness and light. They have seen troubles aplenty—the Korean and Vietnam wars, race riots, generational conflicts, breakdown of our cities, energy problems, a recession, and frightening inflation. So, if it is true that we have been living through a golden age, it is gold with a good bit of tarnish. And, some say, it contains the seed of its own destruction; the golden age will be vanishing during the rest of the century.

They see two possible scenarios. The first we might call the Mother Hubbard scenario, and the second, the Gone Fishing scenario.

MOTHER HUBBARD

Will we go to the cupboard and find it bare? Certainly, we have been using up resources at a furious pace during the golden years. It would hardly have been possible to produce as much as we have, to have improved our material well-being so greatly, without using up vast quantities of resources. And it is true that we have been so preoccupied with our affluence that we have given little thought to the resource base. But will the cupboard really be bare? The answer is no. There will be problems, but these problems can be resolved by putting some old tools to new uses.

The "bare cupboard" view got under way a number of years ago when the Club of Rome decided to sponsor a study on growth. A team of MIT specialists was formed to study the problem. The team ran the whole world and its 3.5 billion people through a computer and found that they were multiplying at a rate which would bring about a collapse of civilization in a hundred years, if not sooner.

So great is the world's complexity that everything is related to everything else. Consequently, the study called for not just one set of equations and one run through the computer, but about a hundred runs. Various assumptions were fed into the computer in hopes of finding a brighter future, but invariably the printout was a disappointment. For example, what would happen if unrenewable resources were doubled as a result of new discoveries and new technologies? The answer: greater industrial output but only at the cost of intolerable levels of pollution. Or, feed the computer with "unlimited resources" and pollution held to a fourth of its present level, where do we come out? Answer: food per capita sinks to the subsistence level, the death rate rises, and population growth grinds to a full stop. The scenario left us freezing to death from lack of energy, starving because of world population growth, or choking on a highly polluted environment.

If the MIT team did its homework properly, a limit on exponential growth seemed inevitable. Either we impose it, or nature imposes it for us.

Shortly after the study was published, the United States began having difficulties in the energy area. Although a number of economists were highly critical of the MIT study, for many laymen it seemed the conclusions of the study were stunningly accurate. Other experts have calculated the amount of energy and other resources available on earth and have concluded that if we continue devouring resources at current rates, we will indeed face some shortages within the next one hundred years or so. An end to the golden age and a dismal future for mankind seemed to be in store.

Have we really eaten our seed corn? Looking at the problem from an economist's point of view, I again must answer no. Almost two hundred years ago, another futurist, the Reverend Thomas Malthus, painted an equally dismal portrait of mankind. Yet, here we are in a golden age. As a number of economists have pointed out, he made the same erroneous assumption that underpins the current view— that resources are fixed in quantity.

One of the important facts that Malthus missed was that resources make up an *expanding* pool that depends on technology and relative prices. The amount of minerals on earth is fixed, but many of these minerals have no value anyway until technology comes up with a use for them. Iron ore was not viewed as a resource until someone put a fire under it. Oil was so much black goo that impeded agriculture where it seeped to the surface, until man, through technology, found a use for it as a lubricant and fuel. A more modern-day example is uranium, a commodity of little value until the nuclear age. And now technology is exploring how to give us a resource that's entirely independent of our own planet's indigenous fuel stock—solar energy.

Closer to home are the minerals and organic materials that comprise roughly five-sevenths of the earth's surface but are relatively untapped. Hidden in and beneath the sea, for example, is a myriad of potential resources ranging from valuable minerals and oil to drugs and food protein. Many of these are incredibly abundant. About a fifth of the floor of the Pacific Ocean is covered by tons of potentially valuable resources including manganese nodules which contain enough aluminum to meet the world's demand for the next twenty thousand years and enough manganese to provide for the next four hundred years. In addition to these minerals which lie on the ocean floor, even greater amounts of resources—gold, diamonds, oil, and gas—are believed to rest beneath the seabed. Sea water itself and the life in it are both sources of large quantities of resources—food, pure water, chemicals, and drugs. Although estimates of the sea's abundance are incomplete, it is clear that the magnitude of potential resources sequestered in the sea is tremendous. To get at them we need technology and a rise in their value to justify the effort.

Our economy is capable of working out a solution to these resource problems as it has done in the past, if we let it. The

economy has built-in mechanisms to employ new technology efficiently and to expand our resource base. For example, as I write
this, Congress is in the throes of deciding how to deal with energy.
Advocates of a flexible price system say we have the solution built
into our economy. When there is more demand for something than
supply will support, its price will go up. This induces some to cut
back on their demand and stimulates others to increase supply. As
resources eventually begin to run out, prices not only will ration
what's left but will induce some producers to find alternative ways
of meeting the demand. In the case of oil, for example, rising prices
will induce car drivers to cut back on gasoline consumption and
encourage producers to sink new wells. As we begin to run out of oil,
rising prices will help conserve the remaining supply and encourage
the development of, say, solar energy.

This seems so simple that you ask why it doesn't happen. The
catch is that for the process to work, for this automatic carrot-and-
stick method to be effective, some people will seem to gain and
others seem to lose. In the case of oil, the oil companies may gain
windfall profits and the small farmer may have to pay much more to
run his tractor. So the problem of *inequity* raises its ugly head. The
average American has such strong feelings about fair play that it is
hard for him to let an impersonal market system work out a
solution. You may argue with him that it is all for his own good and
that if producers are not given some incentives to produce, there will
be nothing for him to consume. But I suspect a good many
Americans would rather line up at the gas pump than see oil
companies get windfall profits.

A second problem is that market prices do not always accurately
reflect the total costs of production and consumption to society.
Why? One reason is that many important costs of using resources
are not brought to bear on the individual who makes consumption
and production decisions. As a result, the *private cost* associated
with his use of resources differs from the *social cost*. It is this
difference that gives rise to the pollution problem and to an
inefficient use of resources.

The move to develop ocean resources illustrates this point on an
international scale. The ocean has been, and still is, everyone's
garbage dump. And one country's "national garbage"—nuclear
waste, mercury, and plain old sludge and sewage, for example—can

be another's poison. These pollutants may destroy marine life that is of economic value to another country or result in injury to people who come across them during mining operations. Dredging or deep-sea mining itself is a source of potential pollution. "Dust" from these operations could drift thousands of miles, clouding water and destroying marine life. Thus, the private cost of exploiting resources may not represent the true cost to all societies.

Although this problem now appears quite small because of the vastness of the sea and the limited scope of current ocean operations, it is likely to become increasingly troublesome as nations pick up the pace of their efforts to tap the sea's wealth.

All this poses a real dilemma for policy makers, but not an irreconcilable one. The price system can do a much better job than controls in dealing with resource problems. It should be allowed to work. Together with a free rein for development of new technology, it can stretch out existing resources, develop new substitutes, and direct them to the most productive uses. Some have argued that the price system may not give appropriate weight to conserving resources for use by all future generations. While I have some sympathy for this argument, I feel the price system offers the best solution, at least for the time period most of us can foresee or care about.

The equity problem requires taking a long view. At times some producers may have to be rewarded especially well when supplies are short and there is a need to expand them. Over a longer period, however, it should be easier, through government tax and subsidy programs, to prevent gross inequities from persisting.

Environmental problems also require help from the policy maker. Market prices of some resources may need to be modified to reflect the full cost (including pollution costs) of their use. In some instances, a tax on production of a resource may be in order. In other cases, such as with ocean resources, a clear definition of "rights" to their use is needed if they are to be exploited efficiently. In the late 1960s we began clearly specifying and enforcing rights to environmental resources. And, to date, significant progress has been achieved in cleaning up our rivers, lakes, and skies.

Obviously, these kinds of solutions are trade-offs. Completely controlled prices in the interests of equity and the environment can create havoc. Complete laissez-faire without regard to equity or the environment will not be accepted by the American public. Policy makers must steer a course in between.

I believe that this can be done with some degree of success. If it can, the Mother Hubbard scenario need not be in our future for a long time to come. I see no need for it to foreclose many more golden years.

GONE FISHING

Another alleged threat to the golden age is that the American economy could become so unproductive that its growth would stop or, at best, continue at a sluggish pace. Underpinning this view is the belief that, because the welfare state has so stifled incentives, signs reading "Gone Fishing" soon will grace corporate doors. It is true that during the past couple of decades government redistribution programs and the taxes that pay for them have grown. In addition, businessmen have been concerned with what they see as slipping profit margins and ever more regulation. Although these developments can impact worker and business incentives to produce, I do not think they have yet spurred sales of fishing tackle. But the threat is there and it bears careful watching.

The horrible example held before us is England, where, it is said, factories are inefficient, managers incompetent, and workers preoccupied with afternoon tea. The welfare state attempts to give everything to everybody from cradle to grave, but no one is interested in producing enough to make it all possible. Proponents of this view believe we are well on our way to becoming such a society.

They cite growth of the government sector as evidence of this trend. In 1950, combined federal, state, and local expenditures amounted to 21 percent of gross national product; by 1977 this figure had shot up to 33 percent. During the same period, the number of civilian employees of government more than doubled. Now one out of every six working Americans is employed by government. And the fastest growing area of all has been in social welfare expenditures, which jumped from $23 billion in 1950 to over $286 billion by the mid-1970s.

It is argued that this growth of government redistribution programs in particular has blunted incentives to work. The low-income population, it is said, has less incentive to work because of food stamp, rent supplement, health, unemployment, and welfare programs. These redistribution programs must be paid for with higher taxes, which can produce a disincentive for work among people with higher incomes.

Further compounding the problem, according to this view, is the surge in business regulation in recent years. Between 1970 and 1975, some thirty significant pieces of regulatory legislation were added at the federal level alone, bringing the number of pages in the Code of Federal Regulations to 72,200. This mass of regulation is said to have so tangled business in a web of paperwork and administrative delay that costs are climbing, innovation is stifled, capital formation is slowing, and employent opportunities are being reduced.

Costs associated with increased regulation are claimed to be enormous. One example is the Environmental Protection Agency's estimate of $32 billion to reduce noise to the 85-decibel standard in manufacturing plants. Another governmental agency pointed out that this recommendation comes out to over $19,000 per involved worker. Yet, earplugs or hearing protectors could achieve the same result at much less cost to industry and consumers. It is claimed that capital formation and, hence, economic growth are slowed by regulations that divert funds to environmental and safety expenditures, force "substandard" plants to close, delay construction of new facilities, and raise the minimum wage.

In sum, opponents of big government see productive efforts of both individuals and business being increasingly blunted by government efforts to redistribute income and regulate business decisions. The outcome in this scenario is economic growth grinding to a halt in the not-too-distant future.

How realistic is this outlook for America's future? Although I see a threat, I do not think the process has gone so far as to predetermine our economic fate. There are two aspects to this scenario: the impact on individual incentives and the impact on business investment.

Economists have long recognized two conflicting impacts on individual incentives. Suppose, for example, government increases tax rates. First, people may decide to work more to maintain their old standard of living (incentive effect). Second, they may see that a higher marginal tax on income means a smaller return for extra hours of work, and because the price of leisure has fallen, may choose to take more leisure and less work (disincentive effect). Economic theory cannot tell us which effect will dominate. Economists are continually doing empirical studies to find out what the facts really are. Results are still tentative, but there is evidence that work incentives *are* damaged by overambitious governmental regulation, taxes, and welfare programs. The incentive to work is weakened among individuals eligible for unemployment and welfare benefits as well as among high-income individuals facing steep marginal tax rates.

. Yet we have long had in the United States an attitude toward work that we label the work ethic. This attitude is credited with many of the advances in well-being that we enjoy. We want more things and are willing to work for them; we work hard and so produce more. Despite the disincentive effects that I have cited, on balance, I'm inclined to believe that the work ethic is still strong.

Evidence is hard to come by, but there is some. For example, over the past thirty years we have experienced substantial growth in our work force, and with the exception of the retail trade sector, the average number of hours worked per week is about the same as it was thirty years ago. The percentage of the working-age population employed right now is higher than at any other time since World War II—around 58 percent. Partly responsible for this figure is the entrance over the last few decades of a major new group to the work force—women. In 1947, women accounted for about 28 percent of employment. Today they account for over 40 percent. Further evidence of the American work ethic is the action to move the mandatory retirement age back to seventy or to eliminate it entirely. This movement is occurring here while in many other industrialized countries the mandatory retirement age is being lowered.

The work ethic gives grounds for optimism. There is, of course, much dissatisfaction in Middle America with tax burdens ratcheted upward by inflation and made necessary by governmental welfare programs. And there is always a possibility that this trend could bring a breakdown of the tax system. The IRS sees some $9–10 billion of income going unreported. According to some, there is a growing underground economy where transactions are conducted in cash and no written records of income are kept. One estimate places these transactions at $195 billion or about 10 percent of 1977 GNP.

How can we maintain the trend toward more income equality without all being driven off to the fishing hole? One step in the right direction is to achieve more efficiency in our redistribution programs. Milton Friedman has popularized the notion of a negative income tax as an alternative to existing redistribution programs. The idea is to eliminate all government agencies engaged in such programs and replace them with direct cash payments to individuals who fall below a particular income level. Some have argued that the savings in administrative costs (government employee salaries) would permit greater income equality without increasing tax burdens. The poor would be able to spend the cash supplements on items they need. In addition, thousands of government employees would be added to the private-sector work force. I am not fully convinced that this particular reform is workable, but it does show the kind of imagination the situation calls for.

In short, I believe, we can achieve our old goals of more income equality and economic growth by rethinking some of our current policies. Implementing policy changes of such magnitude is not easy or costless, but the possible alternative of a stagnating economy, worker apathy, and taxpayer revolt can be a much more costly outcome for all.

A second and perhaps larger threat to continued economic prosperity comes from disincentives to business investment. A key ingredient in economic progress is continued capital formation. For progress we need not only to replace worn-out plant and equipment but also to continue adding new productive capacity. Yet there is a fear that high rates of inflation, increased uncertainty, and the growing regulatory morass may be slowing the rate of capital formation.

What prompts businessmen to invest in capital projects is the expectation of making profits. Reported profits have shown tremendous growth over the last few years, but they are distorted by inflation. Costs of inventory and capital depletion occurring in the production process are usually accounted for on a historical rather than a replacement-cost basis. Thus, during an inflationary period, the cost of producing is understated and profit is overstated. This means a smaller *real* rate of return on investment than current profit figures indicate. The lower the rate of return, the less incentive there is to invest.

In addition to inflation, several shocks to the economy during the

1970s seem to have increased uncertainty about investment prospects. For example, the imposition of price controls in the early 1970s and the quintupling of international oil prices are shocks that depressed profits and increased uncertainty about what the future would bring. Added uncertainty means added risk that requires a higher-than-normal rate of return. If the prospects for such returns are poor, then investment decisions are postponed, or short-lived assets, with quicker recovery periods, are selected. With enough uncertainty, even businessmen whose job it is to take calculated investment risks will sit on the fence.

Although the 1970s produced bouts of inflation, unhappiness with corporate profits, and waves of uncertainty, several recent studies indicate that things are not really that bad in the board room. One study finds that once the rate of return on corporate capital is adjusted for business cycle disturbances, there is little reason for believing that the rate of return on corporate capital is in a long-term slide. And if adjustments are made for the fact that corporations will be repaying their debt with cheaper dollars because of inflation, then the after-tax return on equity capital during the 1970s is running at about the same rate as it did in the 1950s. Supporting this point is the fact that the ratio of capital formation to GNP in 1977 is about what it was in 1960.

Nevertheless, I have an uneasy feeling about the investment environment. The uncertainties about inflation, energy prices, and resource availability are much greater than they were in the 1950s. Thus, a rate of return compatible with the 1950s may be insufficient to spur investment in the 1980s. If this is true, then policy makers need either to reduce uncertainty or to adjust corporate taxes to produce an adequate return on investment.

Clearly, equity is an important element of any policy decision aimed at affecting profits. If profits are taxed too heavily, then investment will slow and so will our ability to produce goods for future consumption. Yet if profits and investment are substantially boosted through government actions, we may end up with a greater flow of goods and services in the future and a reduced flow in the present. There is no easy answer as to how much we should forgo now so as to have more in the future. My own feeling is that while we may have struck an appropriate balance in the past, there is a pitfall ahead that could swing the balance toward too little productive investment.

I see a potential threat to business investment from the rapid growth in government regulation of business. A recent study found that pollution and safety regulation have cut deeply into productivity growth during the 1970s. By 1975 these measures reduced the average growth rate in productivity by roughly 20 percent.

I am not suggesting that we do away with regulation per se. A cleaner environment and less hazardous working conditions are benefits to all of us. The question that needs to be asked is this: how much are we willing to pay in terms of fewer goods and services, higher prices, and slower growth to obtain these benefits? In short, what is called for is a cost-benefit analysis of existing regulations. Those that can't pass the test of benefits exceeding costs should be phased out.

Although I see the rise in regulation as a potential threat to capital formation and economic growth, I remain hopeful. The cost of regulation has not gone unnoticed. "Deregulation" seems to be a word gaining political currency in Washington. For example, airline regulations are being reduced, and the Commerce Department is beginning work on a "regulatory budget" whose purpose is to show the impact of federal regulation on private-sector expenditure. These are healthy signs, for they are indicative of a growing awareness that economic growth can be smothered by too much regulation.

CONCLUSIONS

So I am optimistic. Intelligent action by those in responsible positions in the private and public sectors can continue whatever goldenness we may have enjoyed in the last thirty years. That is to say, economic growth can continue to be rapid, technological advances can proceed apace, resulting enhancement of material well-being can flow to society.

This is *not* to say that life will be just the same. We will be increasingly conscious of the Mother Hubbard problem. We can no longer be so profligate in our use of resources or abuse of the environment. And I suspect we will be well enough impressed with the Gone Fishing scenario to go fishing more often. Studies suggest that there is not always a clear relationship between happiness and affluence. I believe the American people will continue to seek more material things, but increasingly they will be seeking happiness itself and whatever else in addition to material things may be needed to produce happiness—leisure, contemplation, or escape from the rat race. Over a century ago a great economist, John Stuart Mill, envisioned a time when we could turn our minds to "improving the Art of Living" rather than being "engrossed by the art of getting on." In this sense, we can look forward to a truly golden age.

—DAVID P. EASTBURN

---◦◦◦◦---

CHAPTER 4

Democracy and
Persistent Inflation

I welcome the opportunity to contribute a chapter on the subject of inflation and to be able to express my views on the significance of the effects of inflation on democracy and on democratic government under which we have the privilege to live in the United States today.

My prime motive in being concerned with inflation is that I am convinced of the profoundly adverse effects it has on all aspects of modern society; and, clearly, the political process is one of its most important aspects. I believe that inflation, if it is allowed to persist, erodes the political process and undermines the foundations of democracy. If the process lasts long enough, it will destroy democracy.

INFLATION AS A THREAT TO DEMOCRACY

In the following pages I shall explain the reasons for my concern about the effects of inflation on the political process and the economic future of the United States within a worldwide political and economic context. Before doing this, however, I would like to point out that I am not expressing a new view of mine. I have written before on this subject[1] and, while I learned a great deal from

1. Irving S. Friedman, *Inflation, a World-Wide Disaster* (Houghton Mifflin, 1973; available in various translations), and Irving S. Friedman, *Recovery and Growth Without Inflation,* an address delivered before the International Monetary Conference, San Francisco, California, on June 17, 1976 (published by Citibank, N.A., New York, 1976).

my fellow economists and from economic history, my own views on inflation are mostly derived from experience with countries all over the world which I gained during my career with the International Monetary Fund and the World Bank, and now in private international finance.

Among the most dramatic experiences was the way in which inflation undermined the national government of China. In that country inflation began before the World War II years, accelerated steadily as the war progressed, and became explosive by 1948. Another very dramatic experience was the way in which inflation brought the Brazilian government to a state of great inefficiency, if not collapse, in the early 1960s. Another example presents itself in Indonesia, where inflation completely demolished the political process under the country's first president, Sukarno (leaving aside here whether one agrees with his politics or not). Explosive inflation eventually led to President Sukarno's government being replaced by a military government (which in its own way has proven to be efficient). In the interval, however, between presidents Sukarno (then) and Suharto (now), the country suffered under a highly destructive civil war.

There are many other illustrations of how in the post-World War II period the political process of countries was severely affected by rapid inflation, and these examples are not restricted to the developing world. When one thinks of inflation in industrial countries, the experience of Germany with hyperinflation in the early 1920s comes to mind immediately. Inflation then actually wiped out the German middle class with ultimately disastrous political consequences. In post-World War II years, inflation in several industrial countries contributed much to the instability of governments and to grave social disturbances. One such instance is France, where repeated republican governments proved unable to achieve stability as they failed to cope with strong inflationary pressures. The French governments of the 1950s simply could not control inflation, a development which contributed to the downfall of the Fourth Republic.

In the United Kingdom, the destabilizing impact of inflation on the political process was demonstrated in the 1960s. In those years, the Conservative and Labour party governments successively became unpopular with the electorate and lost the next general election. In the United States today, public opinion polls list inflation as the number-one concern of the American public. It has been cited by the Gallup Poll as the main reason for the low public esteem of President Carter.

The significant characteristics of the post-World War II inflation are—whether we look at the industrial world or at developing countries—that inflation is not any longer a national problem but has become *global,* and that it is not anymore temporary in duration but *persistent.*

Peoples of most countries used to believe that inflation was a temporary phenomenon. This belief was based on one hundred years of experience during which inflation had largely resulted from specific historic events. Inflationary price movements were caused either by wars—the Napoleonic wars in Europe, the American Revolution and the Civil War in the United States—or by a sudden increase in the world supply of gold and silver following the discovery of the New World in the sixteenth century and the gold strikes in California, Alaska, Canada, and South Africa in the nineteenth century. However, once these specific events had passed and their effects had been absorbed, prices tended to move back again to earlier lower levels. This experience led people to expect that the general normal situation was one in which the average level of prices moved up and down, usually relative to the expansion and contraction phases of the business cycle. Secularly, prices tended to decline, reflecting the long-run trend in the increase in efficiency of modern production.

Even the dramatic experience gained in some European countries (Germany, Austria, Hungary) in the early 1920s following World War I did not give people the impression that inflation could become a generalized long-range problem throughout the world. Inflation that persists through a slow continuous process lasting years and undermines steadily established societies and institutions is novel with no historical precedent in recent centuries, if ever. In my opinion, governments and people—the general public and experts alike—in the 1950s and 1960s were not prepared intellectually to assess the inflation which had begun during World War II and never ended, and were therefore not sufficiently concerned with the new phenomenon of *persistent global* inflation. They did not pay adequate attention to it and the world is paying a heavy price for their errors.

THE NEW PHENOMENON OF PERSISTENT INFLATION

I use the term "persistent inflation" to describe a process with two major aspects. The first is a *rise in the general price level*—either in the national economy or worldwide—*which occurs continuously, over a long period of time,* and over successive business cycles. People become convinced at some point in time that cyclical downturns in business activity will not bring the phenomenon of rising prices to an end. The second aspect of this process is that the *structure of prices* increasingly *reflects these expectations of an indefinitely continuing general rise* in prices, and no longer can be understood as the result of changes in the real economy. As a consequence, changes in the general level of prices or in the structure of prices can no longer be predicted from historical experience. Policy prescriptions used in the past for dealing with temporary inflation do not operate as expected.

Persistent inflation produces drastic changes in personal values and in society. Although this is essentially a slow degenerative process which can extend over one or even more generations, it threatens ultimately, if not stopped, to result in the destruction of the foundations of human society as we know them today. As the process goes on, the changes in the attitudes of people are as much the effect as the cause of persistent inflation, and these effects become a major factor in their economic, social, and political behavior.

The phenomenon of transition from temporary inflation, and the assumption by the public that inflationary price increases are only temporary, to persistent inflation, and to people's expectations that inflationary price trends will persist, is essentially simple: at some point those who had assumed that inflation would be temporary find that they have been wrong, while those who expected inflation to endure have been right. Expectations of persistent inflation become an independent force in perpetuating inflation. In other words, inflation is feeding on people's expectation of continued inflation and the very defense mechanisms people create against past forms of inflation contribute to an acceleration of the process, because they do not deal with the special nature of modern inflation.

At first, the effects of persistent inflation are hidden as a silent deterioration takes place which might be compared to the steady process of soil erosion, but gradually the effects become more visible and dramatic. This process of erosion of society and of its institutions is, if left to itself, irreversible because there does not exist an automatic or self-correcting force or mechanism to stop or reverse it, unless worldwide massive unemployment or exploding inflation and paralyzed societies are regarded as correcting mechanisms.

Governments trying to cope with the problem of continuously rising prices, wages, and other costs have achieved only temporary successes, at best. In general, the record has been one of repeated failures as rising prices and inflation continued and most governments proved themselves incapable of bringing persistent inflation, including expectations of its continuation, to an end.

Many policy measures taken by governments have proven to be inadequate because inflation was considered to be the phenomenon described in textbooks—a national and temporary problem—when it was not. Inflation was seen as caused only by temporary factors like the impact of excessive credit creation, artificially low interest rates, large budgetary deficits, bottlenecks resulting from over-full employment and overutilization of plant and equipment, wage increases, changes in exchange rates, increases in oil prices, etc. Policy measures were designed on the basis of a fallacious understanding of continuing inflation.

Whether they called them monetary, fiscal, Keynesian, classical, controlled, or interventionist and so forth, all governments failed to see that the success of their policy prescriptions was based on the false premise that people regarded the inflation as temporary, and that changes in credit conditions, taxation, public expenditures, public enterprise pricing, etc., could halt it. The low positive rates of inflation in the industrial and many developing countries were only hiding the fact that inflation was a serious problem. Instead of continuing to rise, prices should have been declining during cyclical downturns and should have secularly been trending downward. False comfort was taken in the relatively low rates of price increases. The significance of *persistency* was overlooked.

The novel character of modern inflation is evidenced by the

Irving S. Friedman

experience that policy variables which might be appropriate and successful under conditions of temporary inflation do *not* work under conditions of persistent inflation.[2]

Among the tools considered the most effective in dealing with inflationary price increases is *monetary* policy. Monetary policy, used at the right time and to the appropriate extent, can prove effective provided it is exercised in a "healthy" economy. Under conditions of persistent inflation a tightening in money supply can be at least partially offset by an increase in the velocity of money; an increase in interest rates can be taken as a sign that inflation is getting worse; instead of reducing demand it can lead to increased debt assumption and credit buying by the public in anticipation of even higher interest rates. The purpose of monetary policy, e.g. to achieve an increase in the *real* rate of interest, can therefore be defeated by people's expectations of continuing inflation.

Fiscal policy can also become less effective or even counterproductive. Any increase in taxes, with the purpose of reducing the after-tax income of individuals and corporations and thus reducing demand, can under conditions of persistent inflation be interpreted by the public as a sign that inflation is worsening, or otherwise the government would not increase taxes. People do not expect that the government can bring inflation to an end. Therefore, they may well choose to offset the expected depressing effect on demand from increased taxes by borrowing or use of savings. Postponed consumption or investment has too often proven very costly. Similarly, any lowering of taxes can increase consumption by much more than intended by the policy makers if such action is taken as a sign of future acceleration of inflation.

Unemployment/inflation trade-off policies are limited in their application because of the growing insistence of organized labor upon defending the purchasing power of current and *future* incomes as well as future jobs. Labor endeavors to strengthen its defensive mechanisms. The greater inflexibility of labor, in turn, results in

2. In the 1950s and early 1960s, so-called creeping inflation was found acceptable by many economic policy makers and economic theoreticians as a tool to ease the structural transformation of the economy. The acceptance of creeping inflation was based on the assumption that inflation could be stopped at any time by adopting a slower rate of structural transformation. Inflation was by some considered as useful, by many as terminable with the same policies and instruments which had been used to control temporary inflation.

lower productivity and higher per-unit labor costs. A higher unemployment rate, on the other hand, leads to larger transfer payments to the unemployed and to further growth in welfare and "unearned" incomes.

Depreciation of the currency will, under conditions of temporary inflation, make imports more expensive and exports more competitive. A country's current account position can thus be improved. If, however, the public expects inflation to persist, and even to accelerate, a depreciation of the currency's foreign exchange rate can have a contrary effect on the economy. Capital flight may increase and the public continue to hoard imported and domestic goods (flight into material values). Thus domestic demand may be augmented instead of being curtailed. The increase in prices of imported goods should have only a partial effect in raising prices because such goods usually account for only a small fraction of total goods consumed in an economy. Instead, the increase in import prices may well spread quickly to all domestic prices. Wage demands are made in order to offset the rise in the general price level rather than the limited impact of the rise in import prices alone.

In the extreme case of the *imposition of controls on prices and wages,* persistent inflation, and the expectation of persistent inflation, will prevent controls from doing any more than suppressing inflationary pressures temporarily. Once controls are removed, the wage and price spiral will reappear with renewed force. Rumors of controls create anticipatory price and wage increases. Successful use of price and wage controls during World War II reflected the assumption made by all that the suppressed inflation was a form of temporary inflation to be followed by a period of normal noninflationary conditions after the immediate impact of the lifting of controls had been absorbed. Money owned during the war could be used after the war with only a small loss of purchasing power, if any.

Considering the failure of governments to diagnose the problem correctly, it is not surprising that of the various policy prescriptions tried all proved inadequate to end inflation.[3] In various countries,

3. Governments (and people) react to their frustrations by redefining inflation or putting consoling adjectives in front of the word. Six percent inflation becomes "not inflation" or "tolerable" inflation, even though it means a decline in purchasing power of more than one-third in five years and two-thirds in ten years—the life span of many a decision to buy or not buy a consumer durable, or make an investment in plant or equipment.

governments even tried to maintain themselves in power and to remain popular with the electorate by continuing to pursue policies which, although strengthening inflationary trends, were politically and socially acceptable to, or even demanded by, their people. For years in some countries, and among some groups, and today more strongly than ever, such policies have contributed to the widespread conviction that inflation is inevitable and that governments cannot and, in the opinion of some people, even should not bring rising price trends to an end. It is implied that instead people should try to protect themselves against the effects of persistent inflation and if possible to profit from them.

Questions should be raised immediately in this context: What are the causes of this worldwide and persistent inflation? Why have governments repeatedly failed in their efforts to halt persistent inflation? What are the consequences for, and the effects on, society and democratic institutions if persistent inflation is allowed to continue into the foreseeable future?

Before attempting to answer these questions, a brief look at the history of inflation in the United States is in order.

HISTORY OF PRICE INFLATION IN THE UNITED STATES

In the nineteenth century, the general course of prices in the United States was downward and the value of money was probably higher in 1900 than one hundred years earlier. Chart I shows that external shocks, caused by the War of 1812, the Civil War, and both World Wars, resulted in sudden and very steep increases in the consumer price level. In the decades following the conclusion of the wars—with the exception of World War II—prices, however, trended sharply downward and declined secularly, reflecting the improvement in productivity in the United States economy.

After the end of World War II, however, prices continued to rise steadily despite cyclical fluctuations. At first, and until the late 1960s, prices increased slowly but steadily at a faster rate than at any other comparable period in history. Since the late 1960s, the rate of increase has sharply accelerated. By 1968, the general public and business enterprises had become convinced that they had to assume that prices would continue to rise in the future irrespective

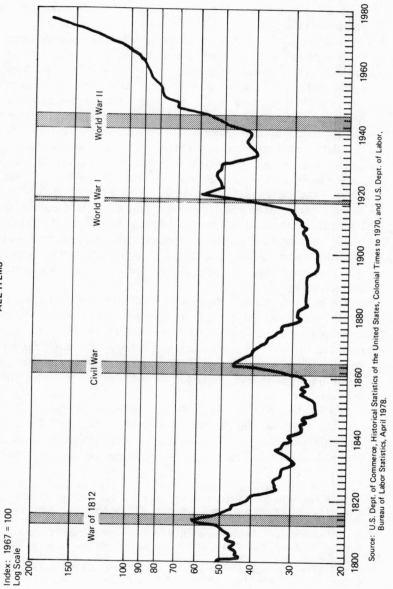

Chart I
UNITED STATES: CONSUMER PRICE INDEX (BLS), 1800-1977
ALL ITEMS

Index: 1967 = 100
Log Scale

Source: U.S. Dept. of Commerce, Historical Statistics of the United States, Colonial Times to 1970, and U.S. Dept. of Labor, Bureau of Labor Statistics, April 1978.

of cyclical conditions and economic and monetary policies. The United States had moved into an unprecedented and unknown era of persistent inflation.

Around the secular downtrend of prices in the nineteenth century there occurred, of course, up- and downswings in price movements reflecting the expansion and contraction phases of various business cycles and special causes.[4] Among the causes of upswings in prices were the sharp increase in the gold and silver supply in the United States in the 1840s and 1850s and the technology-related boom in economic activity that took place at the turn of the century. During the short-run expansions and contractions of economic activity in the nineteenth and early twentieth centuries, prices, output, and employment in the United States tended to rise and fall together. In the contraction phase of the cycle, prices in most sectors of the economy declined in absolute terms. This experience deeply conditioned thinking about inflation and does so to this day. Inflation was nearly universally regarded a temporary phenomenon caused by cyclical or special causes. Decades of experience would be needed with modern persistent inflation to see its novel character and extraordinary societal effects.

The business cycles of the post-World War II period in the United States with their declines in output and employment were not accompanied by an absolute decline in prices.[5] In the six recessions[6] recorded by the National Bureau of Economic Research during the past thirty years, the decline in output was usually accompanied by a slowing in the rate of price increases but not by an interruption in the rising price trend itself.

During the past two recessions—the milder recession of 1969–70 and the most serious postwar recession of 1973–75—both gross domestic product (in constant prices) and industrial production declined in absolute terms yet prices continued to rise. Chart II

4. The National Bureau of Economic Research (NBER) recorded for the United States eleven cyclical peaks and troughs in the period June 1857 to December 1900, and eight cyclical peaks and troughs between 1902 and the Great Depression of the 1930s.

5. The Bureau of Labor Statistics (BLS) consumer price index (CPI) shows that consumer prices declined by less than 1 percent in 1949 and by less than one-half of 1 percent in 1955.

6. The seventh contraction period, which occurred in 1966–67, was not officially designated a "recession" by the National Bureau of Economic Research.

Chart II

UNITED STATES: CONSUMER PRICES AND BUSINESS CYCLE INDICATORS

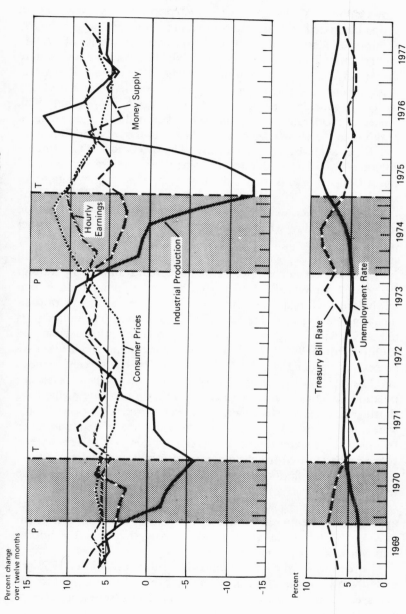

P, T = Turning points of the business cycle, (Peak and Trough).

Source: U.S. Dept. of Labor, Bureau of Labor Statistics (BLS), and U.S. Dept. of Commerce, Bureau of Economic Analysis (BEA).

shows the rate of change in consumer prices over a twelve-month period compared with the rates of change in money supply, hourly earnings, and industrial production from the first quarter of 1969 to the last quarter of 1977. Industrial production declined much more sharply in the 1973–75 than in the 1969–70 recession. The movement in consumer prices lagged the movement in industrial output by several quarters. The rate of inflation began to slow in mid-1970, started to accelerate again in the second half of 1972, and reached a peak in the fourth quarter of 1974. At no time were noninflationary conditions achieved and at no time did expectations of continuing inflation in the foreseeable future come to an end. On the contrary, since 1976, it seems that inflationary pressures have again increased.

The acceleration of the inflation rate since World War II is even more clearly shown when subdividing the period into three distinct time spans. In the period from 1954 to 1968, i.e. the period after the shock effect of the Korean War on the domestic price level had subsided, the consumer price index increased at an average rate of 1.7 percent per year. Persistent inflation was beginning to take root, but before 1968 many, still impressed by the relatively low rates of inflation, held on to the inherited conviction that inflation is temporary and would be followed by periods of price decline and stability. From 1969 to 1972, the rate of increase in the CPI was 4.7 percent, and from 1973 to 1977 averaged almost 8 percent. A peak of 11 percent was reached in 1974, mostly the result of persistent inflation though to some extent the aftermath of a worldwide food shortage and the fourfold increase in world crude oil prices. People were now convinced of the indefinite existence of inflation, even though policy makers did not act as though they recognized that the economy had moved from temporary to persistent inflation.

After 1968 inflation began to accelerate in almost all of the industrial countries and throughout the world generally, as everywhere people consciously or unconsciously moved from attitudes appropriate to temporary inflation to attitudes reflecting persistent inflation. Rates of inflation varied greatly, but in all countries inflation was now persistent.

The reasons for the acceleration of world inflation after 1968 are undoubtedly complex. The acceleration cannot be attributed to any one specific cause but was the consequence of a series of developments which followed each other over time or occurred simultaneously.

Chart III compares the increase in consumer prices since 1954, worldwide and in the United States. In the period from 1954 to 1968, the increase in consumer prices averaged 3.8 percent worldwide and 1.7 percent in the United States. After 1968, the average rate of increase accelerated to 10 percent worldwide and 6.7 percent in the United States.

In 1977 the inflation rates in almost all industrial countries were lower than the peaks reached during the last cyclical upswing. Expectations of continued inflation have, however, not been eliminated or even weakened. Conversely, current inflation rates are generally higher than the low points during previous downswings, thus indicating the long-term acceleration.

Government initiatives in the past have included "jawboning" and imposing price and wage controls (or at least issuing guidelines). These approaches did not prove successful; they all implicitly assumed that expectations of persistent inflation could be ended by treating inflation as a temporary phenomenon. Most anti-inflationary policies were based on the simplistic notion that the only effective way to control inflation was to restrain growth and maintain relatively high rates of unemployment.

The easing of inflation rates in 1975 and 1976 was achieved after the United States and a majority of the industrial nations *simultaneously* gave top priority to inflation fighting, based on the theory of the unemployment/inflation tradeoff. Their determination was attested to by rising levels of unemployment and sharply curtailed domestic production. Widespread concern that recession might deepen into a global depression, like that of the 1930s, however, prevented the governments of industrial nations and their peoples from accepting prolonged and severe unemployment as the way to end inflation.

CAUSES OF PERSISTENT INFLATION

A successful attack on persistent inflation must begin with the recognition that it is not a special case of temporary inflation but a different disease—both produce a fever for societies, but, just as in

Irving S. Friedman

Chart III
CONSUMER PRICE INDEX: WORLD AND UNITED STATES

Index: 1954 = 100
Log Scale

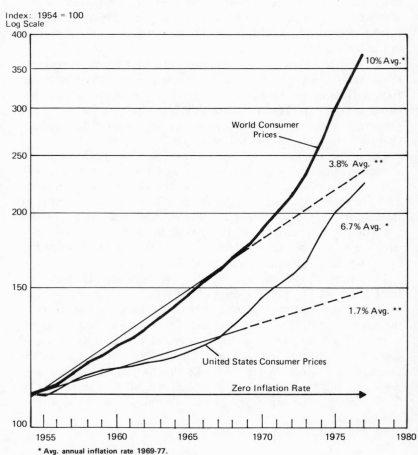

* Avg. annual inflation rate 1969-77.
** Avg. annual inflation rate 1954-68.
World excluding centrally planned economies.
Source: International Monetary Fund and U.S. Dept. of Labor, Bureau of Labor Statistics, April 1978.

medicine, not all fevers are symptoms of the same illness or indicators of the gravity of illness. I believe the problem of inflation not to be a technical problem that affects only prices, nor to be merely a question of proper or improper monetary management.[7] It is rather a phenomenon created by a myriad of specific events in a dynamic process of social and political change with all-pervasive consequences. I have accordingly developed what I have called a "societal" approach to inflation.

The societal approach was extensively discussed in my book on inflation, published in 1973.[8] In the Introduction I emphasized the societal causes and effects:

> ... the twentieth century was intellectually ill-prepared—
> and still is—to understand the modern phenomenon of persis-
> tent inflation, its world-wide scope and its societal causes and
> societal effects. It does not probe its causes to get much
> beyond an understanding of the relation between money and
> prices. Yet the persistent world-wide inflation that now exists
> is stronger and more pervasive. ... It is transmitted from
> country to country as depression was in the 1930s. If inflation
> were temporary, its causes and effects would be easily ex-
> plained in terms of money and prices. Its control would be
> relatively simple. But the persistence of inflation makes it
> necessary to look deeper for causes and effects. Unless these
> are understood, we will not understand why persistent infla-
> tion is a destroyer of modern societies and we cannot know
> how to begin to deal with this problem effectively. ... The
> investigation of the social and political as well as economic
> effects of persistent inflation entails our entering into unex-

7. Theoretical explanations of inflation emphasizing one cause to the exclusion of others are not satisfactory. It is more appropriate to use a multivariable approach to explain the process of persistent inflation. I do accept the monetary explanation of inflation to the extent that, based on observable facts, a sustained rise in the price level has always been accompanied by a parallel sustained rise in the quantity of money. However, in my view, the question really is what are the elements in political and social conditions which lead to the rise in aggregate monetary demand and to a sustained increase in the price level. The purpose of inflation analysis, the way I see it, is to determine the forces which bear on prices and on monetary behavior and policies. Similar comments apply to other approaches to inflation.

8. Irving S. Friedman, *Inflation, A World-Wide Disaster* (Houghton Mifflin, 1973), pp. 6–7.

plored territories. . . . to tackle persistent inflation in the same way as temporary inflation is not only to invite failure, but to make the problem much worse and more difficult to solve.

In the same Introduction I also presented the reasons why I consider inflation to be a societal problem.

> . . . . the problem is societal, not in the narrow sense that all people are affected and involved; in this sense the discovery of a new medicine or the invention of a new camera is societal. The approach is societal because the causes of persistent inflation are just as much social and political as economic; so are its effects. Solutions, therefore, have to deal with these social causes and aim to eliminate the unwanted societal effects. It means that it is a subject not only for economists, or even only for all social scientists; it involves all who participate in the political process.

My own experience with countries all over the world led me to the conviction that I had to look for the causes of persistent inflation in the social and political systems of modern societies; each society, and each country, differs from the other, but nevertheless all societies have certain general aspects which are common to virtually all of them.[9] The most important societal cause of inflation today is secular worldwide scarcity created by rapidly increasing secular demand everywhere exceeding our global capacity to produce and deliver goods and services.

What is meant by "scarcity" and how is it brought about? One decisive factor has been the acceptance by all societies of the desirability of a material well-being and a better life for all people in the industrial nations, whether in the United States, Western Europe, or other industrial nations, and in the low-income developing countries. High levels of unemployment and persistent economic stagnation are considered socially intolerable and politically unjustifiable in modern societies. Instead, peoples of the industrial coun-

---

9. It was pointed out above that "the investigation of persistent inflation entails our entering into unexplored territories." I am fully aware of the fact that I am venturing here beyond the narrower field of economics into the much wider field of social and political behavior. I would like, therefore, to apologize to my fellow behavioral scientists for the shortcomings with which I approach the subject.

tries are taught by society to expect a steady improvement in their real incomes irrespective of gains in employment, output, and productivity.

People demand that their governments achieve these objectives which society has taught them should and can be achieved. Governments have accepted this unachievable responsibility. To say that it cannot be done is to court a "thumbs-down" verdict in modern societies. People are often blamed for not understanding the implications of their demands. Politicians are blamed for responding. Blame is useless and destructive. History explains how it happens. The need is to explain what can be achieved and what cannot and how, by trying to achieve the unachievable, we are gambling the loss of what we hold most dearly.

Rapid improvement in worldwide communications technology has acquainted all peoples of the developing world with living standards, including consumer goods and comforts, so far available to only a few nations. The population explosion in the developing world, probably the single most potent force in the world economy, makes these demands for a higher standard of living even more pressing and unachievable.

Thus, among the key causes of inflation in modern society is the fact that we live in a period of history in which society has culturally created a demand for goods and services beyond the capacity of society to produce. Excess demand or "scarcity" is not absolute and unchanging even within one country. It tends to be whatever society defines it to be.

The constraint on people's income was once considered to be the great regulator of demand and supply. Effective demand was essentially based on earned income and, therefore, had to be the counterpart to the production of goods and services. The conviction seems to have spread around the world that, with the help of government, all people—not just a relatively few—can achieve a level of consumption that is higher than their own earned income, or savings from prior income, or inherited wealth would permit. It has become taken for granted that governments have the ability to provide the financial means for additional consumption, as though money by itself added to the real resources of society. It might be provided indirectly through the subsidization of certain kinds of services (free health services, education, recreational facilities, lower utility rates, etc.), or it might be given in the form of direct income payments to individuals (transfer payments consisting of pensions, student stipends, and various types of allowances). In the same view, government expenditures are not seen as alternatives to private expenditures but as optional additions. The naive view is often held that because governments can create the money to finance their expenditures, these expenditures are not costly to the private citizen. Only overt taxes are recognized as being at private expense.

I have been talking about the "societal" causes of inflation because I am convinced the basic problem is that modern society has defined what our consumption standards "should" be, both in terms of private and of public goods. The societal definition of consumption is not related to the supply capabilities of the individual countries, or of the world. There is no automatic linking between consumption and supply capabilities because consumption in modern societies is a culturally or politically induced factor.

Over the past three decades, and all over the world, the societal desires and expectations of peoples have been pyramiding into a highly unstable structure. The instability of the structure is evidenced by persistent inflation.

EFFECTS OF PERSISTENT INFLATION

When studying the causes of persistent inflation I finally came to the conclusion that its effects are far-reaching and devastating to society. If I may quote again from the Introduction to my book on inflation,[10] where I summarized my views as follows:

> ... the effects of persistent inflation are devastating for all kinds of societies. None is immune. To accept the persistent rising trends as inevitable is to accept the inevitability of the devastating effects—devastating because they attack and erode the fundamentals on which any organized society rests, irrespective of political and social ideology and structures. Persistent inflation is a universal solvent of organized societies.
> ... If the problems continue to be underestimated either in the strength of their roots or the harm of their effects, or in the

10. *Inflation, A World-Wide Disaster*, pp. 7–8.

difficulties in achieving successful cures, we will have to live with the costly consequences. For we cannot expect effective political action—which will have to be different in each of the countries—to be taken unless the depth and scope of the problem are much more fully understood and the feasible political alternatives explored and debated, and critical choices made.

In a society which becomes disorganized through inflation institutions will function with less and less efficiency. In the United States, we have inherited a very strong set of institutions, but as inflation persists, society is losing confidence in these institutions and in their leadership. The very objectives and ideals of American democracy are already being questioned; next will come questions as to the ability of democracy to function.

Although in the United States we are not at the stage of *exploding* inflation, we are beginning to experience the effects of persistent inflation in every aspect of our lives. The agreed national objectives of U.S. society—satisfactory levels of growth in output and employment, and an equitable distribution of income—are brought into question. As costs continue to rise, people begin to question the necessity of institutions and practices which represent the highest accomplishments of modern civilization. I am thinking here, for example, of universal education, which President James Madison considered the "foundation of democracy," and which is one of the great achievements of society. Yet, rising costs of maintaining a good educational system have brought people to question the necessity of universal education, at least at the college level.

Universal good health and long life are other examples of the achievements of our civilization. Health services, and services for the aged, are deteriorating with rising costs as people find themselves unwilling to pay for institutions which they themselves regard as desirable. Other institutions fundamental to society, like the family and religious, philanthropic, or charitable entities, suffer from rising costs and the lack of funds because their endowments have shrunk in purchasing power and currently people are contributing less.

Inflation threatens American democracy because it destroys the institutions which are basic to democracy, such as people's belief in the equity of the political and social system, in family responsibility and education, equality of opportunity and social mobility, in the future of their society and their culture. People come to doubt that the values of their society can be maintained into the future, and question the permanence of institutions. They are worried about the educational opportunities for their children, about their financial circumstances in old age, the increase in violence and crime, the deterioration of cities which will cease to be safe and decent places to live. Loyalty to government is being questioned and people do not feel anymore an individual sense of responsibility toward the functioning of the government as an instrument that serves all the people.[11] All the great elements of civilized society, whether we are thinking of peace, security, justice, health services, education, social mobility, and others, are threatened in day-to-day life by the existence of inflation.

The worst effects of persistent inflation fall on the poorest people in the community, those who are not organized, or are incapable of organizing themselves, to build a defense against inflation. In the United States as in other industrial societies, large sections of the lower-middle classes are equally vulnerable. In the early stages of persistent inflation, a certain amount of protection may be secured through trade union membership and indexation[12] of union wages, salaries, and pensions, or through supplementary incomes, or inherited wealth. People with small, fixed incomes are not protected. As time goes on, the defenses weaken and eventually the great majority

11. One example of this development is the fact that in most countries today strikes by public service employees—firemen, policemen, hospital workers, teachers—have become acceptable and are tolerated although such strikes can endanger the lives and safety of fellow citizens. On the other hand, the defensive behavior of public service employees is only to be expected in a society in which persistent inflation has been allowed to take root. These employees are reacting to a situation that has been deteriorating more and more over time, and their reaction is understandable under the circumstances. Modern society is complex and integrated to an extent that large sections of the population are highly vulnerable to the actions of others, even to the actions of a few. The current wave of terrorism around the world indicates how far the process can go. The *only* defense against this process is the loyalty and commitment of the people and their appointed public servants. It is in a climate of general discontent, and of indifference of people to the plight of others, that corrosive forces against democracy can flourish.

12. Indexation is a technique for relating income from any source, or the nominal value of financial instruments (such as government securities), to changes in the cost of living.

of people feel the harmful effects of inflation. Indexation first becomes an engine of inflation and then undermines the feasibility of what it is trying to protect, such as real wages and the purchasing power of pensions. In the "dog-eat-dog" atmosphere which characterizes inflationary situations, indexation, if effective, must be at the expense of someone. This is eventually perceived by these victims, and the defense is not allowed to operate as originally contemplated.

Increased government spending results in inflation and higher taxation, as one phenomenon goes with the other. With increasing inflation, more and more people in a modern tax system find themselves in the higher income brackets of money wages and incomes. As people become subject to higher and higher taxation, their resistance to paying taxes increases, even though they may agree with the purposes for which the tax revenues are spent and bemoan the failure to have social benefits which require the increased taxes they oppose. Cash earnings are preferred to other forms of payment, and the "subterranean" economy (moonlighting of employees who are earning cash from second and third jobs) escapes the national income statistician and is ever gaining in importance.

We should recognize the fact that any kind of inflation means redistributing consumption in a way that is arbitrary, and is penalizing those who cannot defend themselves in the competitive struggle for consumption. Much emphasis has been placed in recent years on the inflation/unemployment trade-off. More important, in my view, is the inflation-caused trade-off between the living standards of those sections of the population that can protect themselves and those that are defenseless and suffering the greatest losses. Persistent inflation is a clear signal that the social system is working in an arbitrary way and against those who are without defense.

CAN WE STOP PERSISTENT INFLATION?

It may be useful to review where we now stand in the United States before considering what steps to take:

• The expectation of continuing inflation has become part of all decision making by consumers, investors, and savers, private and governmental.

- Neither the private sector nor the government has been able to devise effective protection against persistent inflation.
- The private sector has come under increased government controls, with the prospect of more.
- Uncertainties caused by inflation continue to disrupt business and public planning and budgeting.
- Unemployment, both cyclical and structural, is relatively high by historical standards.
- Inflation has so deteriorated many public services that in certain communities they represent a major handicap both to economic growth and the quality of life.
- Inflation has made most difficult the achievement of a satisfactory international monetary system and weakened international cooperation in other areas.

There seem to be two ways of attacking the problem of persistent inflation. On the one hand, governments must stop the practices of the past thirty years of responding to societal demands without explaining the costs to the public in terms of all other uses of resources in private and public sectors, and a process begun of reformulating expectations of improved material well-being to realizable levels—to try to avoid meeting people's expectations through budgetary deficits and monetary expansion. Demand must be realistically related to the productive capabilities of the economy.

On the other hand, the principal thrust of my recommended policy is to increase U.S. and global output. There are over two billion people who live in want and poverty and are eager to acquire the goods and services which constitute modern living. Furthermore, the world population explosion multiplies this demand dynamically and geometrically.

My approach, therefore, emphasizes supply management as well as demand and incomes management. Supply capacity should be increased so that more of people's expectations can be fulfilled. However, as only actual or *real* output and income can be redistributed equitably, the public must be taught to realize that their expectations cannot all be achieved simultaneously. As any kind of inflation redistributes income and consumption in an arbitrary way, penalizing those that cannot defend themselves in this competitive struggle, I am led to a very drastic notion of inflation: the only acceptable inflation is "no" inflation.

Since there are no practical short-term remedies for inflation, we cannot look for success within one or two business cycles. A longer-term sustained approach, as outlined below, should be designed and applied by the governments of the leading industrial nations in a simultaneous and cooperative effort. Such an approach could end persistent inflation within one decade. There would be major benefits, moreover, along the way. First, countries would be tackling their major social and economic problems, which require solutions in any case. Second, inflationary expectations would subside as people saw their basic problems being addressed. Third, the shift from secular accelerating price rises to secular decelerating price rises would allow increasingly more economic decisions to be made without the built-in concern with long-run inflation. The deceleration of inflation rates would need to occur during a period extending over several business cycles hopefully of shallower depth and shorter duration.

I believe that an effective attack on persistent inflation can be mounted if general policies are applied in a long-term nonpartisan manner. As inflation is a process, it is important to establish the mechanisms which will ensure that the fight against inflation, once it is begun, will be sustained, because in the course of this effort there will emerge new and unanticipated aspects of policies and practices. I would like to emphasize the importance of establishing effective mechanisms because the intricacies of the problem are so great and the roots are so deep that a solution of the problem through designing a rigid policy "package" to be executed in a relatively short period of time like one presidential administration is illusory.

I would like to propose the following policy principles to guide the United States and other countries around the world in their anti-inflationary programs.

1. Countries should aim at combined public and private voluntary savings in the range of at least 25 percent to 30 percent of gross domestic product. Where necessary, institutional mechanisms, including tax and interest-rate policies, should be changed to achieve these savings. Voluntary savings should be encouraged by fiscal incentives with recognition given to the general social benefits from such savings. This would achieve desired changes in consumption while encouraging productive activities. Greater

flexibility could be given to financial institutions to attract household savings.

2. Measures should be taken to attract savings into high-productivity investments. Fortunately, our financial institutions and markets are highly diversified and sophisticated.

3. Priorities in public investment must be established. Public investments are not "costless" when they are financed by printing money. The true economic and social costs must be better understood by the public.

4. Private consumption should continue to reflect individual wants and desires, but the costs to society of such consumption should be reflected in taxes and other ways. Public consumption must be most carefully costed out and judged both from the viewpoint of other expenditures and in comparison with private consumption and investment.

5. An investment climate is needed which encourages investors and producers to assume that the pent-up demand by the world will result in strong continuing demand for all kinds of goods and services for decades. This will require a new look at our international monetary and commercial systems.

6. The selection of priorities for spending and distributing the national product lies at the heart of any country's effort to end persistent inflation. What is often lacking, however, is recognition of the tight interdependence of economic units within a country. These interactions must be well understood by policy makers and, in political systems based on public consensus, by everyone. Making and implementing priorities are specific and difficult tasks, whose details can be filled in only at appropriate levels—national, regional, or municipal. It remains for political, business, and academic leaders to provide the overview of anticipated interactions.

7. In setting priorities, value systems are of prime importance, and national priorities reflect value judgments regarding, for example, the role private enterprise or the government should play in such areas as price and wage behavior, public ownership of industry, regulation, and centralized planning.

Special efforts at the national level that I personally would advocate are improving living standards for the poorest segment of the population, creating jobs for the *chronically* unemployed, and channeling savings to areas of production with the largest unutilized manpower. I would also promote greater awareness of the true costs of public services—for example, encourage public utility rates which firmly reflect those costs, and, if needed, openly subsidize the poorest. Indeed, all subsidies granted to enterprises, public and private, should be open and come through the budgetary process. How else can people choose intelligently what they wish to subsidize? In general, I would do everything possible to reduce the relative importance of transfer payments and increase the relative importance of earned income. I would also promote more intensive analyses of such problem areas as education, health services, and transportation. Until these key problems are resolved, we have little hope of coping with persistent inflation.

I do not believe that there is only one set of policies or one approach that can work. Many approaches could work, if based on a realistic assessment of conditions and a realistic assessment of how the proposed policies would affect people and their likely responses to these effects.

Because these responses can intensify frictions among many competing groups within our economy, I advocate the creation of a National Commission on Ways and Means of Ending Inflation, whose members would include individuals representing major concerns and various constitutents of the American public, including the political process. This commission, which could be private or governmental in origin, should formulate basic long-term strategies for ending inflation, identify the issues and alternative critical paths.

Second, in the field of national security, for example, we might have a Cabinet Committee on Ending Inflation chaired by the President in order to deal with areas of greatest concern. This Cabinet Committee should be given the responsibility and authority to deal with basic issues affecting the implementation of an anti-inflationary strategy.

On the global level I would suggest that the world food problem be tackled from many sides in an effort to eliminate shocks to national and world economies from recurring food scarcities. This cannot be done quickly, but it can and must be done because food prices are a key element in inflation in both industrial and developing countries.

The crucial role of energy sources and distribution is a perfect example of a problem that can be solved only on a global basis. An effective attack on world energy needs could help to eliminate inflation. Another area for global action against inflation is nonpetroleum minerals and industrial primary products production. Postponing investments in these areas could produce bottlenecks and scarcities in the foreseeable future with resulting strong inflationary effects on the world economy.

Any concerted attack on global inflation must include effective functioning of the international monetary system. The international capital flows that produce the equilibrium between investment capital needs and surplus savings are an important area for global cooperation. The upsetting uncertainty of erratic fluctuating exchange rates are difficult to eliminate, however, as long as industrial countries are experiencing inflation of significantly different orders of magnitude.

CONCLUDING REMARKS

Modern inflation is the product of modern relationships among people. In turn, it strains those relationships, diverts us from our social, political, and economic goals, and creates inequities we cannot in good conscience tolerate. Because it is a fairly new phenomenon, different in kind from earlier inflations, unprecedented, persistent, and innovative actions are required over many years to end it.

We should recognize that eliminating persistent inflation will *not solve* the other basic issues of modern societies, such as the population explosion, environmental issues, conservation of natural resources, and dangers of nuclear war. We should realize, however, that eliminating the destructive effects of persistent inflation will bring the solutions to many other problems more easily within our reach. The continuation of persistent inflation greatly handicaps efforts to achieve better conditions in all these other areas.

The democratic system of the United States can provide the political framework within which its economic system can work effectively. Through international cooperation with other countries the United States could lead the world back to conditions of monetary stability.

To achieve the end of persistent inflation, we must first of all recognize the need to do so. Then we must recognize that this objective must be national—not partisan—just as the avoidance of large-scale unemployment is a generally agreed national objective. Then, the content of the program to end persistent inflation—the establishment and implementation of priorities—must become the content of our political issues. People must be given alternatives to consider, debate, and choose. Old issues must give way to current ones. Only *after* this debate can a national concrete set of initial policies or measures to end inflation be chosen. Perhaps we should start as suggested, with a national commission appointed by the President, requesting all sectors of society to examine what can be done, and to facilitate the decisions which need to be made. Our democratic process can provide the mechanism to reverse the present inevitable process of persistent inflation which, if not stopped, can destroy democracy itself.

American presidents will not win election without promising to do something effective to end inflation. American presidents will not win reelection unless they have done so. Many continue to take comfort in "lower," "more satisfactory," "lower than other" rates of inflation. The public is too experienced to accept this simplistic, erroneous kind of economics. Public support can be mobilized to *end* inflation if the public is shown how the end of inflation means higher rates of growth, more jobs, and less unemployment. It cannot be effectively mobilized to keep inflation from rising by "X percent" with a promise of more in the future. Likewise, it cannot be effectively mobilized if persistent unemployment is offered as the alternative to persistent inflation.

—Irving S. Friedman

CHAPTER 5

The Plight of Private Enterprise
and a Possible Way Out

In *The Camp of the Saints,* novelist Jean Raspail projects a bone-chilling vision of Europe overwhelmed by starving, unarmed hordes from India. As France is laid waste like a wheatland infested with locusts, the governmental leaders keep mouthing the clichés of popular social theory, refusing to the very end to acknowledge reality or utilize in self-defense the remnants of the military that have survived the attacks of the "peace" movement. The shock element of the book is that the political rationale which invited the catastrophe is an accurate echo of the liberal views which have dominated Western political thought for several decades. As the author notes in his brief preface, "Many of the texts I have put in my characters' mouths or pens—editorials, speeches, pastoral letters, laws, news stories, statements of every description—are authentic."

It does not take a very large brain to decipher the message of this parable. When a society deteriorates to the point that it has no national purpose, acknowledges no principles, and has abandoned all standards of personal conduct, it becomes the helpless victim of passionate zealots and persuasive demagogues. In the absence of generally held concepts of right and wrong, honorable people have no defense against the accusations, the plunder, and the tyranny of those who are in a position to manipulate public opinion.

Raspail's modern apocalypse offers one interpretation of the circumstances which have closed in on private enterprise, circumstances which are frustrating the efforts of businessmen to hold back the tide of regulations, restrictions, and taxes that are exhausting their corporate resources and discouraging their productive initiative. The do-your-own-thing Bacchanalia has muddled the nation's judgment. America has been reduced to government by decibel. In the philosophical vacuum, when spokesmen for private enterprise turn to the legislators and regulators to request help in providing a more wholesome business climate, they are likely to be received as just one more self-serving pressure group with no greater claim to assistance than the lesbians, the colleges, the American Indians, the unions, the veterans, and the hundreds of other special interests all clamoring for protection and privilege. What seems so compellingly persuasive to the businessman—that the health of the economy is critically important to every citizen—doesn't even dent the consciousness of the great body of people who have learned that the government will pay for anything if the advocates make enough noise and become sufficiently unpleasant. "Whatever the cost of what our group demands, it can be added to the deficit" is the prevailing notion. "Why should the government balk at another twenty or fifty million in a budget of half a trillion?"

The plight of private enterprise takes on added gravity when one recognizes that the cultural institutions which shape the values and beliefs of the citizens are dominated by hedonistic or welfare-state views, or both. The live-it-up-and-don't-worry-because-the-government-is-obliged-to-take-care-of-you attitude speaks with a strong voice among the television scriptwriters, the novelists, poets, and playwrights, the literary critics, the teaching profession, rock music, the clergy, the movies, and both the intellectual and popular magazines. In this context, the business forces mobilized to discourage hostile legislation and to conduct programs of economic education are seen to be a mere corporal's guard to contend against the whole range of professions engaged in molding the views of the citizens and manipulating their emotions. The unfavorable balance of opinion-making forces is acknowledged, perhaps unwittingly, by the stance of many industries. The trade associations seem to concentrate their efforts on minimizing the additional territory that will be lost each year to Leviathan, or alleviating somewhat the tyranny of the governmental gauleiters in lands that have already been occupied. How many organized efforts have been initiated to repeal inappropriate laws or to cause to be removed from office bureaucratic functionaries who engage in unauthorized, irrational, and devastating practices?

It is the thesis of this essay that the difficulties which confront capitalism are so pervasive and so deeply rooted that a renaissance of private endeavor will require an altogether different kind of strategy from that which is now employed, a strategy which is rational, affirmative, and comprehensive. It must be derived from an accurate understanding of social and political dynamics; it must be founded upon the just principles which govern a viable free nation; and it must entail a responsible and practical plan for reenlisting the opinion-making forces as allies of true liberty, weaning them away from their advocacy of a spurious concept of liberty which is tantamount to anarchy and license. Such a course of action would seem to offer the best change for diminishing the political expediency, the bureaucratic arrogance, and the erroneous social dogma which are perverting the character of the nation and crippling its productivity.

In order to identify and comprehend the requisite principles, it will be useful to review some pertinent history and focus upon the human values and priorities which undergirded the founding of the nation and which delivered an environment exceedingly favorable for private enterprise. The impetus for the Pilgrims to cross the Atlantic in tiny boats and to create a settlement in the Massachusetts wilderness was the desire to attain liberty. The victims of religious persecution, they sought only the freedom to worship in their own way. It is difficult for those who have grown up in a state of freedom to recognize how powerfully the urge to liberty rises in the human soul. That, of course, is the force which has impelled countless individuals in recent decades to risk, or lose, their lives trying to escape to West Berlin or to Hong Kong from the tyranny of Russian or Chinese communism. And it was the determination to be free of British tyranny that led to the Declaration of Independence and the waging of the long, cruel, arduous Revolutionary War.

During the two centuries since the nation was established, Americans seem to have lost track of a basic fact. *Liberty is not free.* Nor is private enterprise, which is merely the economic dimension of liberty. The opportunity for private endeavor to flourish is directly related to the degree of liberty. The nature of liberty and the price which must be paid to achieve and sustain it have been studied by political philosophers for centuries. Among them, one who had a critical influence on the architects of the United States Constitution was a Frenchman named Charles Montesquieu. His greatest work was *The Spirit of the Laws,* published in 1748. His recommendations for the separation of legislative, judicial, and executive powers and for the provision of checks and balances became cardinal features of our government. Even so, the aspect of Montesquieu's reasoning most pertinent to this analysis is his thesis that each form of government has a characteristic relationship to its people. When that relationship changes, the existing form of government cannot survive and must give way to another kind of government or, perhaps, to anarchy.

In the case of a dictatorship, the relationship is one of fear on the part of the people. When the citizens are no longer afraid of their government, the dictatorship is doomed. In a monarchy it is loyalty that is required. If the allegiance to the crown falters, the throne is endangered. The republic was regarded by Montesquieu as the most desirable governmental structure and the most difficult to sustain because its requisite is a virtuous citizenry, a rare phenomenon among the civilizations of the world. Although latter-day historians and biographers have labored to expose the peccadilloes of the nation's most admired statesmen, those revelations do not invalidate Montesquieu's analysis as it applies to America's past. Montesquieu merits a full hearing.

Consider, for instance, the interaction of individuals in any group or society. Savages are persons who do their own thing. They acknowledge no obligations to anyone or anything and accept no limits on their conduct, doing that which gratifies their whims or passions. By definition, they are incapable of joint endeavor. In contrast to an aggregate of savages, every group or society must have some means to assure a certain conformity of conduct among its members so that common purposes may be served. If the group values human life, then some technique is necessary to keep the members from killing each other. If the group is an athletic team, there must be a high degree of coordinated action. If the group is a nation, the required conformity has countless dimensions.

Among the options for controlling citizen conduct, at one end of the spectrum is the dictatorship. In that instance, the ruler and his adjutants determine what the citizens may and may not do, and those decisions from on high are enforced by the use of spies, compliance officers, harsh penalties, and the other techniques of tyranny. The extent to which the citizens observe the decrees of the despot depends upon the level of their fear. At the opposite pole of governmental systems is what is designated a "free" nation, but it is not a society in which all persons may do whatever they please. Political freedom is not a synonym for anarchy. On the contrary, in a successful free nation, the regulation of conduct is extensive, but the dominant mode of control is the *voluntary observance* of informal codes of conduct that apply to almost every aspect of living. Included are religious commandments, professional ethics, integrity, lawfulness, patriotism, manners, the house rules of each organization, morality, sportsmanship, marital fidelity, civility, philanthropy, and all the other formalized prescriptions which delineate the fundamentals and the nuances of truly civilized conduct. The extent to which the citizens observe these codes depends upon how fully and effectively has been the training of their consciences.

This is the phenomenon embodied in Montesquieu's insistence that a republic can survive only when the citizens are virtuous, that is, self-disciplined. In a free nation when the informal codes of conduct are set aside and the "liberated" conduct of the people multiplies to the point of serious damage to the group, then there arises a cry for the government to set matters aright and that tends to precipitate new laws, new legions of compliance officers, and new penalties. In the process, the power of the regulatory government increases, and the costs go up. And the society engages in a transition from liberty to tyranny. The fear quotient rises. Individuals and colleges and businesses become more cautious about what they say and do, and are forced to allocate increasing amounts of time and money to learn what they are permitted to do, having become fearful of retaliation by the agents of government who have power over them. Montesquieu's theorem inexorably proves itself.

In this regard, it is important for the businessman to recognize how the hedonists' assaults on moral values result in serious consequences for private enterprise. In 1976, about half of the new babies born in the District of Columbia were the offspring of unwed mothers. Nationwide, the percentage is smaller, but the number of such children is very large and it is growing. Some portion of those husbandless mothers may be able to provide their youngsters with a home life sufficiently disciplined and supportive that the children may grow up as responsible and productive citizens, but for a very large percentage of these children, the emotional scars of the upbringing are likely to result in a high incidence of vandalism, arson, shoplifting, auto theft, and other costly destruction as these youngsters reach an age when they are out on the streets.

The theorists who advocate sexual liberation seem to focus their attention upon the pleasure of the individual with a blind indifference to the consequences for the society. Human nature doesn't change. The outcome of this form of self-indulgence is predictable: a generation of adults, or adolescents, bent on exploiting the sexual passions but unwilling to accept the responsibilities and joys of rearing the children, is incapable of delivering succeeding generations of citizens with the self-discipline to sustain a free society. The coinage of the term "life-style" and the insistent use of this term denoting the absence of any moral standards constitute a semantic sleight-of-hand that bids fair to making the family disappear. As one critic has observed, it will eventually be recognized that the smashing of the family is a greater threat to the survival of civilization than the smashing of the atom.

The ethic of the savage, which in its sexual dimension is decimating the family, has spread to almost every other aspect of life. When the families and the other educative institutions of a free society abandon their efforts to train the conscience of the young in such matters as lawfulness and the respect for private property, as has happened to a great extent in the United States, the result is a mounting disregard for laws and for property. The annual cost of vandalism has soared above $1 billion. To put this in comprehensible terms, if the average value of the property ruined annually per vandal turned out to be $200, the number of contemporary American barbarians engaging in wanton destruction would be about 5 million. Turning to another category of "liberated" conduct, shoplifting and employee theft, the cost to American businesses was estimated at $26 billion in 1976. That amounts to a surtax of $500 which each American family had to pay on its purchases as a result of this form of savagery.

It needs to be recognized that the increase in crime is not so much a reflection of deficiencies in the law, the police, the courts, and/or the treatment of prisoners, but rather the consequence of the massive cultural revolution which has taken place. The codes of conduct which distinguish the free man from the savage and the slave are being jettisoned. Having been subjected to an almost uniform chorus of derision by the opinion makers, the principles, morals, and standards which once shaped the society have fallen to such a low estate that even their champions tend to shun principled declarations that certain things are wrong, and hide behind the bibs of children. Following the recent revelations about child pornography, there surfaced a vestige of public conscience of sufficient force to produce several laws banning this category of degenerate "entertainment." Even so, the anti-repression voices are so formidable that instead of a condemnation of commercialized smut, there was only a timid judgment that *little* children should not be lured or dragooned into this profession. One must wait until adolescence. The efforts to restrict immoral, barbarous, and animalistic enactments on television and in the cinema follow the same pattern: the burden of objection turns out to be the protection of the innocent young rather than a principled stand against the escalating corruption of the whole society or even a forthright advocacy of civilized standards of conduct.

Conscientious businessmen who wish to protect the institution of private enterprise face the same overwhelming odds as conscientious clergymen and conscientious grandparents who wish to protect the institution of marriage, or conscientious policemen and judges who wish to protect the institution of private property. When the juggernaut of cultural orthodoxy has rejected the concept of self-disciplined virtue and endlessly defends or glorifies self-indulgence, the efforts to uphold any aspect of liberty are drowned out in the din of "liberation."

Karl Marx theorized that the form of the economy determines the character of the society. The error of his analysis is nowhere more dramatically proven than in the dynamics of the American nation today. It is not the economic system which shapes the destiny of the people. Instead, it is the culture which most often dictates the judgments for the captains of industry as for the highest officers of government. The orchestration of public opinion is what increasingly determines the agenda for management, affecting the conditions of employment, the nature and the amount of remuneration, the race or sex of the people to be employed and promoted, the nature and cost of safety features that must be embodied in the product and in its manufacture, the foreign markets in which the company may sell its products, and even, perhaps, what shall be the energy source of choice in the future. It is the culture which has the principal say in whether a war shall be initiated or waged for victory, whether the errors of a president shall cause his disgrace or be overlooked and subordinated to his accomplishments, which views shall be heard most frequently and most persuasively on any issue, and which shall be suppressed by scorn and token representation.

If corporate America wishes to safeguard what is left of the private enterprise system and deliver it from escalating crime, taxes, and inappropriate bureaucratic interference, then the principal thrust of the campaign must be redirected toward the institutions and the individuals with the greatest power to affect public attitudes. They are the ones that shape the future.

History does not offer much encouragement to hope for a change in the direction in which our society is proceeding. Once a civilization has achieved a prolonged period of economic success, human nature seems to incline the people in power to be more concerned about protecting their privileges than about upholding the principles which animated and prospered the society if, indeed, the later generations are even aware of those principles. There are, however, in contemporary America, two circumstances pertinent to this question, for which history has no precedent. There still exists a dynamic, adaptable, and inventive industrial leadership that has performed near miracles in the face of clear challenge: the retooling and mobilization of American resources for war after the Japanese attack on Pearl Harbor, the rapid and pervasive utilization of new technology typified by the computer, and the crash program in space travel in response to Sputnik I are indicative of the unique genius of the American business community to respond to perils or opportunity when they arise and are understood. The second situation for which history offers no guidance is the capacity of television to affect a whole population, conveying knowledge or misinformation, swaying opinion, shattering old values and establishing new ones at a pace that was simply inconceivable for former generations.

There is nothing inherent in either of these two phenomena to give cause for hopefulness about a revitalization of liberty and private endeavor. Television is simply an instrument well suited to leading the way back to a disciplined society if the corporate leadership, which has the ultimate power over the content of television, could be motivated to use that power responsibly and effectively for that purpose. The obstacles, however, are awesome. The typical American businessman is not much given to concerning himself with political philosophy or cultural trends. Accustomed to perceiving his problems in economic and political terms, he is inclined to search for economic and political answers. In many cases, his voice would be one of the loudest in opposition to the reestablishment of the codes of conduct which circumscribe decadent pleasures and indulgences now widely viewed as part of "the good life." Many businessmen might come to understand that the most powerful domestic enemy of capitalism is the welfare state mind-set that demands a paternalistic government to provide for everybody's needs and wants. Once this is understood, they might lend their support to the reeducation of the people in a commitment to economic self-reliance. However, any movement toward self-disciplined moral conduct would meet the vigorous resistance of those businesses which have a commercial interest in the promotion of decadent, "liberated" values and activities. Montesquieu was correct. It is difficult to sustain republican liberty. Civic virtue is hard to come by and even harder to restore when it is no longer prized and praised by the cultural institutions.

Another category of obstacles derives from the nature of the television industry and the dogma which governs decisions about program content. Television is the campus where America goes to school seven days a week. The educational force of this round-the-clock teaching device is not, however, restricted to the programs which are clearly intended as informational and cultural. A large segment of the presentations—the low comedies, the ever-changing bed partners of the soap operas, the televised dramatizations of outright blasphemy, the sympathetic interviews granted to passionate rebels of every stripe—has a cumulative debilitating impact upon whatever standards of conduct still remain among the adults and render it an almost impossible task for conscientious parents, teachers, and clergy to enlist the young in behalf of civilized norms of behavior. If most parents were to visit a school to determine if it offers a proper program for their children and discovered that the curriculum was composed of the same proportions as occur on television of informative and inspirational materials on the one hand, and cheap, degrading, and sensational materials on the other, they would immediately conclude the school is wholly unfit.

What must be recognized is that the dominating educative force in the nation has its educational content determined not by any concept of what comprises a useful and proper schooling, but rather by what will attract the greatest number of viewers. The dynamics of commercial entertainment now determine the priorities of the foremost influence in shaping the values and attitudes of the people. If one wished to bring about the downfall of a nation, it is hard to conceive of a more effective scheme to accomplish that objective than the education by entertainment which has inadvertently come about in America. The magnitude of this problem is difficult to comprehend. Indeed, when it was brought to the attention of the Federal Communications Commission by a formal complaint, followed by an appeal in 1975,[1] both were rejected on technical grounds without any acknowledgment of the substance of the grievance. This is not a difficulty which will be banished by ignoring it.

Any attempt to rectify the situation will encounter the standard objections of freedom of speech and freedom of the press as those doctrines are now interpreted. It is axiomatic that all points of view may be expressed in a free nation. That net of liberty has too often been stretched to mean that newspapers, magazines, academic platforms, radio, and television are *obliged* to make their channels of communication available to the advocacy of every point of view. There is a distinction here that is of the utmost importance. It is true that some obligations have been imposed upon the managers of the news media by such regulations as "The Fairness Doctrine" and the equal-time provision for rival political candidates, but by and large management still retains the authority to pass judgment on what will and what will not be presented.

In a free nation, that authority needs to be implemented with a responsible attention to the character and the probable consequences of the programming or the printed copy. As an editor, Benjamin Franklin refused to publish in his newspaper scurrilous material that was pressed upon him. He was willing to print the tracts at the writer's expense and under the writer's aegis, but he held fast to the standards of integrity and morality he had set for his *Gazette*. Some media statesmanship is now surfacing here and there illustrating the same point. In 1977, the *Los Angeles Times* made a decision not to accept any more advertisements for pornographic films and the *Milwaukee Journal* removed Doonesbury from its page of comics, not wanting to subject its young readers to repeated scenes of an unmarried couple in bed. There are, of course, theorists who assert that pornography and other far-out cultural products really do no damage to the reader or viewer. A rebuttal to that notion was poignantly phrased in an essay by Irving Kristol:

> After all, if you believe that no one was ever corrupted by a book, you have also to believe that no one was ever improved by a book (or a play or a movie). You have to believe, in other words, that all art is morally trivial and that, consequently, all

---

1. Fairness Doctrine complaint against NBC registered on March 10, 1975 and appealed on April 30, 1975.

education is morally irrelevant. No one, not even a university professor, really believes that.[2]

Art and literature, magazines, movies, talk shows, news analyses, and all the other activities and products of the intellectual-cultural axis leave their imprint on the minds of the citizens and ultimately influence the values by which they live and the votes by which the national political complexion is determined. Thus it is that the partisans of private enterprise would do well to direct their attention to the nature of television programming as the most persuasive determinant of public attitudes. As indicated above, the corporations of America have the power to bring about change in this medium if they should choose to exercise it. Advertising funds constitute the life-giving substance of the video industry. However, the advertising function has been regarded primarily as a vehicle for the sale of goods and services instead of the sale of a philosophy. The result has all too often been that products have been sold and the profits increased through programs which have been undermining the foundation of values upon which capitalism rests. Short-range success is being achieved at the expense of long-range survival. It is not a pattern which can be prolonged indefinitely.

What, then, can a corporation do to change this state of affairs? The first step is to develop a statement of the principles which constitute the company's operating philosophy and which will serve as policy for all aspects of corporate activity, not just the placement of advertising. Such a statement could well begin with a corporate commitment to liberty and an acknowledgment of the integral relationship between private enterprise and all other aspects of freedom. Since this is the fundamental advantage that capitalism has over the welfare state, socialism, and communism, it is the logical point of departure and it is a concept that cannot be registered often enough with the citizens. Presumably, most companies would want to include in the statement their commitments to lawfulness, to equal job opportunities, to the institution of private property, and to economic self-reliance as a basic requirement of human dignity. Whether the list will go on to include corporate support for the church, the family, an expression of patriotism, and other matters will depend on many variables. The extension of

2. *Where Do You Draw the Line?*, edited by Victor B. Cline (Brigham Young University Press, 1974), p. 46.

corporate policy to include the values of liberty should not be undertaken hastily or lightly because of the potential for criticism and contention, as well as the potential for greater corporate strength that are inherent in this endeavor. If effectively conceived, a statement of corporate philosophy can produce, among other benefits, a higher level of operating consistency, simplify some decisions that under other circumstances would be arguable, and raise the morale of the employees. When a leadership commits itself forthrightly to a set of worthy principles, and is proud of them, the long-range consequence tends to be a heightened sense of loyalty and pride among the members.

Once the statement has been authorized, it provides a base point for decisions about the placement of television ads. In the category of situation comedy and serialized drama, it is not sufficient simply to avoid paying for programs which glorify values contrary to those endorsed in the corporate policy statement. The objective needs to be the sponsorship of programs which make a positive case for the specified principles of freedom, depicting protagonists who live by those principles and sacrifice for them and provide attractive examples of responsible citizenship. There are all too few contemporary models in either art or real life for the citizens to emulate. In other types of television fare—talk shows, news commentary, documentaries, cultural presentations, etc.—the judgments are, of course, more complex, but the advertiser's aim needs to be to reenforce responsible behavior and avoid paying for unchallenged or sustained advocacy of the do-your-own-thing and the government-must-take-care-of-you attitudes.

If a company should undertake this course of action, resistance will probably arise first on the part of the advertising personnel who may be skeptical about finding the scriptwriters to develop the preferred themes, since so much of the literary traffic is headed in the opposite direction. Aside from the fact that such an observation emphasizes the need for the undertaking, one should remember that the market still works where it has the chance. If significant sums of advertising dollars are available for certain kinds of programs, the writing talent will surface. The advertising account manager may also suggest that affirmative or straight-laced programs will not draw the audiences to accomplish the sales objectives. This is more a matter of conjecture than fact. The support generated by organizations such as Accuracy in Media, Morality in Media, the National

Federation for Decency, and in Britain by the National Listeners and Viewers Association indicates a very large and growing audience eager for moral, inspirational, and civilized programs.

Another dimension of resistance will be posed by professionals in both the print and electronic media who will perceive any effort by advertisers to affect the content of broadcast programs as an intolerable and even frightening breach of freedom of the entire press. In planning a value-oriented advertising program, this reaction must be anticipated and the reasoning to meet it thought out carefully in advance. An outline to serve that purpose might include the following points:

1. Our company is worried about its survival because of certain trends in our society. Among them are:
   A. The growing frequency of crime with the resulting increase in our expenditures for insurance, security, replacement of that which is stolen or vandalized, etc.;
   B. The burgeoning "transfer payments" of counterproductive welfare-state programs which require higher taxes; and
   C. The multiplication of unwarranted restrictive governmental regulations which divert time, money, and brains from productive effort.
2. All of these troublesome matters reflect certain values and attitudes among the people which seem to be encouraged and reenforced by the publication and broadcast industries.
3. We, therefore, consider it to be a direct obligation to our stockholders and our employees to take such action as we can to develop public support for the values and attitudes that will diminish the problems we have cited.
4. It is not our purpose to dictate to any element of the press how it will run its business, but we do intend to try to use our advertising funds to support the principles of freedom as we perceive them, and we will shop around until we find advertising channels that are willing to have us do so.
5. If the press should judge such a course of action to be inappropriate in a free nation, then please explain to us the grounds for that judgment. Why is it wrong for us to try to reenforce the principles of liberty?
6. Finally, we would like to invite our friends in the media to weigh carefully this effort of ours and the reasons for it, with the thought that the television (or radio or publication) industry is,

itself, subject to the same grievous problems we face. Perhaps you in the media will recognize it is in your own interests to encourage and help us instead of fighting against this undertaking.

Such a stance is not a cause for defensiveness or apology. The struggles for freedom and the efforts to educate people to live by principles constitute the brightest chapters in the history of civilizations. The problem is that the reigning cultural forces seem not to understand the nature of responsible freedom, or not to value it, and have therefore tolerated or encouraged the rejection of the codes of conduct which make liberty possible, oblivious or indifferent to the long-range consequences.

It is to be hoped that the vast reservoir of brains, energy, and organizational talent available in the business community can be brought to a recognition that a flourishing future for private enterprise is dependent upon a renewed national commitment to the principles of liberty and upon the restoration of time-tested standards of conduct. If the corporate leadership could comprehend these requirements, then the prospects for a revitalized America would be much greater than historical precedent suggests.

The formula for averting an American catastrophe of the magnitude of the European collapse envisioned by Raspail has been well phrased by another European author, Friedrich A. Hayek. His challenge: "We must make the building of a free society once more an intellectual adventure, a deed of courage."

—JOHN ADDISON HOWARD

CHAPTER 6

What Price Dependence?

On a recent morning television talk show, a young newswoman was interviewing two members of a visiting Arab trade delegation. She seemed an earnest and sincere young woman, intent on doing her job well. But there was one basic problem: she simply couldn't comprehend what the Arab business representatives were trying to tell her.

They were in the country, they said repeatedly, to buy the American know-how necessary to modernize their nations—just that, and nothing more. The young newswoman, however, wanted instead to pursue the question of Arab investment in the United States, along with what she seemed to feel was an insidious Arab lust for the American dollar.

This made the two Arab representatives somewhat impatient. Because of the condition of our economy, they pointed out, they were increasingly coming to view their American investments as very bad ones. Nor, because of the decline of the dollar, were they any longer particularly enthusiastic about accumulating great quantities of our paper currency. Their message was this: they felt they could not depend on us to put our economic house in order; as a result, they could no longer depend on our dollars; and so, the only thing left to depend on was our technological know-how, for which they would gladly turn over as many of our undependable dollars as we wanted.

The inability of the young newswoman to comprehend this was perfectly understandable. Most Americans still cannot believe that our nation, the first and most basic document of which is the

Declaration of Independence, is in the process of becoming dependent on others, and therefore increasingly undependable in the eyes of the world. And as that process accelerates, we are in danger of ransoming off our future as a free and independent people.

On the domestic scene, this process has been under way for several decades now. Primarily because of well-intentioned but ill-conceived government programs and policies that promise what cannot be delivered, a new subsidized class has evolved, consisting of people who depend totally on their productive neighbors to support them. As this class has grown politicians have come to depend on them as a constituency; thus, it is politically expedient to keep them dependent. The growth of the subsidized class has also spurred the growth of an enormous bureaucratic apparatus which also depends for its continued existence on the continuing dependence of the people it ostensibly serves.

Along with this institutionalization of dependence has come a systematic attempt to make it socially and intellectually desirable. Not too many years ago, it was taken for granted that among the cardinal American virtues were self-sufficiency, self-reliance, and independence. Today, however, aside from the predictable political polemics, these concepts are seldom discussed. And when they are, the references are generally pejorative. Such concepts, we are frequently made to feel, are gauche, trite, even socially undesirable; and those of us in the business community who cling to them are neanderthals or throwbacks to the "robber barons." Instead, the emphasis is on collectivism, cooperation, interdependence—all desirable concepts, to be sure; but when they are the only basic philosophical concepts underlying a given society, then that society of necessity becomes a dependent society.

We have seen this dependence developing in our nation's domestic affairs, as a generation has grown up which not only depends totally on others to provide it with sustenance, but views that dependence as a right conferred at birth. And now, we see the philosophy of dependence intruding into our international affairs. The results are economically devastating; and they have profound implications in the areas of foreign policy and national defense.

Like the young television newswoman, most Americans no doubt still fail to comprehend just how far we have let our independence slip. Our markets and stores are flooded with goods from other lands. We depend on others for iron ore and copper. We are increasingly dependent on others for lead, zinc, and even timber. And most important of all, we have become accustomed to depending on others for our energy supplies. The significance of this dependence cannot be overstated. The industrial civilization we have built is totally dependent on energy. Without that energy, this civilization would cease to exist. Thus, it is an understatement to speak of an energy crisis, for in a very real sense, America as we know it *is* energy. Any significant energy crisis, therefore, is a national or civilizational crisis in the most literal sense, involving every one of us.

Nevertheless, although the stakes have never been higher, we continue to allow our energy independence—and therefore, what could well be our independence as a nation—to slip away from us, our sense of urgency perhaps dulled by the contemporary acceptance of the philosophy of dependence. Consider, for instance, the situation in regard to our oil supplies. In 1973, just before the Yom Kippur War and the Arab embargo, we were importing 36 percent of our oil. Then came the supply cutoff, and the dangers inherent in our growing dependence should suddenly have become manifest to those millions of Americans who suffered from shortages and long gas lines. And for a time, it seemed the message was sinking in. In Washington, with great fanfare, the Nixon Administration announced a crash program aimed at making us self-sufficient in energy—Project Independence, it was called, the precursor of President Carter's Moral Equivalent of War.

What was the result? There was none. For 1977 we found ourselves importing 46 percent of our oil, and paying out $45 billion for the privilege of doing so. At this writing (April 1978) imports are decreasing, primarily because of oil from Alaska's North Slope. But it must be remembered that in terms of long-range supplies, this Alaskan oil is little more than a drop in the bucket. Nor should we forget that the current temporary improvement resulting largely from Alaskan oil has come about *despite* governmental policies, not *because* of them. But the problem here is that various experts will decide that, because of the temporary glut, what they call the "energy crisis" is over, and the American people, just as they did in 1974, will doze off again. In the meantime, the government will continue to devise policies and regulations which discourage domestic exploration and production and encourage heavy dependence on foreign sources. And when we are jolted awake the next time round, we are likely to find ourselves more dependent than ever.

Why is this so difficult to grasp? And why are so many people apparently blissfully unaware of the extent and the consequences of our dependence? In part, as I said earlier, many Americans have come to accept the concept of dependence as not at all undesirable. And in part, it is simply too difficult to understand how incredibly things have changed within a few short years. The world as we had come to know it has lurched violently over the past decade. In the area of economics, for instance, we are witnessing one of the most drastic capital shifts in history, with money from the industrialized nations pouring into the coffers of a small group of oil-producing nations. How many Americans a decade ago could have conceived of the fact that our economic well-being would be so dependent on decisions made in nations like Kuwait, and United Arab Emirates, Qatar, and Saudi Arabia? A hard fact indeed for Americans to digest; but digest it we must, if we are to understand the extent of our dependence and what it is doing to us.

Consider the direct effect of this dependence on our economy. As I write this, the single biggest news story of 1978 has been the decline of the dollar. That decline is directly related to our horrendous balance of payments problem. And that balance of payments problem is directly related to the bills that are rolling in for the oil we import. In 1977, we paid $45 billion for imported oil, and our balance of payments deficit—two years earlier it was a *surplus*—reached $20 billion. Given the current drift toward dependence, there is no good reason to expect that figure to improve. Nor, if the dollar continues its descent, is there any good reason to expect OPEC to continue to accept our dollars for its oil. As the two Arab trade representatives tried to explain to the young newswoman, sentiment is stirring among the Middle Eastern nations against exchanging valuable oil for increasingly valueless paper.

One of the prices we pay for dependence, it is clear, is a growing deficit. And dependence also poses profound problems for us in the areas of foreign policy and national defense. As that portion of the world which can legitimately call itself "free" continues to shrink, a great uneasiness is growing internationally. I remember a very similar international uneasiness during my college days in the

1930s, as Europe became Balkanized. The spirit of militant nationalism burned fiercely, just as it is burning now. The world then seemed to be perched on a powder keg, with a time bomb ticking audibly in the background, and we all walked very carefully in those days, waiting for the explosion. And finally, of course, it came.

I remember that feeling vividly, as all of us who lived through those years always will, and today I fear I hear that same old ticking, still very faint, but definitely there. The situation in the world today is very similar to that situation of four decades ago. But our position with regard to that situation has altered significantly. In the thirties, although our industrial capabilities were still underdeveloped, there was easy access to all the oil necessary for the total and rapid conversion of our industries to an all-out war effort. More than anything else, it was our self-sufficiency in natural resources that allowed us in a very brief period to become "the arsenal of Democracy." (Interestingly enough, what was once called "the arsenal of Democracy" is now called "the military-industrial complex.")

Today, however, things are very different, and if another explosion should come, we might not have time to pick up the pieces. We could quickly muster up all the human enthusiasm and energy we need. But it would be difficult to muster up sufficient energy to fuel our defense systems. Our armed forces, if fully mobilized, would require incalculable quantities of petroleum products, as would our defense and related industries. But given our dependence on foreign oil and the corresponding decline in domestic production, it would require a great deal of lead time even under a total effort; and given the nature of modern warfare, that time might not be available.

The producing nations might supply us with whatever oil we needed, of course. But that does not seem likely. For one thing, it is in their part of the world where that time bomb ticks most loudly; and if the explosion comes there, and if we carry out our foreign policy commitments, they will not want to supply us at all. And if the explosion occurs elsewhere in the world, it is very possible they won't be able to do so.

Through the conscious policy of encouraging dependence, we have ransomed our future to one of the most volatile areas on earth. And in the process, we have stretched our supply lines to the breaking point. Suppose, for instance, that there were an explosion in some part of the world of sufficient magnitude to require some sort of American intervention. I realize, of course, that in this post-Vietnam War period we are no longer eager to think about such possibilities. Nevertheless, we must admit that they do exist. There is one school of thought, to be sure, which maintains that the history of mankind is the history of peace interspersed with periods of war. But the human record could also support another thesis: the history of mankind is the history of war interspersed with brief periods of peace. And there are times when even the most peaceful of nations must take to the battlefield.

Over the past decade we have seen nations and would-be nations battling in many parts of the globe. Sometimes these battles rage nearly unnoticed. Sometimes, as in the Yom Kippur War, they rivet international attention and draw us very close to the brink of all-out war. The full story of the Red Alert during the war in the Mideast in 1973 has not yet been told. But we locked horns with the Soviet Union that October. There was a confrontation, and confrontations always take place on the brink.

The conflicts that draw us toward that brink flare up for various reasons. But they almost always have one thing in common: we support one side, and the Socialist bloc supports the other. The problem, however, is this: given our dependence on supplies of foreign oil, and given the balance of military power in the world today, our support may no longer be worth a great deal, for we may no longer be able to safeguard our supply lines.

In order to do so, we must, among other things, maintain a strong presence in the Mediterranean, for military dominance of the Mediterranean means access to the great oil fields of the Middle East. But the balance of power in the eastern Mediterranean, like our balance of payments, has been shifting drastically. American, French, and British bases have been abandoned all along North Africa. Our Sixth Fleet suffers from growing obsolescence, while the Soviets continue to deploy a modern and sophisticated fleet of fighting ships. A decade ago, the Russian navy was little more than a small coastal defense force. Today it is a deep-water fleet which continues to grow as our own navy shrinks. Over the past decade the number of our vessels has been cut in half, to less than five hundred. And given President Carter's plans to cut back on shipbuilding, that figure will not improve. In the meantime, over the same period of

American naval shrinkage, the Soviet fleet has doubled. As a consequence, the authoritative publication *Jane's Fighting Ships* now says flatly that the Russian navy is the most powerful in the world.

What does all this add up to? There is a very simple point to be made here: our supplies of imported oil must come by sea, and ships transporting oil are extremely vulnerable. The Soviets might never dream of interdicting them. But they are in an excellent strategic position to do so if they choose, and they have the sufficient military wherewithal. The carrier *Kiev* now roams the eastern Mediterranean, with its planes practicing surface strafing of targets. It will be joined by two new carriers now under construction, and sophisticated new weapons systems are being deployed to the Russian naval aviation arm. The Soviet presence in Somalia and the friendly regime in Yemen give them both potential missile-loading bases and effective control of the Red Sea. Add Mozambique to the picture, and we find the Soviets established within easy striking distance of the Indian Ocean. That could mean, in other words, that one day the accessibility to shipping lanes would depend entirely on Soviet goodwill.

And even if we were never required to act against a Soviet client or never slipped over the brink with the Soviet Union itself, there is yet another possibility—renewed warfare between Israel and the Arab nations. Given the history and condition of the region, this possibility must be taken very seriously. But this time around things would be different, for the producing nations now fully understand just how effective the oil weapon can be.

Since 1948, it has been a central principle of our foreign policy that we have a moral duty to ensure the survival of Israel. We met that obligation in 1973 by undertaking a massive resupply of Israeli forces, and the result was the embargo. If war breaks out again, however, given the steady improvement of the Arab fighting forces, Israel might be much more heavily pressed. Our resupply operations would have to be more extensive and our involvement even more overt. If so, we could probably expect a much more comprehensive embargo. They know how to do it now, and they know how well it works. And later, when things settled down again—if they ever settled down—we could probably, as a result of our role, also expect a breathtaking rise in prices and perhaps even a permanent curtailment of much of our supplies.

So what would we do? Would we simply stand by and watch and in the process perhaps let Israel go under? Or would we once more intervene strongly on her side? I do not know the answers to these questions, nor do I like the alternatives they suggest. These are not the alternatives we want to be faced with. But given our dependence on imported oil and the profound effect that dependence is having on all aspects of national life and policy, we may yet have to come to grips with them. It will not be a proud day for our nation when our moral and ethical foreign policy choices are dictated by the politics of oil.

Can this unpleasant prospect and others like it be avoided? My answer is a qualified yes. We can avoid a bleak national future if we force ourselves to renounce dependence on others and once again strive for self-sufficiency. In the case of oil, this means that we must take steps to increase our domestic supplies, and by so doing significantly lessen our need for imported oil.

There are problems here, perhaps the most basic one being that the men we pay to manage our government seem unwilling to admit that we can ever again approach self-sufficiency. Time and time again President Carter, Secretary Schlesinger, and various Energy Department functionaries have taken to the air to tell the American people that, as Mr. Carter puts it, "The oil and natural gas we depend on for 75 percent of our energy are running out," and that "We can't substantially increase our domestic production."

But that, to put it as politely as possible, is simply not the case. True, based on the best estimates of our proved reserves, our existing inventory is being depleted rapidly. But these estimates are made within current economic and technological parameters, and do not take into consideration other sources of oil and gas—among them, tertiary recovery, tight reservoirs, oil shale, geopressured brines, methane from coal and shale seams, coal liquefaction and gasification.

The fact is that no one knows for certain just how much oil and gas can be recovered from these and other sources. In the case of oil, a United Nations report points out that current estimates of supply, because of their rigid parameters, exclude 85 percent of the world's crude oil which could be developed. And the Moscow Academy of Sciences, which can hardly be accused of being in the pay of the oil companies, reckons the crude oil base to be a bit over 12 trillion barrels, or several *centuries'* worth of supply.

Nevertheless, despite the great abundance of sources waiting to be developed, the leaders of our nation seem intent on attempting to persuade us that they do not exist. Why? The answer, I fear, is not an attractive one: they are unwilling to admit that the problem is essentially one of exploration and development, for they know it is the complex web of governmental programs, policies, rules, and regulations that is primarily responsible for discouraging that necessary exploration and development. The government itself, in other words, is a major cause of our real energy problem.

Consider, for instance, the hard fact that we have never actively undertaken a comprehensive search for oil off the coasts of the United States. Ours is one of the longest coastlines in the world, yet only about 5 percent of that coastline has been explored for oil. The reason: the sea bottom belongs to the federal government, and the federal government has not seen fit to allow accelerated development of its property. At this very moment, we should be exploring our coastal areas. But the federal government, amidst the confusion growing naturally out of its perceived role as guarantor of all things to all men, has posted no-trespassing signs along most of our coastlines. Similarly, a no-trespassing sign is being hung out in Alaska, which the government, with its massive and totally unnecessary land withdrawal proposals, is turning into one gigantic national park. We may not be able to develop supplies on federal lands in Alaska and in the West and along our coastline immediately. Nor, at the moment, do we necessarily want to. But we do want to know what resources are available in such areas. Long-range, orderly planning for our energy future demands that, at the very least.

Yet the government, caught in the complex web of its own devising, seems able to respond only by spinning yet another tortuous strand; and when it does allow us to explore and develop, it frequently spins opposing strands which prevent us from doing so.

There is, for instance, the matter of shale oil development in the West. In 1974, along with Gulf Oil, my own company, Standard Oil Company (Indiana), leased a tract of federal land near Rangely, Colorado, for the purpose of developing shale oil. And then, until very recently, we just sat there, unable to proceed, for various experts in Washington had established a set of federal ambient air standards that simply could not be met. It wasn't that *we* could not meet them—the culprit was Mother Nature herself. Because of emissions from various plants and wind-borne particulates, the natural air quality could not meet federal standards. And not even the government can harness the wind or order plants to cease and desist from transpiring.

Thus, as a direct result of several of the complex and contradictory roles government has spun for itself, my company lost several million dollars; we had to convert to a different process; we were finally given a permit to proceed by the EPA in December 1977; in March 1978, the EPA declared the county in which we were operating a "non-attainment" county, which meant that, once again, we were not allowed to do anything; and the nation, which has been waiting half a decade for large-scale shale oil development as a partial solution to our energy problem, is still waiting. And in the meantime, as we waited, our dependence on oil from abroad continued to rise.

In this and scores of similar cases, the government is the problem. But it is inherent in the bureaucratic imperative that you never admit mistakes and never take blame. Therefore, the drill is to find scapegoats: at fault, various federal officials from the president on down tell us, are industry "profiteers" and "rip-off artists," together with a profligate public. "Ours is the most wasteful nation on earth," intoned President Carter in his April 1977 address on energy. And perhaps he has a point. With only 6 percent of the world's population, we do use one-third of the world's oil. But the datum which Washington officials never mention is that we also produce one-third of the world's gross national product.

It is problematical why the government chooses to ignore that fact, but it is perhaps in part because production has no place in the federal scheme of things. If we depend on production, we are depending on the market, and if we depend on the market, we diminish our dependence on government. This may also explain the peculiar emphasis on demand and the lack of consideration of supply in the Administration's energy problem: government can control demand through its various programs and regulations, but it can do little about supply. Thus, the approach is to ignore the supply side of the traditional supply-demand equation and instead devise yet more rules and regulations aimed at controlling demand.

This cannot work, of course. It never does, for when you factor out the supply side of the equation, you inevitably end by running low on supply, at which point demand becomes irrelevant. This, for instance, is what happened in the case of natural gas. For twenty-four years prices for this clean and efficient energy source have been held by government controls well below the natural market level, while the price of everything else in the economy has continued to rise. Because these low prices represent an enormous bargain, consumers naturally increase demand. Producers, however, finding that their profit margins continue to shrink in relation to the spiraling costs in the economy as a whole, either cut back exploration or stand pat. Thus, shortages are inevitable, the natural result of governmental tampering with the market mechanism. And one natural result of federally enforced shortages is increased dependence on foreign supplies.

The government and its spokesmen, with unlimited access to the communications media, would have us believe the only alternative to this dependence is conservation. That, however, is not the case. There is another clear-cut alternative to dependence, and that alternative is readily available to us if we are willing to pay the price. It is not an exorbitant price, no higher than the price the Administration's tax plan disguised as an energy policy asked us to pay. But the difference is this: higher prices in an unregulated market—rather than higher prices in the form of taxes, as the Administration originally proposed—would encourage producers to invest in domestic exploration and development and would provide the means to do so. If we were to phase out all price controls and let prices rise naturally to the world market level, we consumers—and we are all consumers—would be paying more for energy. But we would also be assured of getting the energy we were paying for.

The economic principle involved here is a very simple one: the price received by producers must be greater than the costs of exploration and development. Admittedly, it seems extremely radical in these days of dependence and cooperative collectivism to propose a method of increasing investment capital that relies on the free-market system. That is what I propose, however. And I would like to carry that radical proposal a step further: not only should producing companies be paid enough to cover the costs of production; they should also be allowed to make enough to return a bit extra to their stockholders. As I write this, the President's proposal for a well-head tax on crude oil is being hotly debated in Congress, where the solons seem to see only two choices: Rep. Al Ullman says the tax is essential; Sen. Henry Jackson says it is dead and that the President must therefore be prepared to implement oil-import fees, thereby still further complicating federal regulation of the industry. Again, however, there is that third alternative—remove controls and let prices rise to their natural level. I can think of no coherent argument to justify our current willingness to hold the average price of domestic oil in the United States at about $8.50 per barrel, while paying out approximately $14.00 per barrel to foreign producers.

I am, I realize, discussing a sensitive subject here, for I am referring to profits, and you seldom hear the word "profits" mentioned in Washington these days unless it is modified by the adjective "obscene." But that is something that should require no apology from any American, for the day upon which we apologize for advocating a reasonable profit is the day upon which we will be apologizing for the economic system that built this nation. Perhaps that makes those of us in industry "profiteers" or "rip-off artists." But I prefer to think it simply makes us typical American businessmen who believe the profit motive to be the best incentive to production, progress, and a humane society yet conceived by the mind of man. And as proof of that, we need do no more than compare our achievements with those of nations in which profits have been outlawed. In fact, I trust the profit motive a good deal more than I trust the power motive. Seekers after profits seldom attempt to abridge personal and economic freedoms: to do so would be counterproductive. Seekers after power, however, who gravitate toward government, tend to attempt to abridge those freedoms as a matter of course.

Winston Churchill once had this to say about profits: "It is a socialist idea that making profits is a vice. I consider the real vice in making losses." It is perhaps a measure of just how far down the road we have traveled that today so many Americans associate profits with vice and are unable to understand that whenever the government intrudes massively into the economic sphere, it makes losses. And when our government makes losses, we all lose. We lose not only economically; we also, as is the case with energy, lose much of our independence as a people.

Down through history, the siren song of dependence has been one of the most insidious to be sung by the power seekers. Give up some of your independence, goes the refrain, and we will give you security. But in the process the singers of the song have invariably concluded that to build the totally secure society, they must abridge economic independence. And that, of course, is the ultimate irony, for the history of our nation proves that the only true security comes from economic, and therefore political and personal freedom. Freedom and security are not mutually exclusive terms. They are, instead, synonymous, and there can be no true freedom when we are dependent on others.

Thus, in a very real sense, our energy dependence is symbolic of the ultimate problem facing us as a people. We can continue to proceed along the path toward total dependence, be it dependence on foreign nations to supply our energy needs or dependence on the state to provide our sustenance. This is what many of our politicians and officials and functionaries would have us do, for they have a vested interest in keeping us dependent. Or we can attempt again to raise the tattered but proud banners of self-sufficiency, self-reliance, and independence under which the citizens of this republic once marched. To do this in the economic sphere also means dependence—that is, we would once again depend totally on the free market to guarantee our security as a people. But in the end, that form of dependence is really the most independent of all, for we are all the market, and to depend on the market is to depend upon ourselves. And that is something that we as a people very much need to do once again.

—JOHN E. SWEARINGEN

CHAPTER 7

Challenges Confronting
American Banking

A conventional approach to the implicit question posed for this chapter is to picture banking as an embattled industry, fragmented by the operation of outdated statutes, supervised by a multitiered system of federal and state regulatory agencies, and watching almost helplessly as near-banks and other financial institutions nibble away at its business, while at the same time major foreign banks cast increasingly covetous eyes at the still lush American market. In broad outline, such a picture is not far from reality. Yet merely to sketch in the details would produce a picture that is both distorted and incomplete. For example, a recital of the bits and pieces of banking authority that legislators seem likely to give also to competitor institutions would place undue emphasis on the fact that banking is beset with problems—and would cause one to overlook the fact that it is also faced with some magnificent opportunities. Perhaps even more importantly, the challenges facing banking today stem from deeper forces at work than any particular statute or regulation that may be currently under debate.

Before turning to these challenges, it will be useful to identify the industry that we will be discussing. This is not an easy task. The American banking system, one assumes, must be utterly bewildering to most foreign observers. For that matter, many American bankers would be hard put to describe or analyze what is meant precisely by the banking industry, or how it came to be what it is. The term "banking industry" typically refers to the more than 14,000 institutions designated as "commercial banks," and this in turn is usually intended to mean those banks that accept demand deposits from the public and that number business firms among their more important customers. This definition is intended to distinguish "banking" from those depository thrift institutions whose liabilities are mainly savings and time deposits and whose assets consist principally of real estate-oriented loans or, in the case of credit unions, consumer installment loans.

As a working definition, this is probably reasonably satisfactory, unless too much pressure is applied to it. However, among the institutions that would be classified as commercial banks, there are many which, if judged solely by their balance sheets, would be difficult to distinguish from the depository thrift institutions. Nevertheless, whether commercial banks are viewed in the aggregate or in terms of what one might call the "typical" commercial bank, the identifying characteristics are demand deposits and commercial loans. And if not every bank engages in such businesses, at least it has the authority to do so whereas most of its competitors do not.

It is still possible to speak of an American banking industry using the criteria just supplied, although how much longer this will be true is not so clear. If stress is put upon the word "American," then perhaps one should deduct, for analytical purposes, the approximately 120 foreign banks operating in the United States through various types of facilities, ranging from agencies to full-fledged deposit-gathering branch banks. As of early 1978 the assets of these foreign institutions amounted to $65 billion, or approximately 6 percent of all commercial bank assets recorded for the United States. And these figures refer only to branches of foreign institutions, as distinguished from domestic banks under foreign ownership.

If stress is put upon the word "banking," there exists a large number of institutions which the public at least perceives as doing a banking business, and which in many ways have as much right to the term "bank" as do the commerical banks. There are, for example, the 469 mutual savings banks, concentrated largely in the northeastern states, with a history as venerable as that of the commercial banks and rivaling, if not exceeding, commercial banks in importance in a number of states in New England. Other depository institutions include some 4,858 savings and loan associations, the vast majority of which are mutual in form (as are the savings banks) but all of which offer deposit facilities to the general public and engage in lending activity which duplicates some of the same kinds of lending done by commercial banks. Rather similar in most ways, although smaller in size, are the 22,400 credit unions. All four types of depository institutions recently had aggregate deposits of about $1,450 billion, of which the commercial banks accounted for 62 percent.

And then there are the investment bankers, comprising an industry perhaps as difficult to define and measure as commercial banking. Nevertheless, those firms whose principal business consists of the underwriting and distribution of corporate or government securities do constitute an identifiable "industry," many of whose members rival the largest commercial banks in tradition and in the scope of their financing operations for business and governments. But even here the line cannot be drawn too sharply, since many commercial banks are also active participants in the investment banking business, except to the extent (since 1933) that Congress has prohibited their underwriting and distribution of corporate (and some government) securities.

In one sense, the only real challenge facing the commercial banking industry is the same as that facing every other financial and nonfinancial industry, namely, that the world within which it operates—economic, technological, or political—is changing rapidly and often in unanticipated ways. But to say this is to say everything and at the same time nothing. It is possible to narrow the focus a bit and to suggest that the challenges that the banking industry faces come essentially from three sources: government, the economy, and from within the industry itself. To a considerable extent these three sets of challenges are interrelated, but it will be useful to examine each separately.

A FRAGMENTED FINANCIAL SYSTEM

It is probable that the relationship between government and banking in the United States is unique in the modern world. It is founded in substantial part on a basic fact of American political life, namely, a deep concern over the concentration of financial power. Why this is so, and how it played a part in the development of the American banking system, is a story too long and too detailed to recount at this time. It is sufficient to observe that early in its history this nation opted for a fragmented commercial banking system. This was obtained by providing that entry into the industry would be open to all comers and that its institutions would be restricted in the nature of their operations, not only functionally but, even more importantly, geographically. To this has been added a set of government policies which, through deposit insurance, assure confidence in the vast majority of institutions, and another set of policies which make mergers particularly difficult when banking firms are involved. The result is the more than 14,000 banks that do business today.

The American public has always cast an equally suspicious eye on any concentration of financial power in government hands. No single governmental institution has ever been entrusted with the regulation of the commercial banking industry. Even the central bank, the Federal Reserve, was established in 1913 (and still continues) as a group of twelve regional banks, with a board of governors in Washington. And again unique to the modern world, in this nation each of the states shares with the federal government the authority to charter commercial banks, while their supervision is distributed among three federal agencies in addition to the fifty state chartering agencies, depending upon the particular bank's charter and its membership in the Federal Deposit Insurance Corporation or the Federal Reserve System. There is also a cluster of other agencies, primarily federal, that possess limited but often important supervisory roles when it comes to commercial banking. Most important in this regard would be the Department of Justice in the case of bank mergers and acquisitions, and the Securities and Exchange Commission when dealing with banking organizations that are bank holding companies.

The result is fragmentation of banking power whether in private or governmental hands. This situation is strengthened by government action in the past whereby depository institutions that specialize in one or several of the activities also engaged in by commercial banks are chartered and supervised under quite separate and different agencies and rules. Savings and loan associations and credit unions may also be chartered by either federal or state agencies, but at the federal level, and often at the state level, these agencies are quite separate from those chartering commercial banks. Supervisory and insurance functions also, at the federal level, are provided by separate agencies, namely, the Federal Home Loan Bank Board and the National Credit Union Administration. Investment banking firms look to still a different federal agency, the Securities and Exchange Commission, for oversight at the federal level.

Only with respect to the savings banks has some consolidation of authority been achieved at the federal level, since those savings banks that desire federal deposit insurance (comprising substantially all of them except in Massachusetts) are supervised by the Federal Deposit Insurance Corporation, which also supervises commercial banks. Fortunately for the sanity of those charged with tracking or describing this system, no savings bank is also a member of the Federal Reserve System (although they are eligible to become so) or is chartered by the federal government (although this, too, may soon be possible if present legislative proposals are enacted into law).

Despite the intricate interrelationships between government and banking, there is no deep philosophy that guides government in its relationship to the industry, except for the underlying concern over financial power noted earlier, and an equally important belief that banks must be sound. The first concern has been largely allayed by fragmenting the industry and its regulators. The second concern— stemming from the fact that banks have had an annoying habit of failing—has largely been allayed through pervasive supervision and regulation. But notwithstanding this close government oversight, a fragmented system will necessarily provide some number of bank failures, so in 1933 the gap between two inconsistent pieces of public policy was bridged by federal deposit insurance. It is against this background that government today is posing a variety of challenges for banking. At least two are of major significance.

THE ALLOCATION OF CREDIT

Because of their wide range of permissible activities, commercial banks are crucial allocators of credit. Other depository institutions also allocate credit, but their role is of less significance. A savings and loan association, for example, has a much narrower band within which to make its credit allocation decisions, since the major portion of the funds it receives will go, in one way or another, to support the residential housing market. In recent years government has become increasingly interested in the ways in which credit is allocated and, not surprisingly, particularly so in the case of commercial banks.

In the past, government's interest was directed primarily at the quality of assets acquired by depository institutions, on the reasonable ground that the granting of credit to risky borrowers held out the prospect of possible borrower default leading to failure of the institution. But recently, government has concerned itself with proper procedures to be followed in the granting of credit, enacting statute after statute and regulation after regulation intended to protect consumers by assuring that they have full knowledge of rates, terms, and the like. A result has been time-consuming and costly procedures which themselves constitute an important challenge to bank managements. But the far more serious challenge being posed by government today is whether the banking industry shall continue to have freedom to allocate credit on the basis of business judgment or whether this decision-making process shall be shared with government, or perhaps even completely usurped by government.

The case for more government involvement in the allocation of credit is both attractive and reasonable to many legislators. It is attractive primarily because it provides a relatively painless way of achieving what are thought to be desirable social objectives. To put the matter in its crudest form, if $X billion is thought to be needed for some worthy purpose (say, inner-city housing or energy-related loans) the need to increase taxes or increase government deficits in order to obtain the necessary funds can be avoided entirely if banks can only be compelled to divert a specified portion of their resources to the indicated usage.

Rather than compulsion, it has appeared that similar results could be more satisfactorily obtained by simply making the desired course of action more profitable. Since government officials have long been intrigued with this possibility, guarantees or tax advantages have often been dangled before banks and other depository institutions if they invest in certain types of obligations (residential mortgages, for example). A cruder form of credit allocation can be found in the decision to restrict the nature of the investments of savings and loan associations and, at the same time, to restrict the ability of commercial banks to pay competitive interest rates on savings, all of this for the purpose of causing more funds to flow to housing than the market might otherwise direct.

The financing of solutions to social problems will almost certainly continue to be in the forefront of legislators' attention in the future, and the urge to tinker more extensively, and perhaps more firmly, with the freedom of banks to allocate credit is likely to become even more irresistible. If this were all that commercial bankers faced, the challenge in the future might not be so difficult. The case for allowing market forces to work relatively unimpeded is, after all, a strong one, and the experience with government allocation schemes has been far from successful. One need only note the erratic flows of funds to housing under the system just mentioned.

As we noted earlier, however, from a legislator's point of view, an increasing government involvement in credit allocation is not only attractive but also reasonable. For banks, after all, are investing other people's money to a very considerable extent. The owners' stake in banking has declined substantially, relative to that of depositors and other creditors. With equity comprising today only some 7 percent of all bank assets, a legislator, particularly one not overly familiar with the industry itself, can rather easily conclude that it is entirely appropriate to see to it that the public's money is invested in ways that he, the legislator, thinks the public might desire. The recently enacted Community Reinvestment Act is illustrative; its language requires each federal financial supervisory agency to use its authority, when examining financial institutions, to encourage such institutions to help meet the credit needs of the local communities in which they are chartered, consistent with the safe and sound operation of such institutions.

There is still another reason for many legislators to be inclined to restrict the freedom of commercial banks to allocate credit, and this is deposit insurance. The recent cluster of major bank failures has driven home to even the most casual reader of the financial press that the government has a large financial stake in the operations of commercial banks. The idea that federal deposit insurance was simply a device to provide limited coverage, primarily to small depositors, was never entirely accurate and today has been shown to be largely fiction. Federal deposit insurance officials have not permitted a major bank (nor even a fairly large-size bank) to close or be merged without assuring that all depositors, regardless of the amounts of their deposits, are fully protected.

One of the early and seemingly irrational arguments in opposition to federal deposit insurance had been the claim that it would lead inevitably to the nationalization of the banking system. Today, almost a half century later, nationalization seems no closer. Yet much of the substance of nationalization may be occurring, and to that extent at least those early critics correctly foresaw the future. For as the relative stake of bank owners shrinks, and as the role of the federal government as insurer against mismanagement or worse increases, it becomes easier to justify heavier government involvement in bank operations, not only in a supervisory sense but in all of the other ways that have been popular recently. Especially with regard to credit allocation, the question of further government involvement in the banking and credit structure is a major challenge facing the American economy and particularly the banking industry.

The whole question of the allocation of credit among the sectors of the economy, through the activities of our entire financial mechanism including the banks, is likely to become increasingly critical during the period ahead. This is because the progress and normal growth of this country's economy will require the mobilizing and the effective and efficient use of very large amounts of funds. In order that the national economic growth which the public in this country wants and expects, and which the country has the physical resources to accomplish, may be brought about, the amounts of funds involved are likely to be larger (even after downward adjustment for the effects of inflation) than have ever been mobilized in the past.

For the desired expansion of the country's supply of buildings and equipment and other capital assets, it is first necessary that the economy should generate a corresponding amount of savings. It is then important that the savings be used most effectively. For this, there is also needed the best possible system of financial intermediaries through which these savings can be channeled to appropriate end uses, and it is in this connection that an economically sound mechanism of credit allocation is so vital.

COMPETITION IN FINANCIAL SERVICES

An entirely different challenge, or perhaps set of challenges, is being provided by government in the area of competition. In complete contrast to the early 1930s when competitive excesses were considered to be of serious concern in many fields, restraints on competition among banks, and between banks and other depository institutions, are distinctly unfashionable today. Congress, the courts, and the regulatory agencies themselves are all essentially of one mind in the objective of attaining a more competitive banking system.

By itself, the prospect of enhanced competition poses a considerable challenge to banking, particularly to those segments that believe they benefit from present limitations on the ability to compete. This is a matter discussed a bit later in this chapter; for the moment it may be useful to assume that over the longer run competition can be only beneficial for the banks as well as for their customers. The more immediate problem is the way in which the anti-competitive structure erected in the 1930s will be dismantled.

In the wake of the collapse of the late 1920s and early 1930s, when there was a widespread belief that excessive competition had been a basic cause of the depression, government acted decisively upon this belief and applied competitive restraints to virtually all industries. For the most part these restraints were dropped or substantially eliminated in subsequent years, but they remain in place for banking. The anti-competitive restraints took three forms. First, restraints on geographic expansion by banks were confirmed, with only modest liberalization, in an effort to assure the continued viability of small banking institutions. Second, rather clear lines of demarcation were erected between various industry groups, separating out, as noted earlier, important investment banking functions as well as establishing for the depository thrift institutions (savings and loan associations and credit unions primarily) separate spheres of activity and regulation. And third, limits were placed on the rates of interest that banks could offer for deposits, on the supposition that excessive interest payments prior to 1934 had compelled banks to seek high-yield, riskier assets, thereby contributing to bank failures.

With the increasing emphasis of government on the desirability of competition in general, it can certainly be expected that the trend of governmental moves in the period ahead will be toward the elimination of these restraints in the banking field. However, as a realistic matter, the elimination of restraints on geographic expansion is likely to come more slowly, while earlier attention is likely to be focused primarily on the other two areas indicated above. That is, competition is to be enhanced by relaxing and eliminating many of the interest rate regulations, and by extending to the depository thrift institutions some of the powers previously reserved for commercial banks, most particularly the ability to offer demand deposit services to consumers. And, indeed, there is even talk of re-examining the Glass-Steagall Act of 1933 with the idea of permitting banks to compete with investment bankers over a broader range of investment banking activities, such as underwriting revenue bonds issued by states and municipalities.

In contrast with such prospects, relatively little attention is being paid at the present time to any serious change in the McFadden Act which, as amended in 1933, provides that federally chartered commercial banks in each state shall be subject to those limitations on geographic expansion (i.e., branching) that are established by that state for state-chartered banks. Nor is much thought being given to any change in the counterpart provisions of the Bank Holding Company Act of 1956, which effectively prohibits bank holding companies based in one state from entering other states.

No one doubts that eventually Congress will find it necessary to eliminate, or at least alter drastically, the set of constraints on geographic expansion by banks. Developments with respect to electronic funds transfer systems, if nothing else, will ultimately compel such a move and, indeed, tentative and exploratory legislative efforts have already surfaced in that direction. Moreover, some relief has already been provided by the 1970 holding company legislation which, as interpreted, at least permits bank holding companies to operate their nonbanking subsidiaries without regard to state boundaries. Still, it seems almost certain that the dismantling of the entire bundle of restraints on competition will proceed in such order that those related to branching will come off last. For the banking industry, this poses a significant set of challenges, embracing both problems and opportunities.

Perhaps the most important of the various restrictions destined for elimination is the prohibition of the payment of interest on demand deposits. Here the process of dismantling has been under way for some time and for all practical purposes has been accomplished for consumer demand deposits in the six New England states. There is little doubt in anyone's mind that this will spread across the nation, and that it will be followed rather quickly by the elimination of interest restrictions on all forms of demand deposits.

The problems presented by this change will be immense, as will the opportunities. A substantial part of the pricing system utilized by banks is implicit, dependent upon customer balances. Once it becomes necessary for banks to make explicit payment for demand deposits, then it will also become necessary to price their services explicitly, a fact that will almost certainly result in substantial transitional costs. But once the transition has been effected, banks will find themselves in a more competitive posture, where opportunities will be available to the innovative and the efficient, while there will be penalties on those who are not up to the competitive race. In the long run, both banking and the public will benefit.

Another important change will be extension to the depository thrift institutions of the ability to offer demand deposit services, at least to consumers, together with the ability to pay interest on such demand balances. This change is also well under way, presently in the New England states and, like the elimination of interest prohibitions on demand deposits, will spread across the nation. Rather interestingly, outside of New England the drive is spearheaded by the smallest, in terms of average size, of the depository institutions, namely the credit unions.

For many banks the prospect of thousands of depository thrift institutions entering important segments of their business is viewed as tantamount to disaster. But other bankers sense that when the functional barriers between industries begin to crumble, the ultimate winners—apart from the public in general—will be those institutions that are best able to utilize the newfound freedoms and who have the experience and resources to do so. It is not at all clear that commercial banks will not be numbered among the ultimate winners in this race.

A particular problem faced by the banking industry, however, relates to the sequence in which the 1933 structure will be dismantled. The kinds of changes just noted will, initially at least, enhance competition for consumer deposits and consumer loan business. An important part of such competition is the ability to offer consumers conveniently located facilities, and in this instance banks in many states operate under archaic limitations on their ability to branch. Savings and loan associations and credit unions, for example, are subject to different and, in many areas, far more liberal limitations. If it is correct to assume that the restrictions on branching will be the last of the anti-competitive pieces of legislation to be lifted, then commercial banks face the prospect of entering a more competitive world under rather serious handicaps.

PROSPECTS FOR THE FUTURE

Unless one were prepared to make a serious effort at forecasting fluctuations in economic activity over the next five to ten years—a task not envisioned here—then the challenges posed by the economy for the banking industry can be discussed only in broad outline. So far as one can tell, governments generally have solved rather successfully the problem of avoiding deep and catastrophic depression, but are finding it far more difficult, and perhaps impossible, to solve the problem of endemic inflation. One may assume, therefore, that the prospects are for a continuing burgeoning economy, both in the United States and in the world, but one beset with serious problems.

The challenges facing the American banking industry differ, depending upon which segments of the industry one is discussing. The very largest banks, faced with fairly serious statutory impediments to domestic expansion (particularly on a retail basis) have tended to look increasingly to the world market as an outlet for their resources, and as a source of income. To a more limited extent this has been true also of the major regional banks. At a number of the larger banks, earnings from operations abroad now amount to half, or close to half, of total net earnings.

Inevitably, however, the attention of the major banks must become increasingly redirected to the domestic market. Some relief to the barriers that they face was provided with passage of the Bank Holding Company Act Amendments of 1970, and the subsequent expansion by major companies into other states through bank-related activities such as consumer finance companies, mortgage banking companies, leasing subsidiaries, and the like. However, the major banks, whether or not operating through holding companies, are still largely precluded by statute from two important activities when conducted interstate: deposit gathering, primarily on a retail basis, and extension of credit to the so-called middle market, i.e. the market comprised of business firms and other borrowing entities that are not of sufficient size to have access to national markets.

The inevitable push by the largest institutions to develop these two types of business, through more intensive utilization of the tools already permitted (such as loan production offices) and through seeking relaxation of statutory barriers, will have its most immediate effect upon the major regional banks, and also upon those banks, typically with deposits of at least $100 million, that do a sizable commercial business. Banks in this tier, constituting perhaps 500 to 1,000 institutions, will of course be torn politically by concern on the one hand over increased competition and a desire on the other hand to utilize the same methods to facilitate their own expansion. One result of the challenge faced by such banks, particularly the major regionals, is already apparent, namely, the development of an increasingly higher level of sophistication in the handling of large commercial borrowers, and giving close attention to innovative ways of improving, or protecting, retail or so-called core deposits.

For the great mass of banks, mostly of quite small size and heavily retail oriented, the fact that a growing economy is likely to enhance the expansionist tendencies of larger banks should not be a matter of immediate or even long-run concern, except perhaps for those institutions whose very existence may depend on rigid insulation from competitive forces. The great competitive wars of the future will be largely among the top 500 to 1,000 institutions. However, the emotions of the small banks are likely to be caught up in the political struggle, with results not easy to predict.

Among the economies of the world, the United States remains a particularly strong and desirable market. Moreover, it is a fragmented market and therefore, absent a statutory ban, relatively easy to enter. In recent years foreign institutions have not been slow to appreciate these facts. As a result, apart from branches of foreign banks in this country, there is also a very significant and increasing

number of American banks that have become subsidiaries or affiliates of foreign institutions, including several banks in the states of
New York and California with deposits exceeding $1 billion each.
Like other banks of similar size in those states, these banks combine
a significant volume of wholesale-type business with substantial
networks of retail branches. Their wholesale operations may tend to
be meshed or integrated with the international operations of their
affiliated institutions abroad.

It remains to be seen whether foreign entry may bring still
another set of competitive considerations into the picture, in such a
way as to affect especially the medium-sized and smaller banks
rather than just the larger American institutions where wholesale-
type business is important. While in the case of large banks the
increased competition from foreign institutions should, at least in
theory, be offset by the ability to move into other nations, this is not
really relevant to smaller banks. Up to the present, however, retail
business by foreign banks has not become important except in the
states of New York and California. In those states the smaller banks
have already been in competition (and mostly with a fair degree of
success) against the branches or affiliates of giant domestic banks,
and the prospects of foreign banks developing any substantial retail
business in other states are not at all clear.

Finally, the economy in the future will pose a continuing challenge to bank management because of the inflationary bias mentioned earlier. Banks no less than any other set of institutions must
be able to deal intelligently with the inevitable distortions and crises
that will arise in an economy beset with inflation. Some experiences
can be traumatic, as in 1974–75.

A final but most important challenge is posed by the banking
industry itself. Specifically, the question here is whether banking
will ever be able to put itself in a position to control its own destiny
better. It is not in such a position today. Indeed, a detached observer
might well conclude that the industry is in the process of tearing
itself apart. Obviously, the functions of commercial banking will
continue to be performed, by some group or groups of institutions,
but the banking industry as we know it today may be markedly
changed, or even disappear.

Probably the root of the problem is found in the structure
established by government. A system fragmented by law is one for

which it is difficult to identify or establish a sense of purpose. Illustrations abound of the fissures and divisions within banking which, time after time, render the industry immobile when faced with new developments, and easy prey for competitor groups.

The situation with respect to electronic funds transfer (EFT) systems is perhaps as good an example as any. It can only be a source of amazement to any observer that the industry that has perhaps the greatest need to make effective use of the new electronic technology, and the one that is perhaps most experienced in its application, is completely tied up on the matter of just how or when it will be able to make full-scale use of the new equipment. The problem, of course, lies in the divisions within banking over financial power, branching power, and related matters. And while commercial banks struggle to disentangle themselves from the growing mass of regulation, court actions, and the like stimulated by EFT, there are beginning to be moves into various aspects of the banking business by competitor depository institutions as well as by major enterprises in other lines that are heavily dependent on consumer business.

Technological developments, including EFT, obviously present a remarkable field of opportunity for American banking. But the problems of making the best use of these opportunities will pose a significant set of challenges.

Banks are captives of the very structure that makes it difficult for them, as an industry, to meet the challenges faced by the intermixture of technological advance, government policy, and competitor incursions. Through an extensive correspondent network, substantial amounts of deposits at larger institutions are hostage to the political views of the many small banks in the nation. At stake also are all of the other interrelationships resulting from the correspondent system, whether they be fee services, arrangements for loan participations, or whatever. The dependence is not all one way, of course, since smaller banks are as dependent upon a well-functioning correspondent system as are the larger institutions. But the net result is that when a particularly compelling challenge appears, banking is often incapable of reacting as an industry, since whatever the challenge, it is certain to be viewed differently among the different segments of the industry, either on economic or emotional grounds. As a consequence, the industry's responsiveness to such challenges, to say nothing of its ability to establish its own set of priorities, tends to be smothered by a fear of upsetting existing legislative as well as business arrangements.

It is primarily for this reason that the banking industry has a reputation, largely deserved, for being wedded to the status quo, and for reacting to change in a defensive manner. Still, one must assume that there are many issues on which an industry position can be identified that is in accord with its best long-run interest, as well as the best long-run interest of the public. What seems to be lacking, or perhaps impossible given existing structural arrangements, is strong industry leadership. Or, perhaps, after all, the banking industry as we have defined it is in reality a mirage, and commercial banking in this nation is in essence a loose confederation of separate industries. As we move into an increasingly uncertain world, where the pace of change is accelerating, we may find the answer.

—CARTER H. GOLEMBE

CHAPTER 8

Are We Losing the Freedom to Decide?

Individual freedom is an ideal which is cherished by virtually all Americans. It is no coincidence that we celebrate "the land of the free" in our national anthem and that the expression "it's a free country" is commonplace, to the point of cliché. The trouble with clichés, of course, is that we tend to use them without thinking. I'm afraid that, in the midst of all the real and imagined crises of our time, we haven't been thinking enough about freedom: how important it is; how fragile it is; and, perhaps most significant, how indivisible it is.

I emphasize indivisibility because recent public policies affecting freedom seem to point in opposite directions. In some respects the people of the United States enjoy more freedom today than any people in the entire history of mankind. Emerging law has removed virtually all restrictions on public expression and private moral behavior. We speak, with justification, about a "permissive society." At the same time, our economic freedom, as consumers as well as producers, has been increasingly restricted. We probably still have more of it than any other country in the world, but it seems to be fast eroding.

It is an unfortunate, but perhaps inescapable, characteristic of the human condition that we tend to be far more sensitive to threats against our own freedom than to those that affect the other fellow. Business people are not immune. We are sometimes vocal on the subject of economic freedom, but have too often been complacent about religious freedom, or freedom of the press, or academic freedom. Only recently, with the rising emphasis on prosecution for so-called white-collar offenses, have many businessmen taken a real interest in the administration of criminal justice.

Deplorable as this relative indifference may be, the so-called personal liberties—and particularly freedom of expression guaranteed by the First Amendment—are thriving. They have been vocally and effectively championed by the communications media and by the intellectual community. At the same time, many of these same groups have been in the forefront of the movement toward greater government restrictions in the economic area.

A provocative article by Professor Ronald Coase in the University of Chicago's *Journal of Legal Studies* has commented on the intellectual inconsistency of those who attach unique importance to the First Amendment liberties and neglect the others:[1]

> [The argument] lays great stress on freedom of expression as leading to self-fulfillment. No doubt it does. But freedom to choose one's occupation, one's home, the school one (and one's children) attends, what is studied at school, the kind of medical attention one receives, how one's savings are to be invested, the equipment one uses or the food one eats are surely equally necessary for self-fulfillment—and for most people are considerably more important than much of what is protected by the First Amendment. . . .
>
> Why is it that intellectuals who, one might think, would be made uncomfortable by such inconsistency seem to be unaware that there is any inconsistency in their views, or that their justification for the special position accorded freedom of expression is little more than phrase-making "full of sound and fury, signifying nothing"? Aaron Director has given the answer to the question. It is self-interest. The market for ideas is the market in which the intellectuals operate. They understand the value of freedom where their own activities are concerned. "Freedom of expression" is freedom for them. The market for goods is, however, the market in which the money-

1. Coase, "Advertising and Free Speech," Vol. 6, *The Journal of Legal Studies* 6:14–15 (1977).

making businessman operates. Regulation in this case is directed at the activities of another group and is, no doubt, made more attractive because intellectuals see themselves as doing the regulating. . . .

It might be worthwhile to ponder Professor Coase's comments when we hear facile distinctions drawn between so-called individual liberties and "mere" economic rights by those who make their living communicating ideas. My objective here, however, is not to question motives: the rightness or wrongness of things is not determined by whether people are self-interested. My objective is to emphasize that economic liberties are not matters of interest just to businessmen. They are vital to all of us in our capacity as consumers and, like free speech, their exercise is an important instrument of popular sovereignty.

Essentially, America's economic system is founded on what Adam Smith, some two hundred years ago, termed a "system of natural liberty." It is the freedom of a customer to choose from among a variety of differently priced products and services. It is the equally basic and complementary freedom of a producer to compete for the patronage of that customer. It is the freedom to invest in an enterprise, or not to invest. It is the freedom to risk in the hope of reward.

Economic freedom has worked wonderfully well in the United States. It has provided more of the world's goods for more people than any other system in any other country or at any other time in history. More than that, the abundance that most Americans are able to enjoy in material things contributes to our personal fulfillment in other areas, such as education and the arts, and enhances the whole quality of our lives.

Finally, a free economy has built-in corrective processes that generally work if given the chance. A free economy works so well, in fact, that we tend to take it for granted and forget what a fragile mechanism it really is. We think we can "fine tune" the process with a slight judicious nudge here and there. We forget that the cumulative effect of these individually small interferences may create progressively more serious distortions, which will in turn lead to further "correcting" regulation, and so on until the economy becomes controlled by bureaucratic rather than popular will. A centrally directed state is not intended, but it comes about anyhow.

Let me illustrate the contrast between free-market solutions and regulatory solutions by reference to an example close to my own experience: the redesign of the American automobile. American manufacturers are now engaged in an extreme modification of the size, weight, appearance, and utility of a product which, probably more than any other, symbolizes modern American society and which provides a degree of personal mobility so valued by individual Americans that Walter Reuther could well describe it as "America's Fifth Freedom."

General Motors, as it happens, is leading the way in the redesign of the automobile. In 1977 our so-called standard-size cars were dramatically downsized and in 1978 our intermediate-size cars were similarly redimensioned. In the 1980s we'll be doing the same with virtually all of our remaining vehicles.

This is no easy trick. Our designers and engineers have been asked to provide more room for passengers and for luggage in a smaller overall package; to meet or exceed all the standards for emission control, fuel economy, and safety; to maintain levels of comfort, convenience, and performance; and still manage to turn out these cars in a necessary variety and in lines that are pleasing to the eye and within the means of our customers. The whole endeavor has been called one of the biggest gambles in the history of American enterprise.

What does this illustration tell us about the free marketplace? Let me offer a few thoughts:

First, contrary to popular impression, these redesigned, more fuel-efficient cars are not coming about because of any government directive. They were conceived before the Arab oil embargo, before lines appeared at gas stations, before the imposition—or even discussion—of federal standards for gas mileage, and long before our people were called to the colors in our current "moral equivalent of war." The timing and the details of this redesign program have clearly been affected by these developments, but the basic idea preceded them. In our minds, as auto men and businessmen, it was the consumer who—as always—was calling our shots. These redimensioned, more efficient cars were brought to market because we concluded that the marketplace would be demanding them as early as the late seventies. And, in our business, these kinds of decisions have to be made many years in advance.

Auto manufacturers are often pictured as short-sighted and stubborn. It has been said we persisted in making big "gas-guzzling" cars just because they were more profitable, and that we chose to ignore the "real" public demand for smaller, more efficient vehicles. That's nonsense. No businessman in his right mind sets out to market products that the public doesn't want to buy, and there is no way unwanted products can be more profitable. Sometimes our predictions are wrong and we produce the wrong products at the wrong time, but no one ever sets out to do it deliberately.

In taking this massive risk to downsize our product we could easily have been wrong. To begin with, we didn't know what our competitors were going to do. As it turned out, they read the market a little differently. Consequently, we at GM sold our redesigned models for two successive years in head-to-head competition with the more conventionally sized cars of the other manufacturers. The final verdict of the market has still to be heard at this writing, but overall we believe that our risks will be rewarded. It appears that consumers, acting freely in what they perceive as their own best interests, are accepting the lighter and more fuel-efficient cars that also coincide with the nation's interest in energy conservation.

Suppose, however, that government policy makers—as some have proposed—were to try to accelerate this trend toward lighter, more fuel-efficient cars. Suppose they were to try to "force" the market by mandating a stepped-up schedule of more drastic product changes, not only for General Motors, but for our competitors as well.

There are two possibilities. Under one, the regulations would merely codify or ratify the kind of product mix which the public would be willing to buy anyway. In this case, regulation would produce nothing except bureaucratic overhead. Alternatively, the regulations would prescribe a product mix which consumers would *not* freely select. When people don't like what the government orders, or a manufacturer offers, they just won't buy. Fewer cars would be sold. Jobs would be lost, and the prosperity of a major sector of our economy would be weakened. These economic consequences would be considered as political calamities, and the sorry but predictable prescription would be a further dose of regulation.

Nor would an attempt to force the market conserve energy. Quite the opposite. If people don't want the more efficient new cars, they

would continue to drive their less efficient old cars. These, with
proper care, would run for a long time. Because you can't force a
product on an unwilling public, the overall result of government
action—apart from economic hardship and intrusion on the consumer's freedom of choice—would be to waste rather than to conserve
energy. The air would not be made any cleaner either. Again, in all
likelihood further regulation would be forthcoming.

Let's look at another proposal for government regulation which
could also have unintended effects. There is a lot of talk, particularly in Washington, about the so-called problem of concentration in
some American industries. Companies in those industries which are
labeled as concentrated are supposed to be reluctant to engage in
tough competition and reluctant to innovate. And, the theory goes,
these companies are easy to spot. The relative market share or
profitability of leading companies in concentrated industries—you
might say, their success in satisfying customers—can be taken as
presumptive evidence of an undesirable degree of market power.
The proposed remedy is that these companies, selected for their
success, be dismembered.

Suppose that the law were to be so changed, and a company were
retroactively penalized for its success in winning market share or
earning profit. If success had carried such a penalty, what do you
think would have been the likelihood of GM's undertaking the
expensive risk of redesigning an already successful product line?
The new designs might be even more successful than we expected
and might result, at least temporarily, in a substantial increase in
GM's market share and profitability. Would we have been as willing
to take on that considerable risk if success could only have led to
dismemberment? I think the answer is self-evident.

I do not mean to suggest by these comments that all regulation is
necessarily bad. No one questions the need for government intervention in situations where one person's unrestricted freedom can
seriously inhibit the rights of others. Some standards in such areas
as safety and environmental protection are necessary. The issues in
these areas involve the levels of particular standards—whether their
benefit exceeds the cost which, wherever it first falls, will ultimately
be borne by society as a whole. We do need to remember, however,
that the areas in which the market itself will not make the optimal
adjustment are far more limited than government planners commonly assume.

To the extent that government interferes with the marketplace unnecessarily, individual liberty is not only diminished but popular sovereignty is also impaired. This is so because the marketplace is a far more responsive and finely tuned instrument of popular sovereignty than the political process. In the political system a citizen must delegate his sovereignty first to elected officials and these officials in turn delegate it to the actual administrators. A citizen— at least twice removed from these administrative decisions—can express his displeasure only periodically in elections, and then his particular disagreement may be obscured by a host of other issues embodied in the broad platforms on which political candidates run.

In the market, however, the citizen in effect participates directly in a continuing referendum on every single item in a finely detailed platform. Moreover, unlike the political system, "voters" with different ideas can each win. The market will therefore respond to individual desires far more accurately and promptly than government planners can ever do—*and* with greater regard for individual choice.

I realize that all this talk about freedom of consumers to express their preferences in the marketplace and freedom of producers to compete for their patronage is considered impolitic in today's intellectual climate. But, as history demonstrates, the most important time to speak up for freedom is precisely when the subject is unpopular.

Let's make no mistake about it—a substantial body of our freedom is under attack today: the freedom of talented individuals to apply their skills to their best advantage and the freedom of enterprises to organize themselves to serve their customers most efficiently. Even more important is the freedom of consumers to buy what *they* want, and not what someone else thinks would be good for them.

An increasing number of government regulations, which ostensibly control the products that business can sell, are really designed to limit the kinds of products that consumers can buy. We are told that people are so gullible or so ignorant that they cannot make prudent choices in the marketplace and that accordingly they have to be protected against themselves—an idea that would appear intolerably authoritarian if applied, say, in the areas of religious or electoral choice. An influential coalition of journalists, intellectuals, social "reformers," and government officials—the "new class" described by Irving Kristol—has been able to translate its own paternalistic, and indeed patronizing, viewpoint into public policy. And it is individuals, not just businessmen, who are losing their freedom to decide:

> The real ire of the new class, and the firepower of its social policy, are directed, not merely at those in business who (in Lewis Lapham's marvelous phrase) "go around making things without permission," but also, and perhaps especially, at the mass of Americans who go around doing and enjoying things without permission.[2]

I think we have been lulled into accepting massive intrusions on individual liberty because we have too readily accepted the myth that the free marketplace is incapable of ameliorating pressing national problems. Faced with an apparent crisis, we are too quick to say "there ought to be a law." In fact, however, laws are very apt to make things worse.

In a time of energy shortage, moral exhortations and a hodge-podge of regulation will do little to conserve natural resources. But the forces of a free market, resulting in freely determined price levels, will conserve energy and will bring forth additional supplies of energy as well. Legislation based on vindictiveness or on a nostalgic preference for small-scale enterprise will not create more capable and responsive businesses. In the normal course, the businesses—large or small—that best serve the people will survive and will grow, and those that do not will wither away. The free competitive market system is still the best mechanism we have for encouraging inventiveness and effort, for rewarding the successful, for expanding personal choices, and for enriching individual lives.

Freedom has sometimes been lost all at once—overnight—but more usually it is lost piecemeal, and almost always for what look like the best of reasons: to serve national security, or to enhance public safety, or, perhaps, to protect the environment. But a precious freedom, once surrendered, is seldom regained. We understand this lesson very well as it applies to freedom of expression, but it is also important to remember it whenever a well-meaning public figure, in

2. Paul H. Weaver, "Regulation, Social Policy, and Class Conflict," No. 50 *The Public Interest:* 60 (1978).

or out of the government, tells us that we can no longer afford to act or to choose freely in the marketplace.

It's time for us to reaffirm the indivisibility of liberty. Even if it is argued that freedom to say what we want is a more basic right than freedom to buy what we want, we should remember that our society has many more consumers than speechmakers, and restrictions which cut broad are just as offensive as those which cut deep. Above all, as free citizens we should be on our guard against *paternalism,* wherever it may be found. Justice Brandeis said it best many years ago: "Experience should teach us to be most on our guard to protect liberty when government's purposes are beneficent. . . . The greatest dangers to liberty lurk in insidious encroachment by men of zeal, well-meaning but without understanding."

—THOMAS A. MURPHY

CHAPTER 9

Can Capitalism Survive?

I

Optimism historically has characterized the attitude of Americans about their prospects. And there have been good reasons. This optimism has had a strong ideological component. There has always been a firm American belief that our own nation was formed on the basis of noble concepts and ideas that were destined to move mankind forward. Other nations were geographic and historical accidents, determined by factors of such fundamental inconsequentiality as rivers or mountain ranges that were hard to cross or winds that happened to blow that day in a direction favorable to the king's navy.

Not so our own country. Our forebears "brought forth upon this continent" a new nation committed to principles that would inspire the world and alter the course of history. And perhaps the generous supply of eloquent bicentennial rhetoric in 1976 has by now receded sufficiently in our memories for us to recall again with a sense of awe that prose in the Declaration of Independence or the Constitution which articulated what this nation was to be all about. Our Founding Fathers, of course, had their own fallibilities. Thomas Jefferson, for example, could pen the words "that all men are created equal, that they are endowed by their Creator with certain unalienable rights" without at the same time doing much to extend this concept to his own slaves. They were not, however, meaningless words. Indeed, they and that new nation set in motion powerful

134

forces producing a vast extension of the range of freedom within which people could live their lives in ways that to them seemed good.

Our traditional optimism, however, has been based upon much more practical matters than noble sentiment. The American economy has, quite simply, worked. It has had an awesome track record of demonstrated capability for raising material levels of living and diffusing the fruits of this progress more and more widely. If the National Income Division of the Department of Commerce had existed at the turn of the century, it is estimated that the Division would have reported a GNP for 1900 of $19 billion. By 1977 our GNP was $1,900 billion. Now that hundred-fold rise would be impressive indeed, except for the awe-restraining thought that much of it is to be explained by higher prices. And the U.S. price level has been on a decidedly rising trend in this century. As best this can be measured, and our ability to do this is far more limited than seemingly precise index numbers imply, the dollar of the year 1900 had by 1977 lost about 90 percent of its purchasing power. To be precise, the U.S. price level has had about a ninefold rise since the turn of the century. That still leaves us, however, with an elevenfold increase in real output and real income during a period when our population did not quite triple.

To put all of this into more meaningful terms, the American economy has been delivering a doubling of material levels of living every generation. A quick mental glance around the world or back through history is enough to remind us that such a doubling has not been the lot of any consequential proportion of humanity since the beginning of time.

II

What is this economic system which has delivered such a performance through history? Will it survive? What are the developments raising questions about its survival? These questions are now being asked, and with a growing sense of unease.

While terminological arguments are never interesting, a troublesome problem must be clarified at the outset. Our economy is often referred to as capitalism in action, but this word has a variety of meanings. There is the technical fact that as more and more capital is used per person at work, production becomes more "capitalistic." In that sense all economies, including communist economies, are becoming more capitalistic and in that technical sense capitalism will certainly survive. The second edition of Webster's unabridged dictionary alludes to this technical meaning for its first definition of capitalism. The word capitalism also ranges into meanings with a pejorative implication, and Webster alludes to this for its second or moral meaning—namely, a state where capital, power, and influence are in the hands of a few. The first definition is true and not particularly interesting. The second is defeated by definition.

It is only with the third definition that the word starts to take on the concept of a process or system for organizing economic activity, alluding to economies which depend upon privately owned enterprises operating in competitive markets to produce goods and services.

It is, of course, important that we be clear about what it is whose survival prospects we are examining. The system whose possibilities for survival we are exploring here is capitalism in this third sense, but it could more meaningfully be called the liberal, market-organized economic system. Indeed, it would not be amiss to call it simply the liberal economy, in contrast to the state-organized economic system, which in reality and by its own inherent logic is illiberal in the sense that personal freedom is severely circumscribed. The liberal economy, on the other hand, relies on the preferences of consumers freely expressed in open and competitive markets to determine what is produced, and it in principle accords to people freedom also to decide where they will contribute their productive efforts.

III

Why is there uncertainty about the survival of this liberal economy? If demonstrated capacity to perform and deliver assured survival, the system would certainly survive. It has, as already pointed out, delivered a doubling of material levels of living every generation in this country. Moreover, the inherent or internal logic of the system would lead us to expect this track record of demonstrated performance. And it may be useful for us to explore a bit the reasons for expecting this result. One source of its effectiveness through history is that such a free and open system enables society to take advantage of an aggregate of knowledge and creativity that does not exist in its totality anyplace. This is more fundamental than it seems. In the centrally organized, top-down systems, it is only the limited knowledge and creativity encompassed by those at the top that can be implemented. Yet the lessons of history are clear about the sources of innovative thinking. New and better ideas often do not come from the top or even from so-called logical sources. The automobile industry did not emerge from the wagon and carriage companies. The railroads did not put the traveling public into airplanes. The modern hand-held calculator marvels were not developed by companies that earlier made those mechanical calculating behemoths. Nor did the mechanical watch industry develop and place on the market the digital watch.

The dynamic and innovative economic system must be sufficiently free and open to permit those who think they have a good new idea to try it out even if it seems to have emerged from a quite unlikely source. If the new idea is a dud, as most are, the innovator may lose his all in the venture, but relative to society's resources generally these social costs of the sorting-out process are negligible. We have here also, in short, an efficient weeding-out procedure.

While the proportion of new ideas, ideas and products which their progenitors confidently expect will save the world, that do actually represent an advance (a new product, or a fundamentally cheaper way of making an old product) is low, some new ideas are good, and a few are so fundamental as to revolutionize the economy. The good economic system must also be organized so that the new which is better can prevail. The system must be structured to assure that today's new which is better must become tomorrow's standard, and today's standard, which is tomorrow's archaic, must be expunged from the economy. The liberal, market-organized economic system has an answer for this problem—namely, open and competitive markets. If consumers free to express their preferences in these open and competitive markets like the new product, it will prevail even in the face of an entrenched status quo implacably firm and sincere in its belief that the old, established ways and products are best. The manufacturers of steam locomotives were genuinely certain that diesel motors would never be a practicable source of power for pulling trains, and the diesel locomotive thus was pioneered from outside the conventional industry. It was not the old ice companies who brought forth the mechanical refrigerator.

Economic progress—and, indeed, progress generally—is a process by which the new that people freely choose displaces the old. It is a dynamic process of continuing disestablishmentarianism. Schumpeter called it, in the pregnant title of a chapter, "The Process of Creative Destruction."[1] And if this is all to work freely, the processes of choice and decision must be open. They cannot be under the control of the establishment.

This is one of the inherent superiorities of the liberal or market-organized economic system relative to its major competitor, the state-organized system for managing economic activity. In the liberal economic system those with new ideas are free to try them out (with substantial rewards to those who succeed), and people are free to adopt them—to make them prevail over the old—if they like them better. The state-organized economy, on the other hand, is a system of permits and licenses and edicts from on high—this whether the state owns the means of production, or whether government manages the details of economic life. Inevitably the officialdom and bureaucracies from which a license or permit must be obtained in order to get going with something new would tend to reflect and be a prisoner of the established ways of doing things. And they would reflect the usual establishment aversion and skepticism about a wholly different and new product or procedure. A Federal Department of Watches—mechanical, of course—would not look with favor on a proposed digital watch—with the transfer of status, power, and jobs to another department.

One can almost imagine the colloquy in a state-organized and managed economy (though nominally private enterprise) between the pertinent official in government and an emissary from Hewlett-Packard or Texas Instruments whose company is trying to get the needed permit to go into production with the once-startling idea of an electronic calculator.

"You are applying for a permit to produce calculators?" the GA-12 asks.

"Yes, sir. My company has a product vastly superior to what can be bought today. You see . . .," begins the Company Emissary with enthusiasm.

"Your company," interrupts the Government, "of course, has experience in the production of calculators or you would not be here, though we have no record of having issued to you the necessary license." The tone of voice, a well-practiced blend of condescension and haughty accusation, is not lost on our hero from the company.

1. J. A. Schumpeter, *Capitalism, Socialism and Democracy* (Harper & Row, 1942), Chapter VII, pp. 81–86.

"Well, no," he replies shifting a bit uneasily in his chair. "No, we haven't been in that business at all. You see—"

"Well, I suppose you have a sample of your machine, though I understand, of course," and for the first time there is a hint of benignity in Government's voice, "that you could hardly be expected to carry a heavy thing like that around with you."

"Oh, but I do have it. Here it is," eagerly responds our hero, as he takes it out of his coat pocket.

"That! Young man," clips out Government in his most I-am-a-busy-and-important-man manner, "in my department we collectively represent 2,519 years of experience with calculators. Any one of us could tell you exactly how many shafts and gears and wheels and other parts are required for a good modern calculator. That little box you hold—why, it is not even large enough for the motor. Just take my advice, as one who has spent his professional career in calculators, go back home and don't bother important people here again with practical jokes. Next time we may not be so patient."

Fortunately ours is not an economy which requires such a bureaucratic process, and the result is that these little calculators—which can be put in a coat pocket, do have vastly more computational capability than the behemoths of yesteryear, and whose price tags are a fraction of those attached to the old machines—have become today's standard.

The economy of licenses and permits has more than just an arthritic inability to keep up a fast pace of new things to trouble it. Such a system offers vastly more scope for corruption than one in which the route to success is via superior performance in impersonal markets. If the route to success is through obtaining a permit or license, the grant of such permission has value, and it should come as no surprise that on the other side there will be those ready to pay the price. In all of the heterogeneous array of companies and instances involving so-called improper payments, there has been one pervasive common element. The recipients of these payments have usually been government officials whose nod of approval was the route to success for the sellers.

Illustrations of the corruption that develops around government management of the details of economic life can be drawn from numerous countries. "The Soviet economy," observed a former official of that country, "will continue to be corrupted by an enormous black market in goods and services—a whole parallel, unofficial, illegal economy with its own laws and norms and its crop of Soviet underground millionaires."[2]

"Even if one-tenth of what is said in private is true, the country is in the throes of a moral crisis. . . . It is moronic to imagine that a just society can grow when *les fleurs du mal*—the flowers of evil— bloom on all sides and when parasites, contact-men, fixers and hatchet-men flourish while honest workers find it increasingly hard to make both ends meet."[3] Thus in 1974 did the editor of the *Times* of India comment on the results of that government's detailed management of economic life.

Nor does government management of the details of economic life by licenses and permits produce discernibly different results in the United States. "Hardly a skyscraper is built, scarcely a change is made in the world's most celebrated skyline, hardly a brownstone is renovated or a restaurant expanded without the illegal payoffs, ranging from $5 to $10,000 each."[4]

That these corrupt practices are pervasively associated with an economy whose details are managed by government is to be expected by the inherent nature of the process. That the incidence of these corrupt practices is markedly less in economies and sectors organized through open and vigorously competitive markets is also to be expected since for them performance evaluated by the impersonal forces of markets determines success.

Finally, the record of progress in liberal, market-organized economic systems such as ours has displayed another characteristic that is as notable as it is often ignored or even disbelieved. The major beneficiaries of this progress generated by our market-organized economic system are the people at large, not the patricians of society—the masses, not the classes. We see this intuitively. If such great names in economic history as Messrs. Sears and Roebuck or Henry Ford or Sebastian S. Kresge, or J. C. Penney had gone high-hat and aimed their efforts at the "better people," the carriage trade, they would have faded into the historical oblivion which would have been the ineluctable reward of such foolishness. Because they were smart, they aimed their efforts at the common people generally, where the great markets are. The key to our system, in short, is that we rely on the intelligence of businesses, not their

2. Boris Rabbot, "A Letter to Brezhnev," *New York Times Magazine,* November 6, 1977, p. 60.

3. *New York Times,* February 14, 1974, p. 3.

4. David K. Shipler, *New York Times,* June 26, 1972, p. 1.

benevolence, to assure a particular solicitude for ordinary people and their needs. In Michigan, for example, the Ford and Chevrolet divisions are far more important to their firms than the Lincoln-Mercury and Cadillac divisions.

Whatever the catechistic rhetoric about economic systems, the empirical evidence is overwhelmingly clear that the superior performance in lifting material levels of living and diffusing the fruits of this progress broadly has been turned in by the market-organized economic systems. We see this intuitively in certain pairings of countries. The Korean economic success story is South Korea, not North Korea. Per-capita income in Taiwan is by now a substantial multiple of that in mainland China. The German economic miracle occurred in the Federal Republic of Germany, not in East Germany. Indeed, the Berlin Wall stands as a monument to the failure of state-organized economic and political systems. Some of these countries which represent economic success stories are not political democracies, but countries with state-organized economic systems have uniformly authoritarian governments.

IV

Yet the liberal system of organizing economic activity through open and competitive markets is increasingly on the defensive. It is difficult to look at the broad movements of history during this century or even during the last decade or so and arrive at any other conclusion. There are, of course, a few whiffs of breezes blowing the other way. The overthrow in India of the Gandhi authoritarian government, with its heavily state-organized orientation of economic philosophy, may have nudged that major country in a more favorable direction, but it may also have been an accident of the moment with little impact on the basic direction of history. When people are asked about the prestige of different occupations, businessmen and bankers do not rank well. Their major consolation is that they usually manage to achieve a slightly better score than politicians.[5] There are a few contrary gusts, but the prevailing winds seem clearly to be blowing in a direction lending support to pessimistic conclusions about the survival of the system.

Why is it working out this way when the evidence of experience would seem to be on the other side?

5. See, for example, *Public Opinion*, March–April 1978, p. 36.

The most obvious (and perhaps least significant) reason is to be found in the way the system's record might appear to some. To some, the Great Depression stands as a major monument in history to the way the free and open competitive economy works out if it is not subjected to quite detailed government management. It was the prevailing economic system in the industrial world, and the industrial countries in the 1930s were in grave economic trouble. That is all undeniable. And it is also true that simultaneous problems of inflation and unemployment have afflicted the liberal market economies for much of the time during the last decade or so.

That these developments have not improved the reputation of the liberal economic systems seems clear enough and even understandable. They are not an indictment of the system, of course, since the sources of these problems have been government's mismanagement of economic policy, not characteristics inherent in the economic system itself. It was monetary policy, for example, that permitted the collapse of the banking system and a shrinkage of the money supply to a level by 1933 roughly 40 percent below that which would have been required to continue the reasonably full employment and price stability of the 1920s. And it was economic policies in these countries that interrupted the 1969 to 1971 movement back to a more stable price level and firmly fixed public expectations of high inflation. This has given us both inflation and unemployment. While the charge that these developments "show the way the system works" will not survive careful analysis, it cannot be denied that these developments have contributed to an erosion of public support for the economic system.

V

A more sweeping and fundamental case for the demise of the market-organized economic system rests on what might be called the Hegelian doctrine of inevitable processes. Two names would come to mind here. First, Marx. It is difficult for both Marxians and "the rest of us" to examine carefully the theoretical case that Marx made for the demise of the system. For the Marxians that would be treating sacred scriptures as scholarly writing. For others a careful examination of Marx's theories would seem to suggest respectful and dispassionate treatment of what is inherently Mephistophelian and ought to be denounced out of hand.

Marx's conclusions, however, did have an underpinning of economic theory. His was not just another book of Revelations. It was based on Ricardo's labor theory of value—that the values of products are proportional to the quantity of labor required to produce them. The value (wages) of labor is also the labor required to produce it. Thus there will be a growing surplus value, the gap between the value of output and wages (the value of labor required to produce the labor). Since this labor theory of value means that wages would settle to the subsistence level required to produce the needed supply of labor, wages would thus fall behind the purchasing power required to provide a market for the economy's total output. The capitalist economies, therefore, would experience recurring gluts and depressions and during the expansion phase growing imperialistic pressures to find foreign markets for the surplus output. Thus a relationship was also established between business cycles in the capitalist economies and wars.[6] The inherent nature of the capitalistic process thus, according to Marx, would lead it to its own collapse, ushering in communism.

A thorough analysis of Marx's writings would extend well beyond the scope of this chapter, but it is important to see that amidst Marx's florid phrases and scriptures there is to be found a theoretical analysis, and it is an analysis leading to the conclusion that the liberal, market-organized economic system is inevitably doomed to disappear just as what preceded it was bound to give way to bourgeois capitalism. That his theoretical as well as his theological writings have had a profound effect on the course of history seems evident enough, even if his basic theory of surplus value with its prediction of a growing immiserization (to use Schumpeter's manufactured word) of the so-called working class is quite flatly contradicted by the facts of history. The capitalistic or market-organized economic system by its inherent logic tends to produce a more equal distribution of real income, and the empirical evidence suggests that in fact it has worked out that way.

It was Schumpeter who developed most carefully the theory that the unfolding of the Hegelian process would mean the demise of capitalism—this in his *Capitalism, Socialism and Democracy* (first

6. It was N. D. Kondratieff, of course, who did the empirical work to establish the case for the existence of these long waves. See N. D. Kondratieff, "The Long Waves in Economic Life," *Review of Economic Statistics*, November 1935. It was first published as "Die Langen Wellen der Konjunktur," *Archiv fur Sozialwissenschaft,* December 1926, and translated into English by W. Stolper.

published in 1942, but perhaps more read today than when it was first published). He was not a socialist. Indeed, he was occasionally criticized for being too conservative (perhaps in part because he occasionally spoke a bit contemptuously about the "Keynesian nursery" inhabited by his Harvard colleagues then in the Economics Department).[7] As he himself observed: "If a doctor predicts that his patient will die presently, this does not mean that he desires it."[8]

Nor was capitalism going to expire because it had failed. He pointed out that if real incomes continued to rise during the half century after 1928 (the last year before the descent into the Great Depression began) at historical rates, "this would do away with anything that according to present standards could be called poverty, even in the lowest strata of the population, pathological cases alone excepted."[9] In fact real per-capita income in the United States in 1978 will be within 2 or 3 percent of the level which he projected—a level which would abolish poverty "according to present standards."

Capitalism would not survive not because it has been a failure but because it has been a success, and its success would set in motion forces that would cause its demise. The central actuating process in the drama of capitalism for Schumpeter was innovation—any "doing things differently." It might be a new product, a new method of production, a new approach to marketing. Innovation is not invention. Something becomes innovation only when it starts to have economic reality. The invention of the steam engine had little economic significance until some people put it all together and created a railroad industry. It was not the invention of the internal-combusion engine but the creation of the automobile that constituted innovation. They did not invent retailing, but J. C. Penney and Sebastian S. Kresge with their wholly new approaches to merchandising were innovators just as literally as Henry Ford or Alfred P. Sloan in the automobile industry.

The innovators or entrepreneurs are the prime movers. They are the ones who bring into the economy the wholly new and different. The risks are great, but the rewards of the successful are also large. Moreover, in the heyday of capitalism entrepreneurs received the accolades and prestige befitting the prime movers in society. Cap-

7. I remember his comment that he could learn in a fortnight all of the economics contained in a year's course taught in "the Keynesian nursery."

8. J. A. Schumpeter, op. cit., p. 61.

9. Ibid., p. 66.

italism, the market-organized economic system, then also had the answer to getting the new and better diffused across the economy generally—namely, open and competitive markets in which consumers are free to make their choices. Thus the new and better could supplant and extinguish the old.

What did Schumpeter see in this process, however, that would make it work out to produce its own death? The economy can be understood only if we see it as a moving picture of a process unfolding through time rather than as a snapshot, a still picture. The very success of capitalism has led to the emergence of modern large corporations. These large corporations in turn have the resources in house to do the research and product development that formerly had been the function of the individual entrepreneur. The nonroutine has thereby become routinized. "Since capitalist enterprise, by its very achievements, tends to automatize progress, we conclude that it tends to make itself superfluous—to break to pieces under pressure of its own success."[10] Thus the demise of capitalism would occur because it succeeded, not because it failed.

With this automatizing of the entrepreneurship function, the social role of the entrepreneur would thus also be of diminishing importance as the individual and the function that epitomized the nature of the capitalistic system and its success became obsolescent. Moreover, for capitalism to emerge it had to break down loyalties to the old established institutions, but "capitalism thus broke not only the barriers that impeded its progress but also flying buttresses that prevented its collapse."[11] Thus the growing hostility to the capitalist system and its institutions is not something inexplicably visited upon it from the outside. It is something that could be expected from the internal logic of the unfolding Hegelian process.

Schumpeter's "vision" about the nature of capitalism which has made it so successful in generating economic change and progress is profound. With this vision we can begin to understand better the dynamics of the liberal economy in motion—and why, in spite of rhetoric to the contrary, the liberal, market-organized economic system has been more capable of dynamic progress and of lifting levels of living for people generally than the state-organized economies. There are, however, problems with Schumpeter's analysis. Himself emphasizing the importance of seeing the economy not in

10. Ibid., p. 134.
11. Ibid., p. 139.

static or still-picture terms but as a process unfolding through time, his mind's-eye still-picture of large companies with their research efforts led him to overestimate the extent to which innovation had been automated within existing companies. Some of the major innovations during the decades since his book first appeared have reflected the central role of entrepreneurs and innovation just as he outlined it for the heyday of capitalism. Xerox, Polaroid, Hewlett-Packard, Texas Instruments—these are some of the "new boys on the block" since the publication of *Capitalism, Socialism and Democracy.* And these were not primarily spawned by established large companies but by highly individualized entrepreneurship. The evidence does not yet suggest that societies which try to internalize or bureaucratize the processes of progress within established institutions are apt to be highly successful in promoting economic development.

VI

If the issue is to be decided by an objective comparison of the evidence about demonstrated performance in lifting and enriching material levels of living, the liberal, market-organized economic system has a clear claim to the citizenry's loyalties. Neither the imperfections of its actual operations through history nor even some sort of Hegelian doctrine of ineluctable processes would seem to be sufficient to explain the fact that the system is the legatee of uneasy, uncertain, and eroding loyalties.

Apparently we must probe further. We gain some perspective on this phenomenon if we take a brief excursion into what may seem to be some esoteric matters of philosophy. Traced back to its fundamentals, what we see here reflects the ascendancy in the American scene of what might be called continental liberalism over what is sometimes called classical liberalism. What has been called here the liberal economy traces its intellectual lineage to the latter. Names that would come to mind incident to this philosophical tradition are Hume, Locke, Burke, and Adam Smith.[12] According to this latter philosophy, within the framework of a government of limited power, people would be free to use their knowledge and creativity, with preferences freely expressed through open and competitive markets

12. One of the most lucid expositions is to be found in Walter Lipmann, *The Good Society* (Grosset and Dunlap, 1943).

assuring that the best would prevail. Thus people generally would be the beneficiary of an aggregate of knowledge and creativity that would not exist in its totality anyplace. And there would be a process to assure that the new and better would prevail.

There was, however, an alternative view of the proper route to a good society. Here such names as Condorcet, Voltaire, and Rousseau would come to mind. Thus it is no newer than so-called liberalism tracing its intellectual ancestry back to writers articulating the case for classical liberalism. Indeed, the patron saint of those urging much more detailed government management of the economy might well be Colbert, finance minister in France a century before Adam Smith. While he is widely known for his mercantilistic advocacy of a net export surplus, he really should be known primarily for attempting to administer the most detailed regulations of the economy—with, as usual, good intentions and arthritic results.[13]

This alternative or continental liberalism saw the proper blueprint for the good society as the product or creation of Pure Reason. The Good would be designed and blueprinted by the intellect, by Pure Reason. Government, then, would implement the blueprint. It also believed in political democracy, but not necessarily government of limited scope and power (as in the alternative philosophy).

It is clear that U.S. social and economic policy has increasingly during the last decades come to reflect the so-called continental philosophy, and it is also clear that these two philosophies carry with them some important and different implications. Liberalism in what has been called here the classical tradition does not profess to know what the proper blueprint is for the end result, but it does know the process for achieving it. Within a framework provided by a government of limited scope and power, there would emerge, through the exercise of creativity and knowledge of people generally, a richness and diversity that could never be conceived and designed by any individual or group. The emphasis of classical liberalism is on means, not ends, and on proper limitations to the scope of government so the creative and dynamic process will work. With the continental alternative, since Pure Reason would enable us to know the ends, the emphasis is on sufficient power (including particularly government power) to implement the blueprint conceived by those entrusted with such responsibility. And there will be skepticism,

13. C. W. Cole, *Colbert and a Century of French Mercantilism* (Columbia University Press, 1939).

backed up by the power of government, about things that do not fit the blueprint.

Thus, as the prevailing, contemporary American philosophy has shifted more toward the "continental" variety—though, to repeat, it is really more ancient than classical liberalism—an enormously powerful alliance was forged between intellectuals and government. Intellectuals would consider their own conceptions about the good to be superior to those of the masses. They are inherently, therefore, skeptical about the patterns that would emerge from the free play of people's creativity and preferences generally. Moreover, intellectuals understandably assume that if Pure Reason is to blueprint the good society, intellectuals (being, presumably, the able people in society) will thereby have a disproportionate influence on the outcome.

And the growing scope of government is practically congenial also—at least, so long as we do not actually metamorphose into a state-organized economy run by an authoritarian government. This is true because government becomes a major labor market for intellectuals and for their university products (students).

A major feature of the blueprint for the Good Society has been a growing disinclination to accept the concept of "equality of opportunity" and its corollary that the route to success is through performance in open and competitive markets. The disfavor into which this Protestant Ethic approach to the economy (and to other aspects of life also) has fallen may in part reflect the atrophy of religion, which has robbed our secular philosophy of its moral and spiritual foundation. Its moral rationale has crumbled. Irving Kristol has pointed out that "social critics have been warning us that bourgeois society was living off the accumulated moral capital of traditional religion and traditional moral philosophy, and that once this capital was depleted, bourgeois society would find its legitimacy even more questionable."[14]

Perhaps the basic change has been from equality of opportunity to the objective of equality of end results. Such names as Christopher Jencks, James Coleman, and John Rawls would come to mind.[15] More recently, Arthur Okun in his Godkin lectures presented a

---

14. Irving Kristol, "Capitalism, Socialism, and Nihilism," *The Public Interest,* Spring 1973, p. 22.

15. Christopher Jencks, *Inequality: A Reassessment of the Effect of Family and Schooling in America* (Basic Books, 1972); James Coleman, "Equal Schools or Equal Students," *The Public Interest,* Summer 1966; and John Rawls, *A Theory of Justice* (Harvard University Press, 1971).

tightly argued case for an egalitarian-orientation of social policy.[16] In part this shift reflects the suspicion that a meritocracy tends to be less distinguishable from a system of hereditary privilege than had been supposed. The successful tend to pass on to their offspring the advantages of a better home life, more emphasis on education, more means to finance higher education, and perhaps a higher IQ. And there is now substantial evidence that schooling seems to do surprisingly little to narrow disparities in achievement among children. The great hope for equality in some not fully defined sense, equal access to education, seems to promise less in the way of results than had been confidently expected.

This in turn has led to a growing conviction on the part of some that differences in the material emoluments of life may not after all, as the Protestant Ethic assured us, reflect the rewards for different degrees of diligence and effort and virtue. They more nearly represent random elements of luck. It is the luck of the draw and not their superior virtue that put some children in homes favoring achievement and put other children in a situation where their mothers could not even be sure about the identity of the fathers.

With religion on the wane and with empirical evidence suggesting that the differing material rewards of life are not so closely associated with the degree of access to opportunity, some basic philosophical foundation blocks of our economic system are shaking. "In the nature of human consciousness," to quote Daniel Bell, "a scheme of moral equity is the necessary basis for any social order; for legitimacy to exist, power must be justified. In the end it is moral ideas—the conception of what is desirable—that shape history through human aspirations."[17]

And as the fundamental tenets of the basically liberal economic order have found themselves on the defensive and minus their moral and religious buttresses, the door has come open to new goals and objectives that would gain allegiance and could be implemented only by government power.[18] That equality of opportunity was if not inevitable at least highly probable.

The natural drift of the equality-of-results doctrine is in the direction of a large expansion of state control over our lives.

16. Arthur Okun, *Equality and Efficiency* (Brookings Institution, 1975).

17. Daniel Bell, "On Meritocracy and Equality," *The Public Interest,* Fall 1972, pp. 47–48.

18. See the brilliant paper by Robert H. Bork, "Can Democratic Government Survive?," presented to the American Philosophical Society, April 24, 1976 (mimeographed).

Equality of results is not easily defined (probably, in fact, impossible to define). It is not apt to happen "naturally." The end result of this objective is inevitably, therefore, a large array of bureaucracies trying to define and implement the elusive concept of equality of results (and in the process stepping on each other's toes).

VII

It is this that raises some of the most urgent questions about the survival of the liberal system in the modern world. In most industrial countries the ratio of government outlays to national income has been rising, and for some it is now at or above the 50 percent zone. For the United States the rise in government outlays from 1972 to 1977 was equal to 40 percent of the rise in GNP, and this figure would range up to something over 70 percent for a country like the Netherlands.[19]

These overall budgetary figures, impressive as they are, understate the explosive expansion in the extent to which government has moved toward managing the details of economic life. A crude but probably more accurate index for the United States is the increase in the number of pages in the Federal Register required to print proposed new regulations. Here has been a growth index—rising during this decade at about a 25 percent per year rate, a rate that doubles every three years.

The adverse effects of these developments are apparently already beginning to show up. The evidence seems to suggest that the trend rate of growth in productivity has dropped from its historical level of 2½ percent per year to about 1½ percent. Seemingly small differences loom large over time. If during this century this lower rate had prevailed, the average family today (and with today's prices) would be trying to balance its budget with about half its current income.

The growing scope of government does produce a more arthritic operation of the liberal economy. Smaller and newer firms have less capability to survive the morass of reports and regulations. The larger firms, whose establishmentarian position must be challenged vigorously if there is to be progress, are thereby accorded the more secure market position which, however comfortable, is not conducive either to innovation or to "the processes of creative destruction."

19. See Warren Nutter, "Growth of Government in the West" (American Enterprise Institute for Public Policy Research, 1978).

Bureaucracies inherently tend to play it safe, but safety and security are not characteristics of a dynamic environment.

Moreover, government-implemented blueprints are inherently simplistic. A rich variety and diversity cannot be managed or even conceived by the few at the top. It will develop its own vested interests and honest hostility about the new and unanticipated. Moreover, government is never structured to force a careful and simultaneous weighing of costs and benefits—as is more inherently required of business managements. The FDA will be excoriated before a congressional committee if people die because of an approved drug, but they are not held responsible for people who die or suffer because of delays in approving a needed drug. EPA optimizes its situation by rules for the environment; the adverse energy consequences of its rulings are not its problem.

Finally, to repeat, government-managed economic systems tend toward pervasive corruption as prices get established for needed permits and licenses. Thus a government-managed economy can come to have most of the unhappy features of state-organized systems even if the name on the stock certificate remains John Doe and not Uncle Sam.

Indeed, even the political form of democracy can then come to be of diminishing significance. The right to choose between two people for each of a few elective positions may then begin to appear to the citizen as increasingly irrelevant if *de facto* his life is enmeshed in webs spun by a bureaucracy that is controlled neither by the public nor their elected officials. And the great danger for the liberal economy is not, to paraphrase General MacArthur, that it will receive an overt death sentence from the citizenry but that its form remains while its essence fades away.

VIII

This chapter may appear to the reader to be a bit somber, perhaps even a bit funereal, at times. There are serious questions and concerns about the survival of the liberal economic system, and there is no point in shallow optimism. At the same time we must assume that people are not helpless chips on the ocean. The economic system we have in the future, as in the past, will reflect the choices we make. It will not be the ineluctable result of a Hegelian process. And there are two powerful sets of encouraging omens.

First, resistances against the expansion of government are now beginning to stiffen. The Congress, whose members depend for their survival on sensing vibrations back home, is now following a more disciplined budget process. The process is wobbly and leaky, but it is having some effect. Proposals to impose outright constitutional limitations on public spending are gaining support in states. At the outset the inchoate general public is no match in the government arena for strongly organized and focused interest groups, but when the jelling processes of public determination start, the results can be irresistible.

Second, some refreshing crosscurrents are now blowing across the intellectual scene. Colleges and universities have become beneficiaries of an expanding government with its largesse and power, and this together with the government power that would force us to a Better Society (presumably blueprinted by intellectuals in academe) seemed to be a highly congenial arrangement. But we now find that a government which tells us what to produce and drive and wear also sees no reason not to tell us what to teach and whom to hire in order to have education for a Better World. Educators also, in short, are learning that a liberal society's concerns about the scope of government as well as the form of government are not compartmentalized.

More fundamentally there is now again in the intellectual domain competition of ideas. The idea market was once virtually dominated by papers and articles and books calling for more government programs, more government management of the details of economic life, greater socialization of consumption and investment through public budgets. This orientation has by no means disappeared, but in intellectual circles it is also respectable now to produce articles and papers and books on seeking the realization of objectives through the liberal market-organized economic system.

With competition in the marketplace for ideas becoming increasingly vigorous, capitalism—i.e. the liberal system of organizing economic activity through open markets—may yet survive. Indeed, if it does not, neither will political democracy.

—PAUL W. MCCRACKEN

CHAPTER 10

——————⟨∞⟩——————

The Greatest Threats
to Our Society

Our nation has a religious foundation. The Declaration of Independence is a religious document. The basic institution of any society is the family. Personal morality is essential to good family life and respect for the law. Thus the recent precipitous decline in religious faith, quality of family life, personal morality, and respect for law are our greatest threats.

A grave imbalance in the structure of our society has developed that, if not reversed, will rob us of our freedom, pluralism, and dynamism. It is an imbalance between three sectors on which we rely to solve problems too big for individuals or individual families. They are government, the competitive enterprise profit system, and the nonprofit voluntary sector. In recent decades support of the nonprofit sector has declined. Its recent weakening, if continued, will reduce us to a two-sector society and increase the prospect of an all-powerful governmental sector.

In the area of government and politics our greatest threat is our dependence on a crisis or disaster to develop the public understanding and support for the timely adoption of basic reforms—reforms of the nature needed to solve such vital and controversial problems as inflation, the cities, and energy.

Now let me elaborate. The Bible was the cornerstone of the American society. David Joseph Brewer wrote:

> No nation is better than its Sacred Book. No nation has a
> Sacred Book to be compared with ours. The more this Bible

enters into our National life the grander and purer and better will that life become.

Carlyle wrote, "It is the spiritual that determines the material." The spiritual and moral principles of the Bible were the fountain source of our freedom and unparalleled success.

It has been truly said that the history of the world's civilizations is the history of different people as they moved from fetters to faith, faith to freedom, freedom to affluence, affluence to folly, and folly to fetters.

Our faith in our sacred book, the Bible, and the freedom it inspired have made us the most affluent nation in history. But is our affluence changing our faith and freedom to folly? If so, what can we do about it?

Commenting more directly on American youth, before the counterculture became a newsworthy development, Joseph Wood Krutch wrote:

> The young individual feels a terrible disharmony between himself and the universe when he learns from his parents, teachers, or professors that life is meaningless, that all "morals" are relative, all ethics "situational" and that "eternal verities" are so much religious mumbo-jumbo and obsolete bourgeois nonsense.

Unbelievably, we are being bombarded with efforts to justify nearly every form of crime and immoral conduct. Conduct explicitly and repeatedly condemned by the Bible in both the Old Testament and the New Testament.

Consider the prophetic accuracy of Paul's prediction about our day in II Timothy:

> This know also, that in the last days perilous times shall come. For men shall be lovers of their own selves, covetous, boasters, proud, blasphemers, disobedient to parents, unthankful, unholy, without natural affection, trucebreakers, false accusers, incontinent, fierce, despisers of those that are good, traitors, heady, highminded, lovers of pleasures more than lovers of God; having a form of godliness, but denying the power thereof: ... ever learning, and never able to come to the knowledge of the truth.

Those who are ever learning but never coming to a knowledge of the truth are the intellectuals who substitute man's limited knowledge for God's infinite wisdom. As Clare Boothe Luce correctly charged, it is particularly the intellectuals who precipitated our spiritual, moral, and social confusion and valuelessness by, first, "proclaiming 'the death of God' and scrapping the moral standards by which western society had judged right and wrong"; second, "in the sacred name of free speech defending, in the Supreme Court, the right of publishers, play and film producers to flood America with filth"; and third, making pervasive the view that "although 'crime' existed, there were no criminals—only 'sick' people and 'misguided' reformers driven to commit their acts of protest by the political forces."

Well might those who are rationalizing licentious and immoral conduct be confronted with the Lord's challenge out of the whirlwind to Job:

> "Wilt thou disannul my judgment? Wilt thou condemn me, that thou mayest be righteous?"

For nations and societies the Bible's message is that the spiritual and moral laws of God are as certain and immutable as His laws of nature that govern our physical universe. No sane person doubts the reliability and immutability of the laws of nature. Isn't it unreasonably inconsistent to believe that a Creator would enumerate through his prophets the spiritual and moral laws and then reduce our understanding of them to meaningless confusion by making them flexible and fluctuating? Indeed the Bible is testimony that those who obey His laws prosper and are happy and those who disobey them suffer.

Again, America's accomplishments are preeminent in history because of our sacred book, the Bible. Why?

1. Because it provided the principal inspiration for the founders, reversing the conventional basis for organizing a society. This they did by vesting ultimate power and sovereignty in the people rather than in the government.
2. Because given the opportunity, free Americans, through unique institutions of voluntary cooperation and private, consumer-determined economic enterprise, developed and used their talents more fully and altruistically. It was the American ethic of personal responsibility expressed through private initiative and cooperative endeavor that lifted America out of poverty into fantastic prosperity.

3. Because until recent decades most Americans and most of their leaders considered the Bible's spiritual and moral laws revealed by God as immutable as the laws of nature.
4. Because marriage was deemed to be sacredly ordained of God, and strong families were recognized as the key institutions of society.

Irrevocable among God's revealed spiritual and moral laws are the Ten Commandments. By using them as a measurement we can determine where we are now as a society, where we are headed, and what we should do.

"Thou shalt have no other gods before me." But atheism and agnosticism are now common. People putting economic and social success first are everywhere. Even some churchmen have put other goals ahead of faith in God. Consider Clare Boothe Luce's answer to this question:

"Why do churches seem so powerless today to restore faith in the old moral values, the positive values?" Her answer:

The churches, as formal institutions, have themselves bought too many of the materialistic values of our success-oriented society. The collapse of faith—faith in God—among churchmen themselves is too big a subject to go into here.

"Thou shalt not take the name of the Lord thy God in vain; for the Lord will not hold him guiltless that taketh his name in vain." Blasphemy among adults is general. Even little children punctuate their conversation with the name of the Father and the Son. Channels of communication and entertainment use the name of the Lord as a common adverb.

"Remember the Sabbath day, to keep it holy." Not only has the sabbath become a workday for many, but it is one for every form of recreation, fun loving, and entertainment. Someone has said that professional sporting events have become the average man's Sunday church. Church attendance and holy activities on the sabbath are becoming incidental and secondary and even churches are adjusting their services so as to minimize their interference with the purely secular activities that now dominate the sabbath.

"Six days shalt thou labor, and do all thy work." More and more a spirit of entitlement permeates our land, the psychology that one is entitled to the good things of life without making a contribution.

Government programs designed to help the unfortunate have become a means of the idle benefiting without labor. In combination, these government programs now support millions in idleness and immorality. This is one major reason for New York City's fiscal crisis, and it is carrying the nation down the same road.

"Honor thy father and thy mother." This meant to support them. On every hand children have delegated care of their parents to the state. Children and parents hide property, lie, and cheat to make the parents eligible for government support.

"Thou shalt not covet thy neighbor's wife." Violation of marriage vows is the principal cause of a divorce level that if it continues at its present rate will soon dissolve most marriages. Sex is glorified and both fornication and adultery are held out to youth as sinless. Shockingly, a recent poll disclosed that 82 percent of the mothers interviewed were not opposed to premarital sex for their sons, and 70 percent for their daughters. Abortions, illegitimacy, disillusionment, and misery follow. As a result deterioration of family life is second only to loss of faith in our Creator as a threat to our future freedom.

"Thou shalt not kill." The rate of murder among juveniles has doubled in a decade. Murder in the United States is far more frequent than it is in other nations. Organized-crime killings are now occurring nationwide.

"Thou shalt not steal." Shoplifting is now a multi-billion-dollar problem. Theft, breaking and entry, and vandalism by juveniles has skyrocketed. Police protection inside our schools is no longer news. Drug and alcohol offenses on school property, burglaries of school buildings, and assaults on teachers are common. Every minute of every day some nineteen persons become subject to some kind of crime—be it murder, rape, assault, theft.

"Thou shalt not bear false witness." Every investigation of government programs discloses extensive lying and misrepresentations. In our courts and in everyday life establishing guilt is frequently thwarted by refusal of witnesses to testify or by perjury.

"Thou shalt not covet." Covetousness especially afflicts modern Americans. It accounts to a considerable extent for the rise in violence, crime, divorce, fraud, governmental scandals, and inflation.

In face of these disturbing conditions what must we do to avert the punishment that is bound to come as a result of widespread violation of God's spiritual and moral laws? I do not say *breaking* them, for as Cecil B. DeMille once pointed out, "We cannot *break* the Ten Commandments but they can *break* us." These actions seem a must.

1. We must strengthen our faith and the faith of others in God. God is not dead. He is as concerned with and accessible to His children now as He was in Bible days. This is the most important knowledge we can have—because we live in a "land choice above all other lands" and to retain our freedom we must serve the Lord as its ruler.
2. We must refute the idea that science, technology, and man's learning have repealed the Ten Commandments and other divine laws governing our moral conduct.
3. We must bolster our capacity to obey laws of morality by increasing acceptance of the Bible's assurance that we are all personally accountable to our Almighty Creator and will answer to Him for all we do, think, and say. Without this conviction no moral code is impregnable.
4. We must repulse the attack on marriage and family life and again recognize that our greatest responsibility is that of motherhood and fatherhood; that "no success can compensate for failure in the home."

There is a growing concern about present trends, and this inspires hope that we can reverse them. Toynbee strengthens this hope with this prediction:

> A tottering civilization which has shamefully succumbed to the intoxication of a showy victory over physical nature and has applied the spoils to laying up treasure for itself without being rich toward God, may be reprieved from the sentence— which it has passed on itself—of treading out the tragic path—by being born again as a Republica Christiana which was its own better ideal of what it should strive to be. We may yet live to see a civilization that has tried and failed to stand alone being saved, in spite of itself, from a fatal fall by being caught up in the arms of an ancestral church which it has vainly striven to push away and kept at arm's length.

A vital threat to our society is the diminishing support being given to the nonprofit sector. From the beginning the voluntary initiative of caring citizens in helping others has improved our society. Also, as early Americans faced problems too big for them to solve individually, they turned first to others and said, "What can we do about it?" They did not turn first to government. They cooperated voluntarily in conquering the continent by building roads, dams, homes, churches, schools, and industries.

Since then a vast structure of voluntary organizations has been created to meet cultural needs, solve social problems, change values and morals, and keep government honest. Examples are museums and art galleries, Alcoholics Anonymous and the Salvation Army, abolition and civil rights, taxpayer leagues and the League of Women Voters. This vast nonprofit third sector has been the source of our pluralistic society. It has pioneered many programs now conducted by government and has been responsible for needed reforms.

The nonprofit sector's effectiveness depends on freedom and independence. Both of these require unfettered sources of financial support as well as the contribution of time and talent by tens of millions of unpaid volunteers. Volunteers whose caring motivates those needing help to help themselves.

In recent decades as big government and big business and big unions have become bigger, the nonprofit sector has become weaker. The percentage of the gross national product supporting it has declined by about 25 percent in the past fifteen years. Why?

When confronted now with problems too big for them individually, the initial reaction of most Americans is "What's the government going to do about it?" As government has grown and taxes increased private giving has diminished.

Another reason is the increase in those filing standardized income tax returns. Fifty percent filed them in 1959 but 75 percent file them now. The standardized return reduces the incentive to give. Deductions for contributions are not permitted. Substantial giving comes from those in the standardized category: 54 percent of the contributions supporting the nonprofit sector are made by those with annual incomes of $20,000 or less.

To offset this decline direct government subsidization of the third sector is growing, but this is the wrong answer. Significant government financing will rob those receiving it of independence and convert them into government instruments.

Both governmental and profit sectors can help reverse this trend. Congress can adopt tax policies to offset the effect of the standardized deduction, and under present laws profit organizations can deduct 5 percent of profits before taxes to support tax-exempt nonprofit activities. Yet only twenty-three major institutions were contributing this 5 percent in 1977. The average for all business has been declining and is now just under 1 percent.

As former President Johnson told a group of businessmen in 1971: "You must think the government can spend your money better than you can."

Business should do more to help redress the imbalance that is crippling the independence and vigor of the nonprofit sector because both are rooted in the same soil. The soil of private initiative and enterprise. If the third sector becomes ineffective we will be even more exposed to a one-sector society. One in which ultimate power is vested not in the people but in government.

Our society is unique because the founders vested ultimate power in the people. "We the people" made the covenant that adopted the Constitution. Jefferson identified an essential need if the people were to continue to exercise sovereignty. He said:

> The only safe depository of the ultimate power of society is the people themselves and if we deem them not sufficiently enlightened to exercise that power with due discretion, the answer is not to take it from them but to enlighten them.

Despite public education, a free press, political parties and their campaigns, we have not devised an adequate means of creating an electorate sufficiently enlightened to support the timely adoption of fundamental reforms. We are dependent on a crisis or a disaster, as Lincoln pointed out in his celebrated "House Divided Speech":

> We are now into the fifth year since a policy was initiated with the avowed object and confident promise of putting an end to slavery agitation. Agitation not only has not ceased but has constantly augmented. In my opinion, it will not cease until a crisis shall have been reached and passed. "A house divided against itself cannot stand."

This conclusion on Lincoln's part followed many years of earlier debate and expedient compromise.

Few would contend that public education and a free press have produced an electorate sufficiently informed about the crucial issues of the day. However, most citizens still expect the political parties, candidates, and campaigns to perform that function. This expectation blinds us to the conflict between this educational role and their basic function.

What is the basic function of parties and their political process? It is to nominate candidates who then compete for the responsibility to govern. The winner in that competition must receive the most votes. To do this a candidate cannot discuss specific solutions to basic sensitive issues that are little understood without jeopardizing votes. Thus in campaigns, such issues are usually finessed or avoided. Walter Lippmann stated this point succinctly. He wrote: "You can't be right too soon and win elections."

Being right too soon is to spell out in a specific way actions required to solve highly controversial basic problems that the public does not yet understand.

This was demonstrated in the last national election. Most Americans were deeply concerned about big government. Candidates sought to capitalize on this but they also knew that presenting specific proposals to shrink the government would alienate most members of special-interest groups whose programs would be reduced or eliminated; that the public's concern existed only to the extent that proposed actions would not affect programs benefiting them. Consequently the candidates finessed public concern.

Ronald Reagan said he would cut the federal budget by $90 billion. When asked, "How?" he gave no details but said he would not cut Social Security. Details would have alienated the special-interest groups whose programs would have been affected. As it was, he no doubt lost the crucial New Hampshire primary because the people there realized a federal cut of that magnitude would require New Hampshire to adopt a state income tax. This has been a long time anathema to them.

Jimmy Carter was more adroit in exploiting the big government concern. He talked about the two thousand federal agencies and how he could consolidate them into not more than two hundred. When asked, "How?" he responded: "I'll tell you after the election."

In his book *The Making of the President 1972* Theodore H. White told of questioning Senator McGovern about saving the cities. He asked: "How would you get at that? And he [McGovern] answered bluntly . . . 'How do you talk about that without talking about the race problem?' " White observed, "Without saying it he gave the impression he could not talk about the race problem."

Vice President Nixon and Senator John F. Kennedy engaged in
TV debates during the 1960 campaign. At that time I had not
recognized the risk of prematurely discussing specific solutions to
controversial issues. It seemed to me that the issues they discussed
were secondary at best. The small islands of Quemoy and Matsu
occupied much of their time. My concern led me to write them an
open letter urging them to discuss the real issues. Let me quote from
that letter:

> You are to be congratulated for expending great effort to talk
> to the American people. But what you discuss is of great
> importance.
>
> The hour is late, but you still have time in this campaign to
> enlighten public understanding on certain basic issues which
> will determine our country's future.
>
> These issues are:
>
> 1. Excessive concentration of union and corporate collective
>   bargaining power in the United States.
> 2. The mutual beneficial utilization of unequaled American
>   agricultural technology to alleviate hunger around the
>   world.
> 3. How best to assist other nations in realizing their expecta-
>   tions of higher living standards through rapid economic
>   development.
> 4. Curbing the expansion of federal government power in the
>   United States, so that the American people themselves will
>   grow in character and capacity as a result of shouldering
>   greater political, economic and social responsibilities.

I then elaborated each point, including these predictions about
point one on collective bargaining:

> Just as in Lincoln's day the crucial question was whether the
> nation could exist half-slave and half-free, the key domestic
> issue today is whether economic survival is possible with basic
> U.S. industries on a half-competitive, half-monopoly basis.
>
> Our economic policy is based, in part, on the anti-trust laws
> that foster the principle of competition. It also is based, in
> part, on collective bargaining laws that foster the principle of
> power concentration or monopoly. The two policies are in
> direct conflict. The fabric of our economic life is weakened as
> a result of the concentration of union and corporate collective

bargaining power. Pattern fixing wage settlements resulting from truces between corporate and union power blocs feed the cost-price spiral, block economic growth and produce unemployment, reduce exports and increase imports, undermine the dollar, and expose the nation to centralized economic control.

Subsequent experience made me conscious of the high cost of an uninformed public, and of a candidate's being right too soon. As the first national figure to question what we were being told about Vietnam I was destroyed as a presidential candidate.

By the time I was in the cabinet in 1969, inflation had intensified. The "New Frontier" and "Great Society" programs had expanded federal spending enormously. Massive military intervention in Vietnam increased deficit financing when President Johnson decided on a guns-and-butter policy without an increase in taxes.

In his first State of the Union Message, President Nixon listed Vietnam and inflation as our top priorities. During the first two and a half years that followed, the cabinet on many occasions debated actions required to stop inflation. The economists in the cabinet all advised the President he could stop inflation by curbing demand through a balanced budget and tight monetary policy. Some of us with practical business decision-making experience argued that this was not enough. We agreed on the need to curb demand-pull inflationary forces, but urged him also to curb the wage-cost-price spiral or the cost-push inflationary forces.

As we urged this action on more than one occasion, the President responded:

> You are right, but there isn't the public support and understanding to secure the needed action. Even if I ask Congress to act, they won't act and the people will have forgotten I even made recommendations by the time of the next election.

Accepting the economists' view, he balanced the budget and encouraged a tight monetary policy. Demand subsided, and unemployment rose to 6 percent, but inflation continued. For the first time in the early part of 1971 we experienced high inflation and high unemployment simultaneously. By that time Senator Muskie was ahead in the polls. On August 15 President Nixon did a complete turnabout. He imposed a wage-price freeze. This helped temporarily but not in the long run.

All of this happened before the third major cause of present inflation occurred—the OPEC oil embargo and price hike. Certainly the energy crisis has complicated the inflationary forces but it is not the initial or primary cause of them.

There is another aspect to inflation that must be corrected. Representative government is inherently inflationary and favors policies of consumption rather than savings and investment. Heavier investments are necessary for the research, technology, and facilities required to improve productivity and for us to remain competitive at home and abroad.

Inflation is already reducing our standard of living and undermining our future, but adequate reforms in specific terms are not being discussed by political parties, officeholders, or candidates. Their fear is basically the one implied by Senator McGovern and President Nixon—"being right too soon."

It is urgent that we recognize that basic, highly controversial specific solutions for such problems as inflation and the cities will remain undiscussed until one of two things happens:

First, enough citizens, recognizing our coming peril, subordinate partisan, economic, and other lesser interests and objectively join in determining the true causes of our basic problems, the relevant facts, and needed specific solutions, and after documenting their findings, becoming the catalytic means, through the media, of educating the public. Three hundred thousand concerned, informed, united citizens could shape public understanding. Only an enlightened electorate can overcome the present political dominance of the triple alliance composed of the special interests, bureaucracies administering programs for their benefit, and most members of Congress.

With an enlightened electorate the parties and the candidates would not only gladly compete for votes on the basis of specific solutions for the real issues but they would find it necessary to do so to be successful. Those elected would then have the public support required to adopt needed basic reforms.

Coalitions of concerned informed citizens following the above process have prevented disastrous developments in many communities and states. They can do it at the national level.

The alternative is to continue our present drift toward disaster as inadequate or expedient actions are taken. To date we have been dependent on events to create an enlightened electorate.

The reforms required to prevent the coming disaster are as

fundamental as those adopted in the past only as a result of disaster. I refer to those adopted during the Civil War and the Great Depression.

Unfortunately, the organization of a genuine citizens' effort to deal with our basic problems was delayed by John Gardner and Ralph Nader. As the *Tulsa World* recently editorialized:

> The public is not sufficiently educated . . . to allow its political leaders to make the changes needed to alter the course of inflation. . . . John Gardner and Common Cause could have done it. Ralph Nader could have done it. But . . . both of these movements concerned themselves with secondary or frivolous issues.

Now that this realization is growing there is greater likelihood that a coalition of concerned citizens will organize to avert disaster by informing themselves and others. In a free society governed by a representative government there is need for a continuing cross-section coalition of truth-seeking citizens outside the partisan arena that supplements two strong political parties. Its existence would also strengthen the parties. It would enable them and their candidates to contend on the real issues and then solve them when elected. It would restore confidence in the effectiveness of the political process and preserve the sovereignty of "We the People."

—GEORGE ROMNEY

CHAPTER 11

---◦◦◦---

Challenges to
the Labor Movement

The greatest challenge facing the American trade union movement today is the oldest one: the challenge to secure and defend and extend human rights in our own country and throughout the world.

Our definition of human rights does not end with the formal categories of constitutional guarantees. We believe that political, social, and economic rights are inseparable and that none can be fully enjoyed if any are suppressed or denied.

We believe in the right of people to choose their own rulers and spokesmen and to change them, if necessary. We believe in free speech, a free press, and in the right to worship, to associate, to assemble, and to petition for the redress of grievances.

We believe in the right to decent health care; to quality education for all; to clean air and water; to decent housing; to dignity in the later years of life, and to protection in the marketplace from swindlers and exploiters.

We believe in the right to a job, at decent pay and decent working conditions, for all who are able and willing to work. We hold that the opportunity to live a constructive life, to make or do something useful and of value to others, to pay one's own way, to be a taxpayer instead of a welfare case, is a fundamental right and duty of all free men and women.

And we believe that the right of those who live by selling their labor to join together in free trade unions and to negotiate on a basis of equality with their employers on the terms and conditions of their work is an essential condition of human freedom and a cornerstone of a democratic society.

From the very beginning of our movement we have believed that workers everywhere have a fundamental stake in human freedom, and we have endeavored to help workers everywhere in the world to achieve freedoms and the living standards that we enjoy. We firmly believe that the loss of freedom by workers anywhere in the world is a threat to the freedom of workers everywhere.

Samuel Gompers, the founder and first president of the American Federation of Labor, wrote not long before his death in 1924:

> I do not value the labor movement only for its ability to give higher wages, better clothes and better homes. Its ultimate goal is to be found in the progressively evolving life possibilities for those who work and in its devotion to advancing the basic idea of freedom for all people everywhere.

It was Gompers who led the AFL into the arena of international affairs, into close fraternal ties with the trade union centers of Europe and Latin America, and into direct confrontation with the disciples of anti-democratic authoritarianism. Throughout the half century since his death the philosophy he expressed has remained intact.

That philosophy rests on the view that American trade unionists have a real and vital stake in the freedom of our brothers and sisters overseas and in the defense of free institutions throughout the world.

American labor is thoroughly aware of the imperfections of society in this country and of the need to carry on the struggle for social and economic justice at the bargaining table and in the legislatures. We have been engaged in that struggle for a long time, and the fact that America is and remains a society in which such a struggle can be waged through democratic processes and institutions and in which progress can be made is one measure of our success.

Labor's first struggle after the American Revolution was for the right to vote. The Founding Fathers did not write universal suffrage into the Constitution. The battle to strike down property qualifications and other barriers at the voting booth had to be carried on in every state legislature. For more than a century, right up to 1967, the battle continued to extend voting rights to women and to members of minority races.

Our second fight—the first battle of an infant labor movement on a national issue—was for universal, compulsory public education. That fight, which began in 1828, is still unfinished and probably always will be, because we believe educational programs and facilities should be constantly improved. We achieved federal aid to education less than a generation ago, and we will press for more and better schools for every American, from infancy to old age, until everybody has the opportunity to receive all the education he or she can possibly absorb, at every stage of life.

We have fought for equal rights, in political life and social life and economic life, in public facilities, in the workplace and in the union hall. I know of no other institution that has demanded the passage of laws imposing penalties on itself and its members for failing to honor their own principles, as our unions did in advocating the equal-employment-opportunity section of the Civil Rights Act of 1964.

We have a great many legislative goals—labor law reform, full employment, tax justice, an equitable energy policy, a strong national defense program, a universal health care program, and dozens of others—and we fight for them with great enthusiasm and determination.

We have a strong organizing and collective bargaining program, through which we intend to bring a greater measure of justice, security, and self-determination to every American who works for a living.

We are by no means satisfied with things as they are in this country or any of its institutions, including those we have built with our own hands. We assert the right and the duty of free men and women to build and rebuild and alter the instruments of a free society in every way that will expand the horizons and increase the number of options by which individuals may more nearly realize their potential. For it is the welfare and freedom of individuals, not institutions, that we value.

We have no fear of conflict and confrontation; we look on them as normal and necessary steps to progress. We welcome compromise, if it brings the hope of real progress. We do not pretend that our side is the only one that has a right to life, liberty, and the pursuit of happiness. We stipulate that the rights of management and stockholders are as real and legitimate as our own.

What we cannot stomach and will not concede is that some or all of the rights we assert in pursuing our goals can be denied or suppressed or abandoned or exchanged for other considerations in the interest of some higher good.

Nor do we subscribe to the notion that a hunger for human rights is a matter of taste, or a historical accident peculiar to certain Western nations, and not a universal urge of all mankind.

We have heard it said that the Russian people and others under the control of despotisms of the left or right do not really want freedom, that they don't mind being tyrannized over by their self-anointed masters because they have never known anything else. And we have heard it said that the oppressed peoples of backward nations in Africa and Asia are not "ready" for freedom; that they have no interest in democracy or political rights, but only in immediate physical needs.

We know better. Nearly a century of firsthand, grass-roots experience has convinced us otherwise. Because of our long and continuing contacts with trade unionists and other activists throughout the world, and because of our efforts to help where we can, the AFL-CIO has become a clearing house and receiving station for the oppressed from every quarter of the globe.

It was no accident that Aleksandr Solzhenitsyn turned to the AFL-CIO to provide the forum for his first major statements to the West after being expelled from his homeland. And it is no accident that thousands of others—Kurds, Ugandans, South Vietnamese, South Africans, East Europeans, Latin Americans—have come to us to appeal for support. From them we have heard such passionate and moving expressions of the meaning of freedom and of the innate, universal hunger for human rights as are rarely heard these days in the West.

What greater commitment to human values can there possibly be than for men and women, for the sake of those values, voluntarily to expose themselves and their families to destitution, prison, exile, torture, and murder, which are the standard response to demands for human rights in much of the world? The most telling testimony to the depth and universality of the craving for human rights is the sheer ferocity of the measures that are so commonly used, in this last quarter of the twentieth century, to suppress it.

We have no patience with those apologists for greater or lesser degrees of slavery who make fine distinctions between "political" rights on the one hand and "social and economic" rights on the other.

Unlike some self-styled "friends" of the Third World, who argue that political rights can be and need to be subordinated to "basic human needs," we see not the slightest hope that ordinary people who are denied the right to vote, to speak, to assemble and associate can still, somehow, retain the strength and the means to wrest economic and social benefits from their employers and political rulers, especially when the employer and the ruler are one.

There has been no more fatal illusion in this century than the notion that workers can trust their fortunes to a "benign" tyranny that will discriminate in favor of those who toil and create a "paradise of workers."

There are no more helpless, more oppressed workers on earth than those of Soviet Russia, who have proven the chief victims of the revolution carried out in their name and ostensibly for their benefit. As Solzhenitsyn and thousands of eyewitnesses have attested, the first act of the victorious Bolsheviks was to crush every vestige of independent trade unionism and to erect in its place a monolithic system of state control designed not to represent workers or promote their interests but to coerce and repress them.

Soviet "trade union" officials are not elected by union members. They are appointed by their employer, the state, through its agents, the Politburo and the KGB. They exercise vigilance not against discrimination, exploitation, health and safety hazards, or other violations of the rights of workers, but against any effort by workers to speak up on their own behalf, to protest unfair treatment, miserable conditions, brutal work rules, or inhuman quotas.

The Soviets have gone so far as to reassign the same functionary—Aleksandr Shelepin—from his post as chief of the KGB, the state security and political police, to that of chief of the Soviet "labor federation." The two jobs are interchangeable.

Grievance procedures and arbitration are unknown in Soviet industry, and workers are forbidden to withhold their labor. Such is the human passion for justice and capacity for sacrifice that strikes do, occasionally, take place. A strike at Novocherkassk in 1962 was crushed by machine-gun fire that killed or wounded dozens of workers. Survivors were tried for capital felony and were shot or sentenced to long prison terms.

It takes an Orwellian turn of mind to dignify such a system with the name of "trade unionism" and blind perversity to equate it with trade unionism as it is known and practiced in the West.

But it was precisely on this issue that the AFL-CIO found it necessary to leave the International Confederation of Free Trade Unions and to support the withdrawal of the United States from the International Labor Organization of the United Nations.

Growing agitation for the admission of Communist-dominated labor federations, and increasing exchanges between ICFTU affiliates and the state-run Soviet and Eastern European "unions," led us to judge that the ICFTU could no longer serve as a vehicle for the pursuit of our goals.

The official policy of the ICFTU remains what it was in 1955, when its executive board ruled out trade union contacts with any country that "denies its workers the right of freedom of association and organization, the right of genuine collective bargaining and the right to strike." Unequivocally, the ICFTU declared that such contacts would only aid the Communists in:

1. Winning moral respectability and legitimacy for their state company unions;
2. Misleading the workers of the free world into accepting these organizations, run by the Communist Party, as bona fide free trade unions;
3. Facilitating Communist infiltration and subversion in the free world, and
4. Promoting the expansionist interests of Soviet imperialism.

Too many of our sister organizations, some of them tied to political parties committed to policies of "ostpolitik" or "détente," abandoned the ICFTU's fundamental principles for it to retain its charter as an effective or even viable spokesman for free workers.

In the same way, the subversion of the ILO's tripartite character by the presence of delegations whose members, ostensibly representing the separate and sometimes conflicting interests of labor, business, and government, spoke with the single voice of despotic governments; the reception of spurious delegations such as that of the Palestine Liberation Organization, which represents no one but a handful of conspirators and terrorists; and the conversion of the ILO into a platform for anti-American propagandists made it necessary for us to pursue our goals through other means.

From the beginning, the AFL denied that Soviet "trade unions" have any legitimate claim to represent workers or to sit in international labor councils as bona fide labor organizations. We insisted that they are instruments of oppression at home and agents of Soviet foreign policy abroad.

In 1920 Gompers advised the AFL convention against

> ... any action which could be construed as an assistance to or an approval of the Soviet Government of Russia as long as that government is based on authority which was not vested in it by some popular representative national assembly of the Russian people; or so long as it endeavors to create revolutions in the well-established civilized nations of the world; or so long as it advocates and applies the militarization of labor and prevents the organizing and functioning of trade unions and the maintenance of a free press and free public assemblage.

That same year the Comintern created the Red International of Labor Unions—the "Profitern"—and ruled that all work in trade unions was to be "systematically directed" by the Communist Party and that Comintern members would carry on "a stubborn struggle against . . . the yellow labor unions" of Western Europe and the United States.

"We must be able to agree to any sacrifice," Lenin wrote, "and even, if need be, resort to all sorts of stratagems, artifices, illegal methods, to evasions and subterfuges, only so as to get into the trade unions, to remain in them, and to carry on Communist work within them at all costs."

The intensity of Soviet interest in the international trade union movement springs from two main considerations. First, there is the simple fact that unions, in Soviet eyes, are "where the masses are to be found." Second, there is a recognition that independent trade unions, by their emphatic contrast with the captive unions of Communist states, undermine the ideological basis of the entire Soviet system and challenge its claim to speak for the workers of the world.

So, while he could afford to jeer at the capitalist enemy as a profit-mad fool who would sell the rope with which the Communists intended to hang him, Lenin reserved his most vitriolic attacks for democratically elected union leaders as the "principal social prop of the bourgeoisie," the "real channels of reformism and chauvinism," and the main obstacle to Communist revolution in the West.

To inject a personal note, I take pride in the fact that along with Gompers and William Green, my predecessors as the head of America's trade union center, I have been singled out for more intense Communist vilification than any Western industrial or political figure. This, I concede, reflects no outstanding personal merit on my part—it goes with the territory.

It is as clear to American trade unionists as it is to the Communists that the fate of nations, including our own, hangs on the fate of working people. America cannot survive in a world without freedom, and freedom cannot survive in a world without trade unions.

At the end of World War II, when Europe lay in ruins, the American labor movement took the lead in support of the Marshall Plan—not only in winning acceptance of it among Americans but in overcoming Communist attempts to sabotage its success in Europe. American union representatives were in the front line, on the docks and in the streets and mills of Europe, helping to keep the wheels turning and to rebuild the free unions shattered by Hitler long before the war.

In Germany, in France, in Italy, in Greece, we helped the surviving leaders and remnants of free trade unions to pull themselves together and overcome determined Communist takeover bids.

The massive economic aid that we urged and supported was tied to our vision of a new democratic Europe. Against those who held that Germany should be reduced to an agricultural economy, we urged that it be allowed and helped to reindustrialize and that the restoration of a democratic German trade union movement be made an integral part of U.S. policy.

One of the results was the first step toward "industrial codetermination." We do not view it as any general theory of social reform or as a practice in which we ourselves have any interest, but it was deemed to be a precaution against any revival of the Nazi political-industrial combine that underlay Hitler's power.

If democratic institutions were worth reviving and rebuilding in Europe, they were worth extending to long-oppressed victims of European colonial rule. So the AFL took the lead in demanding of our allies that they divest themselves of their overseas empires. Although we had less than enthusiastic support from some of our European friends, we helped to train, support, and sometimes hide or rescue from prison many who later emerged as trade union leaders and political leaders in the new nations.

We were never under any illusion that political independence alone would solve the problems of the emerging nations. We knew they would need not only economic aid but help in developing modern social and economic institutions—particularly free and independent trade unions—if benefits were to reach the many rather than the few.

Our basic principle was that since, by its nature, an independent trade union movement needs a democratic environment, such an environment must be promoted in rich and poor nations alike as an aid to social and economic progress and development.

The nature and the dimensions of the AFL-CIO's overseas commitments are little known and even less understood by most American businessmen and government officials. Many, indeed, seem offended that labor should even have a foreign policy, let alone carry it out. By what right, they ask, do workers involve themselves in activities that should be left to professional diplomats and policy makers?

The answer is that nobody else is paying attention to this aspect of international affairs. The problems of workers, the aspirations of common people, the perception of masses as to where their interests lie are all but totally neglected by America's foreign policy establishment. If the AFL-CIO did not try to fill the needs we see, who else would?

We have, at AFL-CIO headquarters, a staff Department of International Affairs reporting directly to the president. Policy advice is given to the executive officers and the Executive Council of the federation by a Standing Committee on International Affairs made up of presidents of sixteen of our affiliated unions.

We maintain direct bilateral relations with the trade union centers of the democratic world, such as the British Trades Union Congress, Force Ouvrier of France, the Japanese Domei, the DGB of Germany, and so on. These are pursued through frequent meetings and correspondence and exchanges of delegations.

We have a branch office in Paris where the AFL-CIO European Representative is responsible for our day-to-day contacts with European labor and with the East European human rights movement and endeavors to organize support for the cause of democratic trade unionism in Portugal and Spain, where the survival of newly launched political democracy is closely linked to the trade union struggle.

The AFL-CIO is the leading sponsor and backer of the Inter-American Organization of Workers (ORIT), the coordinating body of the democratic trade union centers of the Western Hemisphere. Our full-time Inter-American Representative works closely with this body and is in constant touch with its affiliates.

To carry out our work in the developing nations the AFL-CIO has created three institutes that serve as the federation's arms in their respective areas of responsibility.

In Central and South America and the Caribbean it is the American Institute for Free Labor Development. In its first thirteen years, AIFLD has trained 257,928 trade unionists at residential centers and in regional seminars in dozens of countries. Two thousand more have completed advanced courses at our training center in Front Royal, Virginia, and 145 selected labor economists from these countries have studied under our auspices at Loyola University in New Orleans, Georgetown University and Mount Vernon College in Washington. Of those who have received this initial training in the responsibilities and techniques of trade union organization and leadership, a great many have risen to responsible office in the unions of Latin America and the Caribbean.

Our African-American Labor Center, since its inception in 1965, has undertaken 245 training programs in cooperation with the trade unions and with the full endorsement of the governments of 37 countries. An estimated 100,000 African trade unionists have benefited from courses on worker education and leadership training, cooperatives and credit unions, social services, economics, and communications.

The Asian-American Free Labor Institute, established in 1968, has sponsored more than 700 seminars on union administration, arbitration, job evaluation, time-and-motion study, mediation, research methods, and many other topics for about 30,000 rank and file union members as well as leaders in Bangladesh, India, Indonesia, Jordan, Korea, Lebanon, Malaysia, Pakistan, the Philippines, Singapore, Sri Lanka, Thailand, Turkey, and South Vietnam.

These three institutes provide the AFL-CIO with a fairly extensive and effective foreign service. They have a staff of 136, of whom 53 are permanently stationed abroad, in 43 countries. Their job is to help trade unions in the host countries to develop their own programs of trade union education, to establish worker cooperatives and health centers, to organize vocational training and worker housing projects, as well as to teach organizing and collective bargaining methods.

These programs offer no threat to economic or political systems or institutions nor do they conspire against governments or regimes. They simply try to give workers the tools of self-help, through tried and proven methods, through which they can build a durable infrastructure of strong, independent trade unionism. Nor do they provide a channel for continuing AFL-CIO influence. All of their emphasis is on self-determination. What the African, Asian, and Latin American workers do with their institutions is up to them.

Along with the international trade union relations and programs for which the federation takes responsibility, our individual affiliated unions work closely with their counterparts in other countries through the various international trade secretariats.

Thirty years ago only a handful of American unions were affiliated with the ITSs. Today more than sixty are actively involved with the international bodies of unions in such fields as metals, education, public service, clothing and textile, communications, entertainment, chemicals, and other trades and industries.

These are organizations through which trade unionists have the best chance of establishing solidarity across national borders to deal with mutual, concrete problems affecting their members, exchange information on their experiences with multinational corporations and on trade and job issues of every kind, as well as organize support for unions that need help.

The rise of multinationals gives the trade secretariats a pivotal role to play in building international labor solidarity.

They provide the machinery through which unions can support one another in disputes with the parent corporation or its branches and subsidiaries through information campaigns, material and financial aid, boycotts or job action to prevent the company from marshaling its worldwide power against unions in individual plants.

They can help establish permanent multinational councils through which unions can coordinate organizing activities involving individual companies on a worldwide scale. Ultimately, they will succeed in compelling companies to discuss their international investment, production, diversification, and other policies as a step toward internationally negotiated agreements on all matters over which central management has authority.

Needless to say, as the international trade secretariats have grown in size and importance, they have become major targets for Communist infiltration and subversion. Both because American unions are heavily represented in the ITSs and because such bodies, concerned with specific issues, are less vulnerable to purely political agitation, those seeking to subvert them have so far made little headway. But in this, as in every other area of international trade union activity, efforts are under way to sow disunity and division among workers and their organizations.

As I have tried to show, the Soviet Union and its supporters give the highest priority to infiltrating, disrupting, and subverting trade unions, viewing them as stepping stones to political power not only in the emerging countries but in Europe and Latin America, as well.

It is unfortunate that American foreign policy has no trade union dimension at all. Our diplomats, like our industrial leaders, are preoccupied exclusively with trade agreements, concessions, and joint ventures that often help to consolidate and perpetuate the power of some who exercise absolute control over the means of production, the marketplace, the armed forces, the police, the teachers, artists and intellectuals, the workers, producers as well as consumers, and whose declared goal it is to extend their power throughout the globe.

Against this poisonous doctrine stands an international labor movement concerned with the welfare of individual human beings in their daily struggle for a voice in shaping their economic future.

Come what may, the AFL-CIO will continue its efforts in the international arena to the best of its ability.

I don't pretend that we are doing or can do all that needs to be done, given the plight of the world's workers and the steady erosion of their rights and liberties.

Measured against the Soviet effort in the international labor field, American activities are small. The AFL-CIO, insisting on its independence of government and political parties, will never have the manpower or financial resources that the Soviet Union deploys. We are not and cannot be their competition in that sense.

I think it is essential for our own government—and all persons, in or out of government, who value human freedom and who give any thought at all to foreign policy—to reassess the role of the international free trade union movement as a force for peace, stability, and democratic values in the world, above all in the developing world.

With all the allies we can get, or alone, if necessary, the AFL-CIO will continue the fight for human rights that will determine the future of working men and women, their countries, and the world we all must live in together.

— GEORGE MEANY

CHAPTER 12

Agriculture—Stumbling Block
or Stepping Stone?

I. THE PATH BY WHICH WE HAVE COME

Certain parts of the earth's surface are especially well endowed for agricultural production. They have that favored combination of soil, topography, and climate that gives them garden-spot status. In this list must be included Northern Europe, the Danube Basin, the Ukraine, the valleys of the Ganges and of the Nile, the Pampas of Argentina, and choice areas in the People's Republic of China.

But none of these favored farming areas approaches, in its natural endowment, that vast American heartland stretching from the Appalachians on the east to the Rockies on the west and from Mexico to the Canadian border. Over the aeons, this land surface rose and fell, the seas came and went, the glaciers advanced and receded, sculpturing and molding a terrain well suited to modern agriculture, laying down a fertile soil that responds to good treatment.

True, there are other superb agricultural areas in the United States, though of lesser size: the Central Valley of California, parts of the Pacific Northwest, scattered spots in the Intermountain Area, productive locations in the Southeast, and some good farming sections in the Northeast. When we think of American agriculture

179

we think of the total. But for sheer magnificence, nothing in the world matches the area between Columbus, Ohio, and Denver, Colorado, between Brownsville, Texas, and Grand Forks, North Dakota, a thousand miles or so in each direction.

Consider briefly how good this area is. The topography, on the whole, is level enough for modern tillage, the soil so deep the plow seldom hits the stone, the natural fertility approached but not equaled elsewhere in the world. It is well watered in the east but drier in the west, relieved in part by supplemental irrigation. Being in the middle latitudes, the growing season is long enough to produce a good crop, and the winter sufficiently severe to minimize the disease and insect problems which beset the tropical areas.

The area is penetrated by great natural waterways. The St. Lawrence-Great Lakes system reaches more than a thousand miles inland; ocean steamers can load at Duluth. The Mississippi system has more than six thousand miles of river transportation, reaching as far inland as Minneapolis to the north, far up the Missouri into the corn and soybean country, up the Ohio to Pittsburgh and beyond, up the Illinois to connect with the Great Lakes, up the Arkansas into the wheat area, and deep into the Midsouth with the Kentucky and the Tennessee.

The frontiersmen who penetrated the American midland had sufficient vision to foresee its possibilities. Think of what they did:

They insisted that it be settled in a pattern of private individual entrepreneurship rather than in the feudal forms of Europe, from which they had fled.

They set apart one section of every township for an elementary school. They set up a land-grant college system to give status as well as knowledge to the farmer-operator.

They began experiment stations, so that they might develop the new knowledge required to best use the land.

They established an extension service, to bring the new fund of knowledge directly to the man on the land.

They criss-crossed the area with roads, railroads, and, in time, airlines. They improved the rivers.

They fought for and got rural free mail delivery, rural electrification, and rural telephones.

They worked and saved and invested: tile ditches, drainage districts, irrigation projects, better buildings, and modern equipment.

They set up markets, elevators, and warehouses. They built stockyards, processing plants, and distributing plants.

A whole new set of agricultural input industries was created: farm machinery, fertilizer, motor fuel, and agricultural chemicals among them.

They set up private credit institutions to tap the Eastern money markets and so bring needed investment capital into the new area.

In managerial capacity, the people who farmed this agricultural empire were the most capable in the world. Good basic education, good agricultural research, good adult education programs, plus the incentives latent in entrepreneurship, all these they had.

The agricultural system they built was fashioned for competition in world markets and there was little doubt in the minds of those early leaders that we could compete. In fact we did so. In 1925, agricultural exports were 48 percent of U.S. total exports. Agricultural exports exceeded agricultural imports by 25 percent.

By the time we were two decades into the twentieth century, most of this infrastructure was either in place or in progress. What we had then was the best natural agricultural endowment in the world, supported by the best infrastructure that man could devise.

And this agricultural plant fit well with national objectives. With our expanding agriculture we fed our growing population, including some 30 million new immigrants. Our agriculture was earning an export balance; with the foreign exchange earned by agriculture we were able to import the capital equipment with which the nation industrialized. Thus we combined natural endowment with entrepreneurial activity and enlightened government action to produce the greatest agricultural success story in the world up to that time.

But trouble was on the horizon. There came the Great Depression, worldwide in its effect. Dependent as we were on international markets, American farm prices fell with those in the rest of the world—from 1929 to 1932 prices received by farmers dropped 56 percent. Gross farm income was more than cut in half. Net income of agriculture fell from $6.3 billion to $1.9 billion. This depression, with some indecisive ups and downs, ground on for a full ten years.

This catastrophe required an explanation, which was not long in being offered. "Overproduction" was an explanation credible alike to farmers and to politicians. Farmers knew that excessive production meant low prices and therefore reasoned that the explanation for low prices must be excess production. Objective analysts had some difficulties with this explanation, pointing out that total supplies per person were no greater than before. A general consensus, some forty-five years after the event, is that the system of money and credit broke down. But explanation of the Great Depression is not our intent in this chapter; the purpose is to trace the consequences of the explanation that *was* adopted.

An idea took hold very power ully—that American agriculture could not compete with the agriculture of other countries. This was in spite of our great advantages, bestowed and created. The idea developed that we should reduce production and create an American farm price structure basically higher than that in the rest of the world. This could not be done by a process of individual decision making; it had to be done by government. The idea fit well into a mood that was then on the ascendancy in the world and in the United States—that government should have a larger and individuals a lesser role in decision making.

So we took decisions out of the hands of individual farmers. By government action we cut production, priced ourselves out of world markets, and subsidized farm income. Without explicitly saying so we began treating our agricultural endowment as if it were a liability, and the fertility of the earth as if it were a force to be thwarted. We conceded the growth in foreign markets to other agricultural exporters.

In fairness, it must be said that those were desperate times. The "remedy" adopted had some favorable short-time results. It did get some new money into farmers' hands, it gave farmers the belief that their government cared, and it may well have precluded worse action; some farmers in the United States were thinking about overthrowing the malfunctioning economic system. Some countries went over the brink to communism or fascism during those terrible days. We did not.

The intrusion of government into the decision-making role was partial only. In general, the crops that were supported and controlled were those that could be stored, those with the strongest political clout, and those whose prices would respond most sharply to a given change in supply. Prominently included were wheat, corn, cotton, rice, peanuts, tobacco, and sugar. A measure of the degree of governmental involvement in agriculture is this: at the peak of government production controls, in the late fifties, the mandatorily controlled and supported crops were bringing in 22 percent of the gross farm income. Omitted from controls were most livestock products, poultry, and most fruits and vegetables. This discriminatory treatment resulted in extreme inequity from crop to crop, from farm to farm, and from area to area. The government shorted the supply and boosted the price of feed to the advantage of the farmers who sold corn, but to the disadvantage of those farmers who bought it to feed their livestock. The government reduced the acreage of cotton but permitted the acreage thus diverted to go into a variety of fruits and vegetables, aggravating the supply problem for farmers who grew these specialty crops.

Unintentionally we encouraged the substitution of manmade fibers for wool and cotton. Once a big net exporter of animals and animal products, we became a net importer.[1] By increasing our prices above world levels, we became an attractve market; to keep from being flooded by farm products from other countries we had to erect a series of barriers to international trade.

World markets were growing with the increase in population and rising per-capita incomes. But this growth we conceded to Canada, Australia, Brazil, Argentina, and New Zealand. We became the residual supplier. Other exporters priced their products a few cents under our support prices. Buyers took the cheaper products first and came to us to round out their needs. Typically this left us with a big carryover. Stocks grew to enormous proportions.

We increased the price of food to consumers by $4.5 billion per year and increased budget outlays by $5 billion per year.[2] We tripled the number of government employees involved in the regulation of agriculture and built a new structure in Washington to house them.

The huge sums of money transferred into agriculture went disproportionately to those large farm operators whose incomes were already above the farm and nonfarm averages.[3]

1. D. Paarlberg, *American Farm Policy* (Wiley, 1964), p. 202.
2. Charles L. Schultze, *The Distribution of Farm Subsidies: Who Gets the Benefits* (Brookings Institution, 1971), pp. 1-2.
3. See W. W. Cochrane and Mary Ryan, *American Farm Policy, 1948-73* (University of Minnesota Press, 1977), pp. 363-371; Varden Fuller, "Wheat, Cotton and Political Arithmetic," *The California Monthly,* July-August 1964; Charles M. Hardin, "Present and Prospective Policy Problems," *Journal of Farm Economics,* 1965; and Luther Tweeten, "Agricultural Policy, A Review of Legislation, Programs and Policy" in *Food and Agricultural Policy* (American Enterprise Institute for Public Policy Research, 1977), p. 52.

The depression, the original reason for governmental intervention, disappeared. But the program continued.

Production costs per bushel or per bale rose above what they otherwise would have been. This came from inefficiencies associated with artificially limiting supply.

In accordance with the well-known Ricardian principle, much of the income gain resulting from the program accrued to those who held the land when the programs began—a gain to the older generation and a loss to the younger.[4]

The long-term effect of supporting farm prices and incomes was to reduce price risk and stimulate production, aggravating future supply problems with ultimate injury to farm income.[5]

This is a substantial series of indictments laid before the public, and documented. The persistence of the program, despite this record, attests the enormous survival capability of government programs.

By 1972, forty years after the government control program began, we were holding out of production 62 million acres, 18 percent of our cropland, at an annual cost of $3.5 billion.

But we seemed hooked, like a man on drugs. We had moved so far from a competitive position on the major crops that a return to the market discipline seemed laden with disaster. One study after another indicated that scuttling the government program would reduce the net income of agriculture sharply. The median reduction in net farm income reported by these studies was one-third.[6] A powerful triumvirate—farmers, legislators, and bureaucrats—worked without stint for the continuation of the program.

Regardless of whether or not it had originally been true, the

4. See M. Gaffney, "The Benefits of Farm Programs: Incidence, Shifting, and Dissipation," *Journal of Farm Economics,* December 1965; and R. D. Reinsel and R. D. Krenz, *Capitalization of Farm Program Benefits into Land Values,* USDA, ERS 506, 1972.

5. See George E. Brandow, "Agricultural Production, Prices and Costs" in *Food and Agricultural Policy* (American Enterprise Institute for Public Policy Research, 1977), p. 78; R. W. Gray, V. L. Sorenson, and W. W. Cochrane, *An Economic Analysis of the Impact of Government Programs on the Potato Industry* (Minnesota Agricultural Experiment Station Technical Bulletin 211, 1954); G. L. Johnson, *Burley Tobacco Control Programs* (Kentucky Agricultural Experiment Station Bulletin 580, 1952); and F. J. Nelson and W. W. Cochrane, "Economic Consequences of Federal Farm Commodity Programs, 1953–72," *Agricultural Economics Research,* Vol. 28, No. 2 (April 1976), pp. 52–64.

diagnosis made in 1933—that American farmers could not compete in export markets at world levels—had become self-fulfilling. At least so it appeared.

Many people had speculated as to how the country might escape from the commodity programs in which we had become enmeshed. Direct confrontation of the executive branch with the farm bloc? Buy back from the farmers the valuable individual production rights that government had conferred on them? A taxpayers' movement? A consumer revolt?

None of these things happened. What happened was a series of phenomenal and unforeseen events, beginning in 1972 with poor crops in the world. Then followed an out-movement of accumulated grain stocks, devaluation of the dollar, the oil embargo, a surge of inflation, and a scare that the world might not be able to feed itself. Market prices soared far above legislated levels.

The Secretary of Agriculture, Earl Butz, used the authority given him by the Congress to suspend acreage controls. Thus our agricultural policy became market oriented. The water rose to float the ship, rather than the ship sliding down the ways to meet the water. In any case, a market-oriented agriculture was launched.

For the four years of this market-oriented policy, from 1973 to 1976, the experience associated with the removal of these restrictions was remarkably good.

Farm incomes during these four years averaged, in real terms, 24 percent above the four years preceding. (This was in refutation of the numerous economic studies previously cited, which had shown

6. See George E. Brandow, "Policy for Commercial Agriculture," Part III in Lee Martin, ed., *Survey of Agricultural Economics Literature,* Vol. 1 (University of Minnesota Press, 1977), p. 249; E. O. Heady, L. V. Mayer, and H. C. Madsen, *Future Farm Programs* (Iowa State University Press, 1972); K. L. Robinson, *Possible Effects of Eliminating Direct Price Support and Acreage Control Programs* (Farm Economics Bulletin 218, Department of Agricultural Economics, Cornell University, 1960); L. G. Tweeten, E. O. Heady, and L. Mayer, *Farm Program Alternatives, Farm Incomes and Public Costs Under Alternative Commodity Programs for Feed Grains and Wheat* (CAED Rep. 18, Iowa State University, 1963); U.S. Senate, Committee on Agriculture and Forestry, 86th Congress, 2nd Session, *Report . . . on Farm Price and Income Projections, 1960–65* (U.S. Senate, Doc. 77, 1960); and W. W. Wilcox, "Agriculture's Income and Adjustment Problem" in *Economic Policies for Agriculture in the 1960's,* Joint Economic Committee, 86th Congress, 2nd Session, 1960.

that with abandonment of the programs net farm income would be sharply cut.)

Agricultural exports averaged, in tonnage, 46 percent above the previous four years. Substantial dollar markets were opened up in parts of the world we had previously thought were of limited potential: the Soviet Union, Eastern Europe, the People's Republic of China, the oil-rich countries, and the developing countries of Asia whom we had formerly considered to be mostly charity cases. These exports helped generate the foreign exchange with which to pay for our oil imports. In 1970, agricultural imports into the United States had been approximately equal in value to our agricultural exports, so that the net contribution of agriculture to our balance of payments was near zero. By 1977, we were exporting $23.9 billion worth of farm products, and were importing $13.5 billion worth, so that the net contribution of agriculture was $10.4 billion. The importance of earnings of this magnitude to a country running an overall trade deficit of about $25 billion was immediately evident.

As a result of our becoming market-oriented, taxpayers were relieved of the $3 billion cost of paying for nonproduction.

Consumers benefited from the suspension of acreage limitations, an action which they rightly associated with an abundant supply of food.

Business firms welcomed the larger volume associated with a policy of full production.

Our capacity to provide food aid to needy nations was enhanced.

Laboring people favored the additional jobs that came from full resource use.

Table 1

AGRICULTURAL EXPORTS: VALUE BY COUNTRY OF DESTINATION,
Year Ending June 30, 1976

million dollars

	million dollars
Japan	3,300.5
USSR	1,863.5
Netherlands	1,755.1
Germany, West	1,618.1
Canada	1,400.2

million dollars

Italy	799.8
India	739.6
Korea, Rep. of	722.4
Spain	655.0
United Kingdom	647.1
China, Rep. of	562.0
Poland	447.3
Brazil	430.0
France	408.1
Egypt	404.7
Mexico	403.7
Belgium-Luxembourg	375.0
Israel	291.2
Venezuela	271.2
Portugal	232.9
Bangladesh	215.9
Philippines	188.6
Indonesia	175.5
Algeria	175.2
Hong Kong	155.9
Saudi Arabia	149.9
Iran	148.3
Pakistan	146.7
Peru	144.1
Switzerland	138.3
Denmark	135.2
Greece	121.1
Dominican Republic	115.7
Nigeria	112.4
Norway	101.9
Sweden	96.6
Chile	87.1
Colombia	86.1
Romania	80.7
Morocco	79.8
Jamaica	75.0
Iraq	70.9
Thailand	70.8
Australia	70.0
Czechoslovakia	69.1
Ecuador	66.7
South Africa	58.9
Trinidad-Tobago	50.3
Singapore	48.2
Bahamas	46.0
Other countries	1,538.6
Total	22,146.9

Source: Economic Research Service, USDA

Table 2

AGRICULTURAL IMPORTS FOR CONSUMPTION: VALUE BY COUNTRY
OF ORIGIN, UNITED STATES, YEAR ENDING JUNE 30, 1976

million dollars

Brazil	801.3
Mexico	633.0
Australia	600.0
Canada	579.4
Colombia	472.7
Philippines	393.2
Dominican Republic	369.6
Malaysia	333.3
Indonesia	332.7
Netherlands	258.5
Denmark	250.4
New Zealand	248.8
France	222.7
India	218.0
Guatemala	211.4
Costa Rica	188.6
Ivory Coast	186.6
Argentina	176.8
Ecuador	176.5
Italy	169.1
Peru	166.3
Spain	164.7
El Salvador	141.3
Honduras	139.8
Poland	136.3
Germany, West	128.6
Nicaragua	120.9
Turkey	113.1
China, Rep. of	109.8
Angola	101.4
Thailand	99.5
United Kingdom	96.2
Ethiopia	82.7
Uganda	74.9
Iran	74.6
Yugoslavia	72.1
Japan	72.0
South Africa	67.2
Ghana	64.9
Madagascar	55.1
Venezuela	53.9

Nigeria	52.6
Liberia	48.9
Panama	48.9
Greece	39.5
China, People's Rep. of	38.4
Switzerland	37.6
Norway	37.0
Kenya	36.2
Guyana	35.0
Other countries	774.8
Total	10,106.8

Source: Economic Research Service, USDA. Compiled from reports of the U.S. Department of Commerce.

Earlier we had believed we could *not* compete in world markets, an idea which became self-fulfilling. After the 1973–76 experience the idea took hold that we *could* compete, a belief that also could become self-fulfilling.

But the euphoria of the 1973–76 period was not for long. The 1976 crop was a large one, worldwide. So was the 1977 crop. Grain stocks were rebuilt, prices came down, net farm income fell; in real terms it came back to and even below the pre-1973 level. Apprehension rose.

In this mood, the Congress deliberated on the Agricultural Act of 1977. What would the Congress do? Continue the market-orientation approach of the previous four years, with a limited role for government? Or return to the governmental supply-management programs of forty years past, with high loans and target prices?

Definitions may be needed here. "Loans" and "price supports" are used interchangeably in this statement. What is involved is a non-recourse government loan on a storable commodity like corn. The government loans, say, $2.00 a bushel on a farmer's corn crop. If the market goes above $2.00 the farmer sells the corn, repays the loan, and pockets the difference. If the market price falls below $2.00, the farmer turns the crop over to the government in full payment of the loan. The effect is to hold the market, in most cases, close to the loan level.

"Target prices" are prices set by government. The market fluctuates more or less freely. If the average market price falls below the target, farmers receive deficiency payments based on the difference; if the market price rises above the target the farmer owes the government nothing. The effect is to put a floor under income, while the market functions in something like a historical fashion.

When the chips were down, the Congress finessed the question. They hedged their bets. They wrote a two-track bill, and they gave substantial administrative choice to the executive branch. If supplies should become heavy and prices depressed, which seemed probable, the stage was set for something like a rerun of the 1933–72 experience. If supplies were short and prices strong, the governmental supply-management machinery could be shelved; farmers would make their own production decisions and sell their products in competitive markets.

We were poised, therefore, to go either way.

II. THE CHALLENGE

American agriculture retains all of the natural advantages cited at the start of this chapter. Some acreage has been impaired by erosion resulting from poor tillage practices, true enough. But most of the acreage has been improved, so that its productivity is greater than before.

Agricultural science has advanced rapidly. And there is this about agricultural science: one may offer it as a principle if not a rule that in its effect scientific discovery generally enhances the position of those areas already more favored. The statistician would say that the relationship among the agricultural input items tends to be multiplicative rather than additive, so that the interaction among high-quality attributes is likely to be exceptionally strong. So during the past forty years the comparative advantage of American agriculture vis-à-vis the rest of the world has probably increased.

Another change has occurred, the significance of which is rarely appreciated. While in the earlier years farm products were generally labor-intensive, today they are capital-intensive. Purdue University has long had a farm accounting project, involving studies of costs and returns on a large number of better-than-average Indiana farms. The capital investment per man in 1976 was more than 30 times as great as during 1935–39. Even after allowing for inflation, this is a sevenfold increase.

What is the significance of the change? We generally think of agriculture as being labor-intensive, a producer of raw materials, an originator of production. An agricultural country is thought to be at a preindustrial stage of development. An agricultural exporting nation is thought of as somewhat laggard; its leaders do their best to push their country into the modern industrial age. Students of economic development divide the countries of the world into three categories:

• Primary producers (minerals, agricultural products)
• Secondary producers (manufactured goods)
• Tertiary producers (suppliers of services)

It is thought that these stages are sequential in time; as it develops a nation is expected to achieve passage from one to the next. And prestige is attached to progress up this ladder. I do not attach much significance to these categories, tending to accept the belief shared by those two very different persons, Adam Smith and the Apostle Paul. These two gentlemen taught that each vocation makes its contribution and that invidious comparisons are unseemly.

The point is that modern agriculture is no longer labor-intensive. It does not initiate production in the sense it once did. It acquires purchased input items and combines these to turn out commodities. Increasingly, the "value added" concept of industry is applicable to agriculture. We should no longer expect agricultural exports to come primarily from underdeveloped countries that are short on capital and long on labor. This may once have held a large element of truth, but not now. There is every reason to believe that the United States, the world's leading exporter of industrial products, should deliberately shape itself to take advantage of a growing world market for farm products. Let us now examine the nature of that market and consider how large it might be.

The world's population, which stood at nearly 4 billion in 1974, is expected to grow to nearly 7 billion by the year 2000.[7] While projections of population numbers are hazardous to make, an increase of great magnitude is virtually certain to occur. The young women who will produce this increase are already born and many of them are already in the reproductive age bracket. Such is the

7. United Nations, *Declaration on Food and Population,* Bucharest, April 25, 1974.

momentum of population growth that no credible family planning program can possibly avert a major increase in population numbers.

The big increase will be in Asia, but all parts of the world will grow.

Not only will population grow, but real incomes are expected to grow as well. As real incomes rise, people wish to improve their diets. This means, usually, more livestock products, which in turn calls for more feed grains and soybeans, two types of farm commodities that the United States is superbly qualified to supply.

The world food market is expected to grow at an annual rate of from 2.3 percent to 3.0 percent during the next seven years, depending on the assumptions made in the various studies.[8] The increase is expected to come both from population growth and from an increase in real income.

Sector by sector, where might U.S. agricultural export opportunities lie?

Historic Markets

Our chief historic agricultural export market has been Western Europe. In 1977 the European Economic Community took close to $7 billion of our agricultural exports. Growth of our agricultural market in Western Europe is inhibited by two main factors.

1. The Common Market Agricultural Policy overstimulates farm production on the Continent and so limits our export opportunities. European protectionism is a consequence, with its special devices for keeping out the products of other temperate countries like the United States.

2. There is a tapering off in the rate of population growth among the European countries.

To those who limit their vision to past relationships (and so largely to Western Europe and to Canada), export prospects are not particularly promising. This is the pessimistic analytical syndrome from which we suffered for so many years prior to 1972.

8. See Economic Research Service, U.S. Department of Agriculture, Foreign Agricultural Economic Report No. 98, *The World Food Situation and Prospects to 1985* (December 1974), p. 36; and United Nations, *The World Food Problem—Proposals for National and International Actions,* Rome, 1974.

Recently Developed Market Economies

But when we look at the opportunities in newer markets, the picture becomes much more optimistic. Chief among the new markets is Japan. In 1976 Japan took $3.6 billion of our agricultural exports. Japan has grown in population and in real income. She has very limited tillable land of her own. Our exports to her have increased very sharply:

U.S. AGRICULTURAL EXPORTS TO JAPAN, YEARS ENDING JUNE 30

millions of dollars

1969	$ 839.5
1970	1089.2
1971	1215.9
1972	1162.9
1973	2258.4
1974	3358.4
1975	3184.7
1976	3300.5
1977*	3600.0

*preliminary

Japan earns enormous amounts of foreign exchange from her exports of industrial goods; she is capable of buying vastly more farm products from us. Her people consume less meat, milk, and eggs per capita than do other people of comparable income status. The chance for increasing our agricultural exports to Japan is very good indeed.

To some degree the Japanese situation is repeated for other countries such as South Korea, Taiwan, and Malaysia.

The Oil-Rich Countries

The OPEC countries surely have the foreign exchange with which to buy food, and many of them are using their new wealth to improve their diets. In 1970, our agricultural exports to the OPEC countries totaled $300 million. In 1977 they stood at $1.5 billion, a fivefold increase. The increase is impressive even after correcting for inflation.

Most of the OPEC countries are not large in terms of population and so have limited export potential for U.S. farm products. But Indonesia and Nigeria are populous countries of the OPEC group and hold considerable export opportunities.

The Centrally Planned Countries

Here is real opportunity for growth.

Our ideological differences with the Soviet Union and with the People's Republic of China long kept us from considering them seriously as major potential partners in agricultural trade. And indeed trading with them does pose substantial problems. They are state-traders and behave like the monopolists they are. They can be in and out of the market abruptly, on a large scale, and so can be an unsettling influence. But they are large, populous countries, they are making real gains in per-capita income, and they are intent on upgrading their diets. Our agricultural exports to the centrally planned countries, which stood almost at zero in 1970, were in excess of $3 billion by 1976.

The ideological controversy over trade with the centrally planned countries has subsided in recent years. The persuasive argument now goes as follows: "These countries are becoming more concerned about improving living levels, especially with regard to food. It probably is good for us that they become more responsive to their consumers. Resources that they expend on food are resources that they can't put into armaments."

The difficulties of dealing with a state-trading nation are not insuperable. The four-year agreement with the Soviet Union is an example of successful coping. They agree to take from us, annually, from 6 to 8 million tons of grain, with escape clauses for each country in the event of unforeseeable circumstances regarding crop production. Specific terms are left open.

The point is that if there is sincere intent to trade, trading will take place. If we are opportunity-oriented it can; if we are problem-prone it cannot.

The Developing Market Economy Countries

The developing market countries in 1977 took about 40 percent of our agricultural exports. And the great bulk of this was for dollars.

The International Food Policy Research Institute of Washington, D.C., published a report in December 1977, addressed to the food needs of developing countries to the year 1990.[9] Chief among these countries are those in Asia, Sub-Sahara Africa, Latin America, and the Middle East. In estimating food needs, production in these countries was assumed to continue to grow at the 1960–75 rates, and population growth was projected at the UN median rate. On top of this, growth in real income was expected to push food needs even higher. Under these assumed conditions, production of staple food crops in these countries would fall short of meeting needs in 1990 by 120–145 million metric tons. This is over three times the shortfall of 37 million metric tons in the relatively good production year of 1975. Asia accounts for 40 percent of the total projected deficit, North Africa/Middle East about 25 percent, Sub-Sahara Africa over 20 percent, and Latin America over 10 percent.

It is difficult to conceive of international food movements at such very high levels. Obviously, food production in these countries should expand more rapidly than it did during the base period, 1960–75. If it does, the shortfall would be less.

Would the developing market economies be able to buy such enormous amounts of food (U.S. $14–$17 billion at 1975 prices)? In the past the appraisal of this possibility has been quite pessimistic. But this also may be in need of reappraisal; they can do better than we have been assuming.

1. These countries are, to an increasing degree, exporting manufactured products into world markets and using the revenues to buy food. During 1960–74, the volume of food imports into developing

9. International Food Policy Research Institute, Research Report 2, rev. ed., *Recent and Prospective Developments in Food Consumption: Some Policy Issues* (July 1974).

countries grew 4.4 percent each year. During the last four years of that period, at a time of rising prices, they grew 6.2 percent annually. Thus, food's share of the import bill rose substantially during 1970–74. At the same time, the oil import bill, as a share of total imports, increased even more dramatically.[10]

2. When PL 480 food was available in large quantities (concessionary sales or donation), we often pushed this food out, based on the finding that the countries couldn't pay. When the PL 480 tether was shortened, greater repayment capability became evident.

For the developing countries to be able to import food and pay for it, they will have to be able to export goods or services of some kind. What can they export? Here, too, the conventional wisdom will have to be reexamined. We have long thought of these developing countries as primarily agricultural; we have not thought of them as having early or significant potential as exporters of industrial products. But with capital now internationally mobile and with managerial skills reasonably transferable, this is changing. Labor is the big cost in industrial production; these countries generally have abundant labor and relatively low wages. It may well be that their comparative advantage lies more with industry and less with agriculture than we have been accustomed to thinking.

Fred Sanderson of the Brookings Institution has done an interesting study of the export performance and export potential of the developing countries. Quoting him:

> Exports of non-oil exporting developing countries have been growing at a rate of 7 per cent, in real terms, during the past two decades. Exports of manufactured products have been rising at twice that rate and now represent more than one-third of the total (compared with one-tenth in 1955). If we project the trend, developing country exports would reach $225 billion, in terms of 1976, by 1985. If export growth slows down to 5 per cent, exports would still approach $200 billion, in terms of 1976 purchasing power, by 1985—a gain of $70 billion. In this case, the projected grain deficit, valued at $5.5 billion, would amount to only 3 per cent of projected export

10. International Food Policy Research Institute, Occasional Paper 2, *Potential of Agricultural Exports to Finance Increasing Food Imports in Selected Developing Countries* (August 1977), p. 1.

proceeds—about the same as at present. Overall, therefore, the balance of payments burden would be no greater than it is now.[11]

If economic development and world trade are to take the directions indicated in this analysis, the case for liberal trade will have to be asserted and defended.

Food Aid

The foregoing export markets are commercial. In addition, there is need for food aid. In 1973, during the concern about the world food situation, the United States supplied $730 million worth of food aid. This was about 60 percent of the world total. The distribution was as follows:

Bilateral	*Million dollars*	
Grants	251.0	
Loans	425.0	
Total bilateral		676.0
Multilateral		
World Food Program	27.0	
Other	27.0	
Total multilateral		54.0
Grand total		730.0

The World Food Council has established a food aid target of 10 million tons a year. Food aid is now, and will be, a legitimate claimant on our agricultural production and exports. If there was any doubt about this point, it should have been dispelled during the 1973–76 period of short food supplies and high prices in the United States. We continued supplying international food aid. The problem is to get the food where and when it is needed, in amounts that alleviate hunger but do not result in disincentives to production. This takes some real doing.

11. Fred H. Sanderson, "The Role of International Trade in Solving the Food Problem of the Developing Countries" in *International Food Policy Issues, a Proceedings,* Economics, Statistics and Cooperatives Service, U.S. Department of Agriculture, Foreign Agricultural Economic Report No. 143 (January 1978), pp. 71–72.

When we add all of this together, what do we see? We see a positive opportunity for increased agricultural exports from the United States to countries that not only need this food but, for the greater part, can pay for it. The expanded exports of 1973–76 were not just a blip on the screen. In some measure they were temporary (poor crops abroad) but in a large part they were the result of forces that can continue and grow (new markets, competitive pricing, full use of agricultural resources, thinking entrepreneurially rather than in bureaucratic fashion).

Is American agriculture capable of meeting the needs of an expanded export market? In 1973 the USDA issued a report on America's capacity to produce.[12] For the major crops, these volumes were deemed likely by 1985, *if land resources were not withheld.*

	Crop Production	
	1977 actual	1985 project-ed
corn, billion bushels	6.4	9.1
wheat, billion bushels	2.0	2.3
soybeans, billion bushels	1.7	2.3
cotton, million bales	14.5	16.4

There can be arguments as to whether we can, should, or will attain increases of this magnitude. But even allowing for some errors of assumption, substantial unused potential in our agricultural capability appears to be a fact.

Of one thing there is no doubt. That is the need for the United States to earn very large amounts of foreign exchange for at least the next decade in order to pay for the huge amounts of high-priced petroleum that we must import. This will be true almost regardless of any conceivable developments with respect to energy policy, environmental issues, or discovery of new energy sources.

In agriculture we have an enterprise that is capable, *if it is allowed to be competitive,* to earn, in the export market, a very substantial part of that chunk of money.

12. David W. Culver, "American Agriculture, Its Capacity to Produce" in *The Farm Index,* U.S. Department of Agriculture (December 1973), pp. 8–18.

A major question of agricultural policy—indeed of national policy—is whether we can be brought to realization of this fact.

III. THE CHOICE

The Agricultural Act of 1977, as was stated earlier, is a two-track bill. Within the parameters of this bill we can either be reasonably competitive or we can return to the restrictive policies of the forty years spent wandering in the wilderness.

Which shall it be?

Advocacy for a strong government role comes from three groups: the commodity interests, the politicians, and the government bureaucrats. This is what John Gardner calls "The Unholy Trinity." If this team makes the decisions, there is little doubt as to what will happen. Loan and target levels will be high, we will price ourselves out of world markets, supplies will pile up in government hands, and we will again impose production controls. Farm subsidies will increase, and there will be jobs for a vast number of government employees to administer these programs. We would turn again inward, we would have to impose import restrictions to keep foreign agricultural products out of the high-priced U.S. market, we would have to subsidize exports to reach foreign markets, we would contribute to the protectionist mood already at large in the world. More decisions would be concentrated in the hands of government.

I have spent sixteen years in the farm policy arena, at highest levels, and there is in my mind no doubt that these unfortunate things will come to pass *if the narrow and immediate desires of the farm commodity lobbies are granted.*

It is not my purpose to impugn the motives of the farm lobby groups. For the greater part, they are earnestly trying to improve the economic position of agriculture, which they hold in high and sincere esteem. The regrettable fact is that the short-run consequences of such governmental intervention are favorable and highly visible, while the long-run results are hurtful—and not clearly evident. A return to strong government participation in the pricing and production of farm products would be a triumph of the short-run over the long-run, of politics over economics, and of the special interests over the general well-being.

Bruce Gardner, describing the actual political operation within which agricultural legislation takes place, puts the matter at its blunt best: "The purpose is to take from those who have less political clout and give to those who have more."[13]

The popular myth is that if private enterprise makes the decisions, the public interest is impaired, and that if decisions are made through public processes, the public interest is advanced. This is the myth that increased the federal government's share of our economic activity from 11 percent of the total in 1929 to 32 percent in 1977.

But despite the forces that incline us toward a rerun of the 1933–73 experience, we need not take this road. The adverse experience with supply control during the years past is present for all to see. The period 1973–76 did serve to provide a glimpse of the good results a competitive agriculture could produce. The law does provide an opportunity to hold the decision-making role of government to a modest level if there is the will to do so. There is enough latent followership in the country so that good leadership could lead.

The plea for government to have a limited rather than a leading role in the pricing and production of farm products is not advocacy for withdrawal of government from all economic activity in agriculture. The role of government, as I see it, is to improve the functioning of the enterprise system, not to replace it. The job is to place a floor over the pit of disaster and to help individuals equip themselves better for their tasks as decision makers.

Many earnest believers in a market-oriented agriculture allow themselves to be backed into a corner and forced to defend not a market-oriented agriculture but a caricature of it. They are forced into advocating a market-oriented agriculture not as it is or could be, but as it once was or as its adversaries contend it would be. I do not intend to fall into this trap. My support for a market-oriented agriculture does not include a defense of those abuses which sometimes occur in markets—for example, manipulation, misrepresentation, gross ignorance, and wild gyrations. These abuses happen in part because government neglects its role as referee and tries to become one of the players.

The supreme tragedy would be for the United States, with the

13. Bruce Gardner, "Agricultural Production, Prices and Costs," *Food and Agricultural Policy* (American Enterprise Institute for Public Policy Research, 1977), p. 64.

best-endowed agriculture in the world, facing an overseas market of assured growth, to turn again inward and to ask government to ration the right to produce.

—DON PAARLBERG

CHAPTER 13

Problems of the Major Cities: What Can Be Done?

This topic is much in the public eye. Some view it as a new challenge. All agree that the solution would have a profound impact on our society. But the topic is not new, nor will its solution, while consequential, necessarily determine the destiny of America. The first step toward reasonable responses might be the development of a sense of historical rather than hysterical perception; and an understanding that, in one form or another, we and our ancestors have been concerned with the problems of cities for a long time. The times were different, as were the details related to those times, but concern with our cities and even the fears of their imminent demise probably started shortly after Jericho was founded.

It would not be wise merely to wish the problem away by anthropological references; but neither is it wise constantly to place the cities' problems in an apocalyptical surrounding. Cities have been charged with being the cesspools of crime, filth, and social diseases of every type since man expressed his gregarious instinct and chose to be closer to his fellowman whether in good health or sickness or in poverty or wealth. The cities will not die (though some will decline and others prosper) nor will they disappear simply because the problems are huge and demanding.

Given this philosophy, what then are some of the problems and some of the possible solutions? And, do they all relate to strictly domestic or internal problems within the power of the cities to solve or must solutions be generated elsewhere? This latter question has macro instead of micro proportions and should be examined at least to a limited degree.

Most Americans possess a trait which is reponsible in a substantial measure for our nation's progress. We tend to approach every problem with a conviction that it is solvable. This is a highly commendable attitude; but the facts are sometimes otherwise. Some problems never really get solved. Or if they do get solved, we do not always provide the answers. For example, it is generally conceded that the key to the solution of city problems is finding an answer to fiscal incapacity to handle increasing capital costs and maintenance and finding an answer to the lack of employment and the consequent poverty of a large percentage of city residents. All of the old-time cures are trotted out, and some are applied with insignificant relief. The problems of the cities are not altogether separable from a list that we confront on a broad expanse of question marks concerning our economy and society. The mention of a few should be sufficient to illustrate the point:

1. Worldwide economic conditions including shifting trading patterns and their effect on the economy of the United States.
2. The city-suburban phenomenon which grew out of the postwar boom, cheap oil and automobiles, and a huge road-building program.
3. The unsolved energy crisis and its impact on employment and growing impact on travel and its cost.
4. The drive for zero population growth and the decline in the birth rate and family size.
5. The intensified effort in human rights with its goal of long-deferred justice for those discriminated against racially, economically, and socially.

These factors influence growth in numbers of people as well as the economy. Growth, which has had a remarkable curative effect, may be absent in terms of prior experience. New social patterns can emerge only out of genuine change. All this and more does not yield appreciably only to local ingenuity and energy. The cities are only a part of the greater problem, but they pay a large share of the price.

Yet, there are problem areas which call for national and local understanding and action. This plus an intelligent use of resources can alleviate and even solve some of the problems of the cities.

There is a tendency to generalize about the subject to such a degree that we forget the cities are diverse. As a result, we devise remedies on a national or universal plan which often miss the mark at the point of need. In doing so, we even discourage local initiative or ignore it. This does violence to our tradition of federalism as well as to mere common sense. As a beginning, it is well to recognize that not all cities are in trouble—not all cities are declining—and even among those in trouble or declining the causes are not always the same.

Some inkling of diversity is gleaned from a survey of 67 of the 75 largest cities. It covered the period of 1970–75 and was based on 1975 population figures. The source is the Joint Economic Committee of the Congress. The cities surveyed were classified in four groups based on population and employment. The results were:

1. *25 cities* in Group I: cities with high unemployment rates (above the national average for 1976) and declining population (1970–75)
2. *16 cities* in Group II: low unemployment rates and declining population
3. *8 cities* in Group III: high unemployment rates and growing population
4. *18 cities* in Group IV: low unemployment rates and growing population

If low unemployment rates are an index to the economic viability of a city, it is interesting to observe that 34 of the 67 cities surveyed had lower unemployment rates than the national average. If declining population is a major cause of city problems, it is revealing that in the period of 1970–75, which included a sizable depression, 26 of the 67 cities showed a population growth. These statistics are merely an index, but even so, they reveal a regional problem and trend. With few exceptions, the growing population is in the South and on the West Coast, and the declines are in the North and Northeast.

Some statistics support the theory that cities have suffered economic dislocation because of changes in the general character of employment. A U.S. Department of Commerce study of the changes in employment in selected central cities by major employment sector over the period of 1958 to 1972 surveyed 25 cities. In manufacturing employment, only 3 cities had very modest gains of up to 9,500 jobs, while the remainder had losses of up to 138,500 jobs. In retail and wholesale trade, only one city in each category did not show a loss in employment, but the aggregate losses were generally more modest than in manufacturing. In the other two sectors surveyed, selected service trades and local government, the statistics confirm national trends. Every city showed an increase from modest to substantial in selected service trades. In government, 5 cities showed a very modest decline in local government employment, while 20 showed increases from modest up to a whopping increase of 126,700 jobs in New York City.

An additional important element of change is our determination to reduce discrimination in economic opportunity and in race. The greatest impact is necessarily in our cities, where most of the poor and nonwhites live. For a long time, it has been popular to condemn our cities as the habitat of the "poor and the black." This seems to be an outmoded formulation, but it persists. Current evidence begins to support the view that much of the resistance to color is breaking down. In the typical city situation the well-to-do nonwhite is not only accepted, but some developers of upper-income housing actually try to prove their broad-mindedness by seeking out qualified nonwhite buyers or tenants. This even applies to affluent suburbs. Obviously, the percentage factor of well-to-do blacks in relation to the total population is sufficiently low so as not to precipitate a discernible problem in schools and other public services and activities. It is the resistance to the typical poverty-stricken families that persists. Color becomes the added ingredient because so many of our poor are nonwhite. Furthermore, the percentage of such families is very high in relation to the total population of our cities.

Controversy arises out of the effort to lessen the problem of poverty-stricken nonwhites by dispersing their residences throughout metropolitan areas. Some of the early bitter fights have been succeeded by more sophisticated contests. Some opponents of fair housing have not reduced the intensity of their opposition, nor have the proponents remained helpless. The courts became the major battleground in instances when administrative agencies and other public bodies took action. No public agency or court can really solve the underlying problem—the unpleasant facts of poverty and the people who make up the nation's poor. Certainly good housing, while a prime necessity, cannot of itself relieve unemployment, underemployment, or poverty.

Of late, new approaches to this challenge have produced modest results. Public programs providing jobs of limited duration and public and private activities to reduce unemployment, especially among the young and the nonwhite, are calculated to produce a transition from unemployment to permanent positions. It is an act of last resort. As badly as it is needed, especially in times of high unemployment, it cannot provide a satisfactory final answer to the needs of these people nor to this basic difficulty of the city in trouble.

Thoughtful leadership has turned to the positive approach of conserving existing jobs, expanding existing employment opportunities, and fighting for new industries. This, too, has its limitations. Our commercial and industrial sector undergoes periodic changes which often change locational needs and even temperature zones. Some cities are destined to lose and some to gain as the evolutionary process in industrial activity continues. Furthermore, the growing competition between cities for a limited pie may begin to look like a "theater of the absurd." It could turn out to be a "no win" contest.

Consequently, a rational approach to this key problem of employment and poverty suggests the following sequence of thought:

1. *The single most important need is an overall growing economy.* The outlook at this writing is blurred by a whole series of complications. There are some signs that our economic posture versus that of other nations has deteriorated. In some industries, our production plant is outmoded and is competing against more cost-effective production plant and equipment. In recent years, even competition from developing countries with low labor costs has grown. Furthermore, the impact of increasing energy costs is not yet fully appreciated. Nevertheless, the nation's economy must grow if the city problems of unemployment and underemployment are to be substantially relieved without "robbing Peter to pay Paul."

2. Recognizing the limitations of local activity, in the absence of a healthy and growing economy, local leadership will have to fight to keep jobs and increase them or be satisfied to shrink the size of

its city. Such an alternative will be inescapable in some instances. This need not be the worst choice if the city plans for its reduction in size and activity. Not everything big or bigger is necessarily better.

3. Since poverty appears to be the single greatest barrier to dispersion of populations and a great barrier to healthy and viable inner cities, public programs within the ability of the nation, state, and city to compensate for this deficiency appear to be an indispensable future necessity. In the absence of economic growth, establishing the public as an employer of last resort may be an inevitable answer.

Certainly the foundation for a viable city is to provide a healthy economic base for it, whether at an existing, reduced, or increased city size, as events may dictate.

No sector of our national life has been more frequently assigned to perdition than our cities. Obituaries have poured out of the pens of academicians, planners, and statisticians at a dizzy pace. Yet a sane overview of our national life renders the demise of our cities unthinkable and undesirable. The reasons are many:

1. Nearly one-fourth of the nation lives in our 100 largest cities, which utilize only three-tenths of one percent of our land.

2. The standard metropolitan statistical area, i.e. the SMSA, includes all suburban communities and counties that depend economically upon the city. The SMSAs in which the 100 largest cities are included account for 60 percent of the nation's personal income, 62 percent of the total payroll employment, 57 percent of manufacturing employment, and 92 percent of employment in real estate, finance, and insurance.

3. As we will say time and again, all of our cities are not the same. In the North and Northeast are older and colder industrialized cities. There are the spreading cities of the West Coast and the burgeoning cities of the Sunbelt. They all face problems of various kinds. Some of these problems grow out of archaic laws at federal and state levels which have eroded the tax base or handicapped the ability to realize sufficient local revenue. Others arise from laws and housing practices which have encouraged more prosperous and middle-class whites to reside outside the city. Additional problems are caused by outmoded laws and

practices which have unfairly burdened cities with social costs, and public and private disincentives to city stability.

4. The United States is essentially an urban society. Modern technology and advanced agricultural practices have reduced the population residing and working on farms to about 5 percent. The remainder, in the main, choose to live in or near large centers of population which provide not only employment and economic opportunity, but also superior cultural and recreational opportunities.

Yet some academicians and planners persist in sounding the death knell of our cities. George Sternlieb, the Director of the Urban Study Center at Rutgers, and a competent authority, made the statement:

> The crisis of the cities is a crisis of function. The major problem of core areas of our cities *is simply the lack of economic value.* . . . The city as we have known it, and the forms of economic and social organization which have characterized it, are simply irrecoverable. The pace of change in our central cities has unquestionably been speeded up by racial tensions and fears . . . but perhaps the greatest cost of the race factor is that it has obscured the real nature of what is going on in the central city.

This is typical of a number of observations. There is a distinguished academic in the Chicago area who, like clockwork, has been issuing predictions of doom for Chicago.

Any extrapolation of metropolitan statistics over the last twenty years would tend to support such apocalyptic conclusions. But a reasoned analysis of available alternatives must abandon such notions. The usefulness of these dark views should be to compel the nation to face up to what could occur if it does not act. In this sense, funereal prognostications perform a genuine service. But in danger and peril there lurks opportunity. And that is what I suggest.

First, let us recognize that other scholars appreciate the limits of the extrapolation process. Edward Banfield, generally accepted as a realist who does not hesitate to condemn when he believes it warranted, observes:

> Most of the "problems" that are generally supposed to constitute the "urban crisis" could not conceivably lead to disaster.

They are—some of them—important in the sense that a bad cold is important, but they are not serious in the sense that a cancer is serious. They have to do with comfort, convenience, amenity and business advantage, all of which are important, but they do not affect either the essential welfare of individuals or what may be called the good health of society.

Karl Tauber in *Social and Demographic Trends* protests the "stereotype of poor blacks moving to cities and rich whites fleeing to the suburbs . . . [as] not only overly narrow [but] . . . largely false." Significantly, this was published in 1974.

The debate as to the future of the cities is essentially a nondebate. We Americans are a practical and yet compassionate people. In a free land it takes time for a problem to emerge as a crisis, but when it does the chances for a sensible supportable solution also improve. The debate is meaningless because there are no practical attainable solutions in our contemporary America other than to make our cities viable to meet today's and tomorrow's need of them. The doomsayers extrapolate practical impossibilities under today's conditions. Even the suburbs that surround our cities are dependent upon the central cities for much of their commerce and the attributes of a good life. But there are powerful economic reasons that in American tradition are conclusive. There is just too much invested in the usable assets of our cities and the desperate need of our nation for the use and reuse of these assets is so great, that there is indeed no alternative to addressing ourselves to this challenge with vigor of mind, foresighted plans, and determined and sustained action. It is toward these ends that I direct my views.

Our people and our private and public enterprise systems must accept the proposition that there is no practical alternative to making and keeping our cities viable and vital. Public and private programs can be generated and executed to achieve this end. It will not be enough to legislate high purpose and intent. We have been down that road before. It will require specific action programs, some of which are identified hereinafter, to achieve desired results. Any student of the events since World War II knows that it was federal housing and development legislation and aids that accelerated the suburban trend. Now it is past midnight to compensate for the damage necessarily done to the cities by constructive measures to reverse the trend. It is the national interest to do so.

It is not a matter of saving the cities for the cities' sake but a sheer necessity for the nation's sake. At the end of World War II, the nation faced problems of unusual magnitude. Millions of veterans were returning home, many of them to new families they had formed but not often seen. The nation was emerging from fifteen years of depression, recession, and war-induced prosperity. The cities had very little improved land available for a new burst of prosperity and family growth. Close-in farmlands were to be had at low prices, and the costs of then permissible minimum improvements were low. Few worried about central water supply and tertiary treatment plans for sewage disposal. Road building was relatively cheap, and automobile sales at relatively low prices met an avid demand for goods. Even underused public transportation was available at reasonable fares.

The Congress authorized a highway system in the 1940s. It ensured its greater growth with the passage of the Highway Act of 1956. An interstate system was programmed for 42,500 miles of highways, which is more than 90 percent complete. This created an enormous trucking industry, but it also further decentralized populations by making suburbs easily accessible.

Federal housing laws also encouraged and simplified the creation of new subdivisions and suburbs. This was aided and abetted by a flight to the suburbs by those who feared the campaign for civil rights just aborning. We did what we needed to do. We met desperate human needs in the best way we could, given the inability, if not our earlier failure, to prepare for the deluge. This sowed the seeds of large-city decay with an impact that later became visible. What the public neglect encouraged and paid for must now be compensated for because the needs and demands call for metropolitan reclamation with vision and certainty.

Why is this so? There are positive and negative aspects of this era which together constitute a compelling case for the cities. Without statistical confusion, let us examine a few obvious and relatively incontestable conclusions.

In spite of years of commitment to a decent home in a good environment for every American family, we are still millions of dwellings away from that achievement. Simultaneously, housing capital and monthly costs are constantly rising to new peak levels. About the only families able to pay them are the wealthy, the upper middle class, and those of low income eligible for subsidy.

The need to reduce total capital costs is of paramount importance. The major elements that constitute cost are land, building, and finance. In 1975 the cost of a new single-family home in the six county Chicago areas ranged from $38,700 to $55,700. In 1970, comparable figures were $36,700 to $42,800. The scarcity of new houses drove used house prices up to a $41,000-to-$50,000 range from a comparable level in 1970 of $32,000 to $34,200. Long-term interest rates still persist at high levels. But, as one builder recently observed, "The increase from 7 percent to 9½ percent in borrowed money is the equivalent of raising home prices by $5,000." Since 1975, costs have continued to soar. Interest rates dropped for a while but are on the way up again.

The cheap land, improvement, and housing costs in the suburbs are generally a memory. With newly enforced and desirable environmental standards, improvement and service costs have gone sky-high. Building requirements to meet competitive demands for lower energy costs have added to building costs. The individual luxury transport of the automobile is rapidly reaching a level which makes commuting exceedingly expensive as well as a kind of conspicuous consumption that is increasingly defeating reasonable energy conservation measures. Public transportation has grown in cost and added public transport is almost impossible to design and construct without major capital and operating subsidies. In short, while the suburbs will continue to grow in a more modest way, some pressing needs for housing must be met in the central city.

Thousands upon thousands of abandoned and underused acres of land are to be found in cities serviced by existing utility systems and transportation. Much of it is near to work opportunities and most of such sites improved at reasonable urban density standards can be made available at effective costs equal to or below today's suburban production. In many cases where job opportunities are near, reducing or eliminating transportation costs, total cost can be much less. What is needed is intelligent security and school planning, which must come in any event. There is no just reason why central-city and even outlying neighborhoods in metropolitan cities cannot compete with or out-compete suburban housing production in today's market. What is required is a determination to do so accompanied by a sensible plan of cooperation between federal, state, and local governments, private enterprise, and those who are deeply involved in the viability of the city, labor and the public at large.

Rising new construction costs have been heretofore mentioned as a deterrent to meeting housing needs. At the same time, this factor has rendered the rehabilitation of old neighborhoods competitive. Aside from the reality that many older structures are more commodious and even more charming than much new construction, the potential savings in costs makes a massive rehabilitation program possible in many places.

We found the way when we needed to do so to use such combined strength to create housing in sprawling suburbs. We can do no less in returning strength to our cities while helping to reduce energy demands and conserving otherwise wasting assets.

Demographic developments favor a push for city reclamation. Our family sizes are shrinking. Predictions of zero population growth are approaching reality. Most recently, the Bureau of the Census reported a major decline in the projected size of families arising out of its periodic survey of potential mothers and their expected family sizes. Furthermore, the percentage of single-person families, both young and old, is growing. These statistics extrapolated would support the propriety of somewhat higher density housing typical of an urban environment.

At the same time, we are witnessing a fast growth in the number of working mothers. The prospect of families with both parents working and one or both commuting two or three hours a day projects some very serious social problems.

The other two significant questions of security and schools are impacted somewhat by the changing population. In the immediate postwar period our child population grew so rapidly that we could not build schools fast enough. Quality disappeared in many places in order to meet the quantity push. It happened first with elementary schools and then with secondary schools and most recently at the higher educational levels. Now in some places elementary schools are already in surplus supply, which makes the next steps with respect to high schools and colleges predictable. In a number of instances, private colleges have already closed their doors. All this suggests that everywhere in America, as far as education is concerned, we can turn from quantity production to the improvement of quality. There is no justification in thinking that such change will leave the city school systems declining in quality—the reverse can and should take place.

As far as security is concerned, recent published statistics tend to show an increase of crime incidents in suburbs with cities beginning to show a percentage decline. We have not arrived at the ideal level, but the deficiency gap between suburb and city is narrowing.

But there is another aspect of this challenge that is equally pressing. As we have already said, some of the distress of our metropolitan cities arises from a decline in jobs within the city. While service trades have generally grown, other work opportunities in important areas have declined. Some of our older and colder cities have lost ground to the Sunbelt, sometimes because the Sunbelt could provide industrial locations at less cost than older and colder cities. With our drive for higher environmental and nonpollution standards, there are many desirable areas in major cities that can be reclaimed for light industry, and even some heavier industry, at competitive costs.

There are other economic aspects which have a public face. A highly respected banker directed attention to an awesome inequity in our national approach to this problem. He made an interesting and plausible argument. He observed that it might be urged that major industrialized cities of the North and Northeast, through the flow of federal tax dollars, may have financed the economic development of both the suburbs and the South and Southwest.

Each year, for example, the federal government receives a net inflow from New York State of over $7 billion more than it spends in New York State. For Illinois, the second largest, the inflow to the federal government, net of reinvestment, is over $4 billion per year. In reverse, California (our largest state), Virginia, Texas, and Mississippi, among others, received inflows amounting to many billions of dollars. At the same time, most of these states have established business development commissions to relocate industry from New York and Illinois by using attractive tax incentives. One could argue that New York, Illinois, and other states in a similar position are indirectly subsidizing parts of the Sunbelt.

This is not an argument against these states attempting to industrialize. It is an argument for the realization that states like New York and Illinois need excess resources to strengthen their own industrial plants and especially the economic base of their large and productive metropolitan areas. We may be unintentionally "killing the goose that lays the golden egg." An outflow of revenues in the amount and manner described above is not sustainable over any length of time.

But there are revenue practices in cities and under their or their states' control that need examination. Recent developments suggest that a good hard look at real estate assessment and taxing practices is long overdue. There is a whole galaxy of proposals that have arisen from time to time, but in the limited space available I suggest only a few examples.

I live high above the central city. It is delightful to look out over Lake Michigan or into the far horizons where details of the ground below are dimmed. On a clear day, looking down to the area surrounding the Chicago Loop is like looking at a mouth where teeth have been knocked out at random. Empty sites of various sizes are either buildingless and vacant or they are used for daytime parking. One-time valuable structures which lost economic value have been destroyed to reduce the tax burden. This has caused some competent students of the problem to question the general practice of assessing land at a low figure and improvements usually at a high figure. Perhaps these practices should be reversed so that central-city landowners could not speculatively hold buildable land off the market at a cheap cost. If land were assessed at real use value and improvements assessed at a value related to depreciable cost, the city would probably gain in total revenues and secure a more efficient use and reuse of its land mass. Of course, this could be debated, but the present tax practices are producing cities with whole areas of toothless mouths. A remedy is needed.

Some municipalities need the revenues and traffic that commercial sites produce. The growth of large-scale regional suburban shopping centers has siphoned off sales tax and real estate tax revenues from cities. These highly desirable and convenient shopping facilities draw many customers from central cities. This need not be. A fine example which can be repeated in proper scale in any metropolitan area is the Water Tower Place in Chicago. On weekends and evenings, it is the usual thing to encounter friends from the suburbs. If such developments do nothing else, they can keep city business and trade within the city.

In brief, the city can and will reclaim its stature when it equals or exceeds its suburbs in all aspects of a good life—housing and job opportunities, transportation and commerce, schools and security, recreation and culture. Then to top it off, it must get its own financial house in order.

This end, I believe, is inevitable. The modern facts of life demand it. The only question that should plague us all is how long will it take? Will every city have to experience the pain of New York's duel with its own destiny? The answer to this depends most on the people who have the greatest economic investment in the cities' viability. The casual dweller can pull up stakes and work where he wishes if he can afford it. There are no visas required for travel, visits, or permanent relocation in our land. But a huge department store, bank, insurance company, printing press, or major hospital— and one could add forever to this list—cannot do so with ease, if at all. Businesses, like people, sometimes stay rooted so long that inertia overcomes the ability to make a decision.

Most suggestions for federal and state aid for the problems of the cities proceed on an assumption that continued overall economic growth is the solution to the problems. This would provide consolation to worried cities if the concept is valid. We have never really enjoyed continued and universal economic growth. Even when the prosperity curve was seemingly ever upward, there were always pockets of dislocation. On the horizon there have been one-industry towns that lost their industry and their hope for growth.

Major changes in consumer and general needs have propelled some cities downward and others upward. The reality of variety is the hallmark of a truly free society. With it come the waves of change which are not to be denied. Yet nearly every proposal for new urban programs, and particularly new or remodeled old programs, rests on the dual premise that (a) money and (b) continued growth constitute the only solution. This is nonsense.

First, it is not at all clear that continued significant economic growth is to be our lot. I am not a pessimist about the future of the United States; quite the contrary. But in the absence of clear evidence, the chances are better for an American economic future with periodic ups and downs, not too much unlike the past.

Second, whether or not we enjoy a never-ending period of upward movement within the totality, there will continue to be areas of progress, areas of decline, and areas of stagnation.

Third, this suggests that in good days and bad our strategy to treat with urban problems must propose solutions that treat either continued growth, stagnation, or decline.

Finally, the notion that all that needs doing is to identify problems, assess the need for solution, and throw money at it is by now demonstrably ineffective. One must never underestimate the helpfulness of fiscal resources, but money without a plan, or money with a patently impossible plan, is waste not progress.

In this chapter, there are suggestions and implications of things that need doing. There are a few key propositions which the experience of the past generation suggests should be given priority consideration. They concern primarily the better understanding and utilization of what we have and the more sensible interaction of those elements that are or should be the prime contributors to the remedies of large-city problems.

1. Governmental Cooperation

For many years, it has been evident that our local governmental structure and performance left much to be desired. The states, with few exceptions, have failed to act. True, the average state legislature is weighted against the typical big city and in favor of the rural and suburban communities. The federal government has tried by using the carrot-and-stick method to encourage some reduction in waste and duplication, but the results have been modest at best. At present, all sorts of ideas are surfacing—most of them too expensive or of the same kind that have not worked. The notion that cities' ills could be cured by more money to meet the increasing demand for services, the costs of which are inflating constantly, is not all wrong, but it has limitations.

A recent study of Dayton, Ohio, and environs illustrates what can be found in and about most, if not all, major cities. In one typical year, 1973, the federal, state, and local governments in the Dayton metropolitan area spent over $1.4 billion, of which $790 million came from the federal government jurisdictions controlling one-eighth of the federal funds. The rest went through 55 state agencies or 122 nongovernmental agencies such as United Way.

The total public expenditures flowed through 270 separate governmental and nongovernmental departments and agencies, with multiple local governmental, state, federal, and nongovernmental administrative units operating programs in the same area. There were 36 separate drug-abuse efforts, 27 efforts dealing with alcoholism, 45 with mental illness and retardation, and 89 with crime and delinquency.

In addition, $628 million dollars was spent by the Department of Defense for salaries and services at the Wright-Patterson Air Force Base, near Dayton, which was identified in the study as a local expenditure on a national problem. The report further concluded that there is virtually no coordination between the base and the city in such areas as minority employment or transportation.

In short, the Dayton metropolitan area, like most such areas, is a public conglomerate involving federal, state, and local funds and units without the kind of planning, coordination, and accountability that a typical business conglomerate would demand even on a mimimum basis. Waste, duplication, and surplus overhead and administration are inevitable.

The notion of throwing more funds into such a pot is appalling in the absence of a sensible plan of consolidation, merger, or contractual arrangements which will make better use of what is already available. The federal government, if it has the courage and laws, could withhold resources until the state and local governments put their houses in order. For too long, voices have cried out that local governmental units could be cut to 20 percent their present number without loss of either local democracy or opportunity. Only the states can do this, by establishing laws which would permit other cities to encompass their suburbs, as Houston has. Or, if this cannot be achieved politically, at least the suburbs which benefit from the central city should contractually assume a fair share of the central-city cost of social and governmental burdens that the suburbs escape. Maybe such steps will eliminate the immediate need for additional money aid, or else substantially relieve it.

Considering the political problems, it must be conceded that this will not be easy to accomplish. Nevertheless, an earnest effort should be made. The federal, state, and local governments should set up a trilateral small commission for each SMSA to develop a workable plan for the utilization of all resources. And if federal assistance was made dependent on reasonable progress in keeping with the plan, it is possible that we could break through this implacable barrier. Certainly there is enough public interest and deep concern about the problems of the cities to provide some hope.

But there is yet another preliminary step that should be required.

2. Improving Productivity in State and Local Government

The proper and effective use of federal, state, and local funds in metropolitan areas needs to be accompanied by a decided improvement in productivity at the state and local governmental levels. Soaring costs of state and local government generally produce political defenses that either taxes must be increased or services must be cut back. It is conceded by all that the services involved are basically important in their own right, and they also have an important impact on the quality of American life generally. But the "either tax more or cut back" approach ignores a third alternative—improving productivity.

It is recognized that this cannot be achieved easily or readily in the public sector without considerable assistance from the private sector, including business, industry, and the residents of the community. Furthermore, legislative restrictions and practices tend to complicate the process as well. However, the resources consumed to produce the local services have grown to a magnitude that today makes state and local government one of the major components of the American economy. From 1954 to 1974, state and local purchases of goods and services grew almost sevenfold, from $27 billion to $192 billion. This increase skyrocketed this item from 7.4 percent of the gross national product to 13.7 percent. During this time the number of state and local employees increased from 4.6 million to 11.6 million, or nearly one in seven nonagricultural workers in the United States.

When the Committee for Economic Development studied the effects of inflation in 1973 and 1974 and its sources, it reached a conclusion that Americans could no longer "look solely to the private sector for productivity increases that will improve economic well-being. Given the shift in national resources to state and local governments and the significance of the service they provide, we must look there, as well, for greater productivity." It issued a statement in March 1976, making a number of general and specific suggestions toward this end.

When one considers the need to improve services and provide for capital investment in order to replace outworn systems of various kinds in the metropolitan areas it becomes doubly necessary to measure productivity and to find the means to increase it. Communities have been driven toward this alternative when perhaps it should have been a practice long ago. Nevertheless, if it is to become firm, fixed, and immovable national policy to find the answer to the current problems of our big cities and our metropolitan areas, then in addition to proper planning for utilizing funds, it is no less necessary to institute meaningful efforts in the metropolitan areas to increase productivity. Both propositions should be essential prerequisites to an increase, if needed, in the level of assistance from the federal government to the localities through the states.

3. The Role of the Private Sector

In a free economy self-interest is a powerful motivation. The private sector has the largest stakes in capital investment in our great cities. Aside from this motivation, much of the talent that is needed to cope with the macro-situations which have been described is to be found in the private sector. Corporate social responsibility has become a regular concern of many of our large companies.

Whether it has to do with the better utilization of funds already expended in a given area or whether it has to do with increasing productivity or in helping to generate the programs for additional jobs or jobs for the hard-to-employ, there is a rich accumulation of experience, energy, and capacity in the private sector that must be appropriately utilized.

Instances can be found across this large country where large companies or combinations of large and small companies have undertaken a whole compendium of tasks which a generation ago were not generally included on the agenda of the private sector. There are recorded cases of major assistance in supplying key personnel to a city like Niagara Falls when it was facing a loss of its credit for municipal functions.

Or, in the case of the city of New York when it faced collapse, it not only called upon the private sector to help with respect to its banking needs, but it went to some of the larger firms for the personnel to help tide it over in discharging key municipal functions.

In one city after another, there have been municipal redevelopment projects, specially financed housing developments, special training programs, and economic development activities in which private enterprises have played a significant role. In some communities, leading businessmen have been co-opted to serve on school boards to help improve the educational facilities in the community.

Without enlarging this simple proposition, it seems clearly desirable in projecting any of the systems or plans that are implicit in ideas herein discussed, that a call be made upon the private sector to collaborate with the federal, state, and local levels of government.

Throughout this chapter references have been made to the economic necessities of the large city and the importance of creating job opportunities. Experience is full of the activities of the private sector to help in this connection. After all, this is where most of the jobs are to be found.

There is a limit to what the federal, state, and local governments can do in connection with the depressing and oppressing problems of our large cities. With a federal budget already over the half-trillion mark and with a large number of programs already addressed to the problems of the cities, it is hardly to be expected that the cities may get large sums of general or categorical grant money beyond the level that is presently maintained.

Certainly there may be need for different facilities such as a properly organized and operating urban bank, as there may be need for an intensification and improvement in many of the programs, and especially the programs that concern employment opportunities. But in the final analysis, the sums that will be available in addition to what is presently being spent will constitute a smaller portion of the total. Therefore, the necessity for the approaches that have been suggested in these concluding pages becomes even more apparent. In light of the nation's fiscal condition, present and anticipated, any additional sums, smaller though they may be in relation to that which is already being provided, should be used as seed money for the improvement of local processes and government operations as well as the variety of other commitments that have already been made. Indeed, this relative pittance as a part of the total could well become the means with which to stimulate the realization of long-neglected and needed changes in the operations at the state and local level. This would be the most effective ingredient in the solution.

—PHILIP M. KLUTZNICK

CHAPTER 14

Government and the Citizen

> Budgets are not mere matters of
> arithmetic, but in a thousand ways
> go to the root of prosperity of
> individuals, and relations of classes,
> and the strength of kingdoms.
>
> —William Gladstone

Discussions of governmental organization and fiscal policy generally conjure up visions of Ebenezer Scrooge, green eyeshades, boring accounting reports, and trivia. Contrary to this view, and in line with the statement of the nineteenth-century British prime minister, decisions on the federal budget and federal programs fundamentally affect our national life and our individual well-being.

Most analyses of the role of government in the United States, however, have missed the central point. It is not so much a question of size of government, although that is not a trivial concern and is worthy of some of our attention. Rather, it is a matter of pervasiveness, "a thousand ways" in Gladstone's phrase.

THE SIZE OF GOVERNMENT

Surely government revenues and disbursements (and often deficits as well) are rising steadily, however measured. Federal outlays are scheduled to cross the half-trillion-dollar point during fiscal year 1979, a doubling since fiscal 1973. In 1973, budget outlays equaled 20 percent of the gross national product. By 1979, the ratio is estimated to be 22 percent. During the same six-year period, federal receipts have been rising substantially, but not at the same rapid pace. Thus, the budget deficit is expected to reach $60 billion in fiscal 1979, a fourfold growth from 1973, and a rising claim on the nation's supply of savings available for investment.[1]

But far more important than the absolute or relative size of the dollar flows is the fact that government is intervening, on an increasing scale, in the daily lives of its citizens. Decisions by one or more federal agencies can alter, influence, or even determine how much money we make, how much we can spend, what we can buy with it, how we can use the goods and services that we own, and of course how we go about earning our daily living. It is no exaggeration to state that governmental decisions also increasingly affect what we wear, what we eat, and how we play.

Before we go into the specifics of these numerous governmental-individual relationships, it is instructive to examine some of the key trends within the federal budget. It has become fashionable to point out, and quite accurately, that government spending is no longer dominated by military programs. Since fiscal year 1974, the various "income security" programs (the transfer payments such as Social Security benefits, welfare payments, and unemployment compensation) have become the largest category of federal disbursements.

In fiscal year 1979, the federal government will spend an estimated $160 billion on income security programs, or 32.0 percent of the budget. In contrast, national defense spending is budgeted at $118 billion for the year, or 23.6 percent of the total, a far lower proportion than a decade ago. Clearly, the United States is not in the "grip" of a military-industrial complex, as uninformed critics continue to charge. The shift in federal spending patterns is an important change. It has begun to receive the attention that it deserves.

But another development is occurring in the federal budget, which has generally been overlooked. The most rapidly growing area of federal spending in recent years is neither warfare nor welfare.

---

1. *Budget of the United States Government for the Fiscal Year 1979* (U.S. Government Printing Office, 1978).

Rather, it is the regulatory activities of the public sector. The budgets of the numerous federal regulatory agencies are increasing from $2.2 billion in fiscal year 1974 to $4.8 billion in 1979, a 115 percent rise in five years[2] (see Table 1). The initial reaction to this state of affairs may be to downgrade the importance of "only" $5 billion in a $2 trillion economy. But that would constitute jumping to a premature and essentially inaccurate conclusion.

There is a powerful multiplier in effect here. The typical regulatory agency generates private compliance costs far in excess of its own outlays. The Occupational Safety and Health Administration, for example, operates with a yearly budget of $100 million. But it takes over $3 billion a year in new capital outlays for companies to follow the many standards that OSHA promulgates. The regulatory functions of the Environmental Protection Agency are budgeted at $200 million a year, but industry's annual compliance cost is over $7 billion.

A recent report prepared at the Washington University Center for the Study of American Business estimates that the aggregate cost of complying with federal regulations exceeded $62 billion in 1976. Direct federal outlays to finance the regulatory agencies came to "only" $3.2 billion that year, for a multiplier of over 20.[3]

As in the case of the activities covered by the other areas of the federal budget, it is not merely a matter of dollars, although the total sums are quite imposing. Rather, it is the staggering arsenal of power that the American society, often unwittingly, has bestowed upon government officials. Let us examine some of the specific impacts of this expansion in the governmental role in private-sector behavior.

THE SCOPE OF GOVERNMENT

2. Robert DeFina and Murray L. Weidenbaum, *The Taxpayer and Government Regulation* (Washington University Center for the Study of American Business, March 1978).

3. Robert DeFina, *Public and Private Expenditures for Federal Regulation of Business* (Washington University Center for the Study of American Business, Working Paper No. 22, November 1977).

Table 1

RISING BUDGETS FOR FEDERAL REGULATION
(Fiscal Years, Dollars in Millions)

Area of Regulation	1974	1975	1976	1977	1978	1979	Increase 1974–79
Consumer safety and health	$1,302	$1,463	$1,613	$1,985	$2,582	$2,671	105%
Job safety and other working conditions	310	379	446	492	562	626	102
Environment and energy	347	527	682	870	989	1,116	222
Financial reporting, and other financial	36	45	53	58	70	69	92
Industry-specific regulation	245	269	270	309	340	341	39
Total	2,240	2,683	3,064	3,714	4,543	4,823	115

Source: Center for the Study of American Business

How Much Money Can We Keep for Our Own Use?

The federal budget is a major income-redistribution mechanism. It determines, to a substantial extent, how much of his or her income a citizen can keep for personal expenditures and how much shall be taxed away in good measure to finance income payments to other individuals. We need to understand the basic income-equalizing nature of the progressive federal income tax. To be sure, many writers claim the reverse, that "the rich pay less, so the poor pay more."

That, very frankly, is the big lie in tax reform discussion. It is a classic case of looking at the hole instead of the donut. To be sure, upper-income classes receive the bulk of the special tax incentives (often labeled with such pejorative terms as "loopholes" or "tax expenditures"). But, despite those special tax provisions, the same upper-income classes also pay a large share of all the federal income taxes collected. On the average, the higher your income, the more federal income taxes you pay, both absolutely and as a proportion of your income. In 1976, for example, the average effective rate (federal personal tax payments as a percent of total income) was 5.5 percent for taxpayers in the $5,000–$10,000 bracket, 13.8 percent for the $20,000–$30,000 bracket, and 30.0 percent for the $200,000 and over bracket.[4] As shown in Table 2, the progressive nature of the federal income tax extends through all income levels. Similar results have been reported for earlier years.[5]

And where do those tax dollars go? As we have already seen, the largest share of the budget is devoted to transfer payments and other programs designed to help low-income people. Unfortunately, the many billions of dollars that the federal government spends to provide food stamps, Medicaid, Medicare, and public housing do not remove a single person from poverty, simply because the official

4. *Statement of Emil M. Sunley, Deputy Assistant Secretary of the Treasury (Tax Analysis) Before the Task Force on Tax Expenditures of the House Budget Committee,* Washington, D.C., February 23, 1978, p. 7.

5. See *National Journal,* March 19, 1977, p. 423; Joseph A. Pechman, "The Rich, The Poor, and the Taxes They Pay," *Public Interest,* Fall 1969; Benjamin Okner, "Individual Taxes and the Distribution of Income," in James D. Smith, ed., *Studies of Income and Wealth* (National Bureau of Economic Research, 1975).

Table 2

THE BURDEN OF THE FEDERAL PERSONAL INCOME TAX

(1976 Levels of Income; in millions of dollars)

Income Class ($000)	Number of Returns (thousands)	Estimated Income	Personal Income Tax Liability	Effective Tax Rate
0–5	25,474	57,557	141	0.2%
5–10	20,109	149,590	8,227	5.5
10–15	16,106	201,036	18,071	9.0
15–20	11,824	205,086	23,009	11.2
20–30	9,907	237,041	32,778	13.8
30–50	3,347	124,836	22,017	17.6
50–100	985	67,484	16,492	24.4
100–200	198	27,371	8,084	29.5
200 and over	49	21,573	6,476	30.0
Total	87,998	1,091,573	135,293	12.4

Note: Details may not add to totals due to rounding.
Source: U.S. Department of the Treasury.

statistics are stated in terms of money income alone. Adjusting for the dollar value of these payments "in kind" reveals that the average income of those officially counted as poor in 1973 was 30 percent above the official poverty line.[6]

The reader should be cautious in applying these averages to individual cases. The data do not mean that each and every family officially designated as being in poverty in 1973 received (including government transfer payments in cash and in kind) far more than enough income to pull themselves above the poverty line. Rather, the data indicate that numerous inequities exist. A great many of the recipients of these federal programs did receive an extraordinarily generous share, while others in similar circumstances obtained inadequate amounts (which is a case for reforming and not necessarily expanding the welfare programs).

In any event, much of the tax payments made by middle- and upper-income taxpayers winds up as income to poorer segments of the society, be they in poverty or not. That is, the distribution of income in the United States is more equal after taxes and government expenditures are taken into account.

What Can We Buy and How Can We Use the Goods and Services That We Own?

Government affects the lives of its citizens in many other ways. There are very few items of consumer expenditures that escape regulation by one or more federal, state, or local government agencies. The following is merely a representative sample:

Category	Regulatory Agency
Air travel	Civil Aeronautics Board
Automobiles	National Highway Traffic Safety Administration
Bank deposits	Federal Deposit Insurance Corporation
Boats	Coast Guard

6. Edgar K. Browning, *Redistribution and the Welfare System* (American Enterprise Institute for Public Policy Research, 1975).

Bus travel	Interstate Commerce Commission
C.B. radios	Federal Communications Commission
Cigarettes	Public Health Service
Consumer credit	Federal Reserve System
Consumer products, generally	Consumer Product Safety Commission
Consumer products containing chemicals	Environmental Protection Agency
Cosmetics	Food and Drug Administration
Credit union deposits	National Credit Union Administration
Drinking water	Environmental Protection Agency
Drugs	Food and Drug Administration
Eggs	Agriculture Marketing Service
Election campaign contributions	Federal Election Commission
Electricity and gas	Federal Energy Regulatory Commission
Firearms	Bureau of Alcohol, Tobacco, and Firearms
Flood insurance	Federal Insurance Administration
Food	Food and Drug Administration and Department of Agriculture
Land (interstate purchases)	Office of Interstate Land Sales Registration
Livestock and processed meat	Packers and Stockyards Administration
Meat and poultry	Animal and Plant Health Inspection Service
Narcotics	Drug Enforcement Administration
Newspaper and magazine advertising	Federal Trade Commission
Petroleum and natural gas	Department of Energy
Physician fees	Professional Standards Review Organization
Railroad travel	Interstate Commerce Commission
Savings and loan deposits	Federal Home Loan Bank Board
Stocks and bonds	Securities and Exchange Commission

The nature of regulation varies by product and government agency. In some cases, the focus is on the price charged to the consumer, as in the case of the Civil Aeronautics Board and the Interstate Commerce Commission. In other instances, such as the Food and Drug Administration and the Consumer Product Safety Administration, the emphasis is on safety in product characteristics. Still other agencies regulate the method of marketing the product (such as the Federal Trade Commission and the Office of Interstate Land Sales Registration) or financing the sale (the Federal Reserve System). On occasion, regulation is aimed at restricting sales to certain types of buyers (Bureau of Alcohol, Tobacco, and Firearms) or limiting the amounts that can be spent (Federal Election Commission).[7]

7. For details, see Murray L. Weidenbaum, *Business, Government, and the Public* (Prentice-Hall, 1977).

A more subtle type of regulation may be in the offing in terms of establishing dietary goals for the American public as part of "the evolution of a national nutrition policy." This is the objective stated by Senator George McGovern, chairman of the Senate Committee on Nutrition, in issuing the committee's new report, *Dietary Goals for the U.S.* The committee report contends that Americans can improve their health by eating more fruits, vegetables, and whole grain cereals, and less animal fat. The report states that the intake of sugar should be reduced by about 45 percent and should account for 10 percent of the average individual's energy intake.[8]

Despite the firm recommendations in the Senate committee report, there seems to be a lack of consensus among nutrition scientists and health professionals. Dr. Kelly M. West of the University of Oklahoma has been quoted as expressing concern that, if dietary sugar is reduced, the calories might be partly replaced by fat. He points out that, under some conditions, low-fat diets are more tolerable when sugar is available as an attractive substitute for the proscribed fat. He sees no hard evidence that sugar is fattening.[9] These are some of the problems that can arise if the federal government attempts to regulate more closely literally what we eat.

How Can We Go About Earning Our Daily Living?

A wide array of federal agencies is involved in regulating the working lives of Americans, in their capacities as employees and employers. From the point of view of the average employee, one or more government agencies are involved in the selecting, training, promotion, and retirement aspects of the job.

Whether an individual is hired or not and whether he or she is retained by the employer can be influenced in many ways by actions of government agencies. The National Labor Relations Board conducts elections governing union representation of workers. Under a "union shop" agreement, workers must—as a condition of continuing employment—join the certified union within a certain time period and pay dues to it regularly. The Equal Employment Oppor-

8. "Revised 'Dietary Goals' Emphasizes Reduction of Sugar Intake for U.S.," *NDSA Bulletin,* February 27, 1978, pp. 1–2.
9. Ibid., p. 2.

tunity Commission investigates charges of employment discrimination on account of race, sex, or national origin and can file charges in behalf of individual employees and groups of employees. If the company is a government contractor, it must follow an approved affirmative action program for designated categories of "disadvantaged" employees, including blacks, women, disabled people, veterans, and persons with Spanish surnames.

Training and promotion of employees are also under the jurisdiction of each of these federal agencies. In addition, the regulations of the Occupational Safety and Health Administration often require substantial training efforts. The work environment, likewise, is subject to regulations or influence of OSHA, EEOC, and the NLRB. Compensation and fringe benefits are affected by each of these agencies, which can file charges for violations of one or more requirements. In addition, the company's pension fund is subject to approval by the Internal Revenue Service. The power to disallow as tax-deductible business expenses employer contributions to pension plans which do not meet federal standards is, of course, a powerful weapon.

From the management's view, basic aspects of operating authority have been taken over, in whole or in part, by various governmental agencies. In some industries, the government must give its approval before a company can go into business. In such specialized areas as nuclear energy, we might expect to see the reversal of the normal process whereby individuals decide who will enter a line of business and market forces determine who will stay. However, such governmental assumption of the traditional role of the market has become commonplace. The Civil Aeronautics Board, to cite an example of required governmental advance approval, has not certified a single new passenger airline since the agency was established in the 1930s.

A more commonplace example is interstate trucking. A potential new entrant must convince the Interstate Commerce Commission that another company is "needed" before it will grant the necessary authority to operate on a given route. As would be expected, existing competitors usually contend, when they are invariably asked by the ICC as part of the approval process, that they are adequately meeting the public's needs and that no additional competition is necessary.

A recent case in point involved Allstates Transcontinental Van Lines, Inc., a small, black-owned, mover of household furniture in St. Louis, operating a fleet of thirteen trucks. The ICC has repeatedly denied the company's application to be certified for handling interstate shipments, thus limiting the company to the far smaller local hauling market. The existing interstate movers contend that there is no "need" for another competitor, that they are capable and willing to meet the requirements of the business.[10]

In the case of other regulatory programs, a company must obtain the approval of a government agency before it can sell a new product. This has become the standard practice in the pharmaceutical area and, as a result of the passage of the Toxic Substances Control Act, will soon become the order of the day in the broader chemical field.

When a company can proceed with producing a new product, it soon finds that a variety of agencies is involved in the production process. The Occupational Safety and Health Administration has established a multiplicity of standards governing an almost infinite variety of production processes and working conditions. Affirmative action programs require redesigning the workplace to make job opportunities available for disabled workers. The Environmental Protection Agency is concerned that production processes do not pollute the environment. The Department of Energy is involved in minimizing the use of natural gas and petroleum. On occasion, that agency requires companies to shift to coal where previously the same companies were forced by the Environmental Protection Agency to switch from coal to petroleum.

The multiplicity of regulators and regulations has, of course, increased the likelihood of an individual firm being caught in the crossfire of conflicting directives. One company attempted to install an elevator for its handicapped workers as a part of its affirmative action program. The company was delayed for six months by the EPA's insistence that it file an environmental impact statement. Federal food standards require meat packing plants to be kept clean and sanitary. Surfaces which are most easily kept clean are usually tile or stainless steel. But these are highly reflective of noise, and may not meet OSHA noise standards. Coal must be combined with

10. Robert L. Joiner, "Moving Experience—Frustrated Trucker Refuses to Yield to Industry Giants," *St. Louis Post-Dispatch,* February 8, 1978, pp. 1 ff.

lime in order to remove the sulfur and thereby reduce air pollution. But this generates large quantities of waste calcium sulfate, the disposal of which contributes to water or surface pollution.

Both OSHA and FDA regard the presence of rats in a food processing plant as an unacceptable hazard. To OSHA, the rats are a danger to employees. To FDA, they are a menace to consumers. But the procedures for ensuring compliance with the regulations differ for the two agencies. An FDA inspector can fine a company if he or she convinces the local U.S. attorney to prosecute the case and if the government wins the lawsuit. In contrast, the OSHA inspector can cite and fine the company on the spot. Thus, because of overlapping jurisdiction and different regulations, the outcome literally depends on who smells the rat first.

Once a product is produced, virtually every aspect of the marketing function is affected by government—advertising, packaging, labeling, and distribution. An examination of the new FDA regulations on saccharin reveals the depth of the governmental intervention. In postponing a ban on saccharin, the Congress passed a statute in November 1977 requiring warning labels on food containing saccharin and specifying that posters be placed in retail stores that sell such food. FDA showed great enthusiasm in carrying out the legislative mandate. It specified the location of the warning (a "conspicuous" place on the label, usually on each principal display panel, and immediately above or below the product name), the type to be used (boldface, with each letter at least one-sixteenth of an inch high), and the exact language of the warning (24 words). For the posted notice, FDA prescribed the minimum size (11 by 14 inches), the number and location of the posters (three: one near the store's entrance, another in the aisle where soft drinks containing saccharin are sold, and the third where the largest amount of other saccharin-containing food is sold), the exact language (75 words), and a requirement that *each* supplier of saccharin-containing food give each retail store the full quota of three posters.[11]

That recent action may be indicative of the shape of things to come, at least under present conditions. The commissioner of the Food and Drug Administration, Dr. Donald Kennedy, stated in the February 1978 issue of the agency's house organ, "I think advertis-

11. "Rules Issued on Saccharin Warning Label," *FDA Consumer*, February 1978, pp. 4–5.

234 Murray L. Weidenbaum

ing is too little regulated now as it relates to health products. There are some very real questions in my mind as to whether some products should be advertised at all, or whether they should be advertised to certain groups of people, such as children."[12]

"Caveat emptor" (buyer beware) is a concept rapidly being relegated to the business history books. As Jules Backman and John Czepiel have written, the marketing strategist of today must be "a broken field runner" covering the field between what his or her company can and wishes to do, what the consumer desires, and what government allows or requires.[13] In a more fundamental sense, the extent of governmental intervention in private activity continues on a growth trajectory, be it in the form of redistributing income or regulating the details of the role of the citizen as producer and consumer.

How We Play

It is no exaggeration to state that the federal government has become involved in how individuals spend their leisure time. Some of the government's activities may be quite harmless, albeit silly. An example is the Consumer Product Safety Commission's safety tips on winter sports. That publication contained such gems of information as "A number of accidents happened when the skier was tired" and "Skiers should use good quality equipment that fits well."

A more serious case involves government directives for the conduct of school athletic programs. The Department of Health, Education, and Welfare has recently ordered the schools in Oak Ridge, Tennessee, to see to it that cheerleaders "cheer equally" for both boys' and girls' varsity teams. As columnist George Will noted, it is unclear whether "equally" means with equal loudness, which can be measured mechanically, or with equal spirit, which cannot be measured.[14] Oak Ridge must also take action to recruit "equal numbers of male participants" or abolish the cheerleader squad.

12. "Better Regulation Through Labeling," *FDA Consumer,* February 1978, p. 16.
13. Jules Backman and John Czepiel, eds., *Changing Marketing Strategies in a New Economy* (Bobbs-Merrill, 1977), p. 19.
14. George F. Will, "HEW Is Ludicrous—But Not Funny," *St. Louis Globe-Democrat,* March 9, 1978, p. 10A.

A LOOK AT THE FUTURE

Human wants are insatiable, or at least that is what is taught in Economics 1. That has been the general case in the federal public sector in the United States. The list of new and worthy "priorities" is almost endless, ranging from a clean environment to safe consumer products to domestic energy independence. In theory, of course, the notion of "priorities" indicates an ordering—that not everything is of equal importance. New and higher priorities thus shove down or out the older, or at least now less urgent, priorities.

But a different type of adjustment has been occurring in the public sector in this nation in recent years. The new federal priorities have not tended to push out older federal priorities, but merely have been superimposed upon them. Tough decision-making choices have tended to be avoided. Thus, in general, new public priorities have resulted in expanding the size of the public sector at the expense of private resources. But there now is a reluctance to increase any further the federal share of gross national product at the expense of the private sector.

Despite the improvements that have resulted from the Budget Reform Act of 1974, there is as yet no effective mechanism for substituting new priorities for old within the federal government. Thus, we are seeing a standstill in public policy, the new federal budget for fiscal year 1979 being a cogent case in point. Virtually no new expenditure initiatives have been proposed by President Jimmy Carter. The emphasis is on keeping down the overall growth of government spending. From some points of view, this may be a happy situation, avoiding a further expansion of the public sector, but it is doubtful whether this is a stable, long-term situation. The possibility emerges of another round of budget expansion contributing, in turn, to an acceleration of inflationary pressures.

The situation in the area of governmental regulation is analogous. Increasingly the consumer is feeling the impact of the ever more costly array of federal intervention in business decision making. In both areas of governmental activity, budgetary and regulatory, the need is for new ways of truly reordering national priorities within the context of the obvious limitations on the willingness of the citizenry to bear ever greater tax burdens and/or reductions in private income flows and living standards.

For specific government programs, both those involving making expenditures as well as using rule-making authority, economics offers a straightforward mechanism for assisting decision makers: benefit/cost analysis. Although looked upon by many as a "green eyeshade" device, the benefit-cost approach can take on more substantive significance when properly used. The basic notion is that governmental decision makers should carefully examine the disadvantages as well as the advantages of their proposed actions.

That examination should be made from the perspective of the society as a whole, rather than reflecting the viewpoint of any specific government agency or private interest. Moreover, in the course of the analysis, the most economical and effective means of achieving the public purpose should be identified. Thus, properly performed, benefit-cost analysis is a useful tool in raising the sights of public policy makers and in assuring that—at least to the extent that the effects can be measured—government does more good than harm in the things that it undertakes.

In the final analysis, it is a new way of thinking about government that is required: the notion that, because society's resources are limited, government cannot attempt to meet every demand of every group within the nation. Those resources, moreover, are more than economic or financial. As has been demonstrated in both military and civilian areas in recent years, there are severe limits to what government can accomplish. Organizational and managerial ability in the public sector, as elsewhere, is in short supply. Society has given government many important responsibilities, ranging from maintaining the national security to providing a system of justice. It is important that government do well those tasks that it attempts to perform.

Economizing and selection devices serve an important role. At the "macro" or aggregate level, budget ceilings serve that function while they simultaneously can contribute to the government's overall economic policy. At the "micro" or programmatic level, various forms of systematic analysis—be they benefit-cost calculations, cost-effectiveness measures, or even nonmathematical arrays of pros and cons—can serve useful functions. Rather than a defense of the status quo, these procedures can help to identify existing government activities of low priority which might be replaced by newer undertakings of higher priority.

A final thought along these lines is that the public policy maker needs to be conscious of what often is an unintentional bias— looking instinctively at government for dealing with the problems of society, while overlooking the capacity of the private sector and market competition to deal with many of these questions. Far too frequently, it has been governmental interference with private markets that has generated or exacerbated problems of rapid inflation, high unemployment, low productivity, and slowdowns in innovation.[15]

—MURRAY L. WEIDENBAUM

15. See Murray L. Weidenbaum, *Government-Mandated Price Increases* (American Enterprise Institute for Public Policy Research, 1975) and *Business, Government, and the Public.*

CHAPTER 15

The United States and Latin America: Looking Ahead

Since the Good Neighbor Policy began under President Hoover, and was implemented by Franklin Roosevelt and Sumner Welles, the efforts of following administrations have been feeble in relation to our important Latin American neighbors.

The Alliance for Progress, under President Kennedy, was a noble effort, but it collapsed because of the inexperience of those administering it.

Latin America in the late 1960s and 1970s received only scant attention because foriegn policy experts in the Nixon-Ford Administration had priorities elsewhere in foreign affairs.

President Carter's policy of intervention in the field of human rights, his nuclear policy, and his attitude toward military dictatorships may prove unfortunate for the United States in Latin America.

Recently, two events suggest the wisdom and necessity of examining critically the status and possible future directions of U.S.–Latin American relations. The first event was a speech delivered in February 1978 to the Center for Inter-American Relations by Assistant Secretary of State for Inter-American Affairs, Terrence Todman. In carefully reasoned remarks, he defended the need for caution and discretion in pursuing the U.S. human rights policy in Latin America. His comments were widely replayed and analyzed in the Latin press. It is interesting to note that the speech was virtually ignored by the U.S. press and public. The differing reactions say a good deal about the American public's perception of the significance of Latin America for the United States and about the degree to which the Latins have become concerned with U.S. human rights initiatives.

The second event was the Senate debate on ratification of the Panama Canal treaties. The necessary two-thirds majority was mustered for approval. Treaty proponents argued that ratification would have a positive impact on our overall relations with Latin America. This is nonsense. Some idealistic persons believed ratification would be welcomed widely as evidence of our willingness to respect the sovereignty and legitimate rights of a small neighbor. In my opinion, it will in no way provide the long-term basis for hemispheric harmony.

These two important events illustrate how the Canal and human rights have dominated center stage in U.S.–Latin relations despite the fact that the great majority of Latin leaders are more concerned with questions of economic development of regional and global significance. Treaty ratification will not build a constructive atmosphere for economic discussions. Latins, themselves, are quick to point out that economic and social rights should receive priority among the several categories of human rights. It seems safe to predict that with the Canal's fate settled, and as human rights becomes a less divisive issue, Latin attention will return to questions of economic development and what the United States is willing to do to meet these future needs.

In the belief that developmental issues will dominate the future Inter-American agenda, I shall concentrate on them. My focus will be on projecting the general context of hemispheric affairs rather than on cataloguing specific issues.

Two little-known documents now lying dormant in the Organization of American States (OAS) probably reveal more about the future shape of the Inter-American system than the much overpublicized Canal treaties. The Draft Conventions on Collective Economic Security and Cooperation for Development were completed in 1976 and evolved out of reform efforts undertaken in 1973. The background of the conventions highlights both the thrust of Latin America's developmental concerns and the problems those concerns present for the United States.

The Draft Convention on Collective Economic Security enshrines the Latin preoccupation with extending the political-military concepts of security and noninterference into the economic area as a means of warding off the detrimental impact of the economic actions of others, especially the United States. The essence of the convention lies in the contracting parties' commitment to "refrain from applying or encouraging measures of an economic or political nature with a view to forcing another state in order to obtain from it advantages of any kind." As developed by Peruvians, the concept included a supranational, parajudicial procedure through which alleged violations could be reviewed and judgments rendered.

The document on Cooperation for Development is overlapping in many ways. However, it focuses more directly on the interdependence of hemispheric development and the responsibility of all states to contribute to shared development "in accordance with the means and possibilities of each of them." Development is defined to encompass its economic, social, cultural, educational, scientific, and technological aspects.

Repeatedly during the reform process that produced the draft conventions, the United States indicated its inability to accept the notion of collective economic security as defined by the Latins. U.S. representatives argued that no system, however well conceived, could guarantee development. Economic security, they maintained, was not comparable to military security, where it is somewhat easier to define countermeasures once the sources of insecurity have been identified. More specifically, the United States insisted that cooperation for development must be voluntary and that the Latin approach implied placing unacceptable limits on the sovereign right of every nation to use its resources as it wishes. Further, stated U.S. spokesmen, the Draft Convention on Collective Economic Security fails to recognize an unavoidable aspect of economic interdependence, i.e. that actions taken by one state in pursuit of exclusively domestic objectives may have a totally unintended negative impact on the interests of another state.

The Sixth OAS General Assembly (June 1976, Santiago) decided that these conventions would be treated during a 1977 Special General Assembly on Cooperation for Development. Such was not the case. During 1977, the conventions were seldom mentioned by the Latins or the United States, and no date has been set for the mandated Special General Assembly.

It might be argued that this apparently strange state of affairs reflects the fact that the documents were the product of a period of hemispheric tensions (1973–76). Bilateral problems between the United States, Chile, Brazil, Ecuador, Panama, and Argentina among others; Latin disappointment with the 1974 U.S. Trade Act; and disenchantment with the course of Secretary of State Henry Kissinger's "New Dialog" had soured the atmosphere. Therefore, it might be suggested, the Latins insisted on radical economic concepts to contain potential U.S. abuses that they now believe are neither wise nor feasible.

It seems just as likely, however, that the apparent consignment of the draft conventions to the OAS graveyard is the temporary result of the priority assigned by the United States to the Panama and human rights issues, the last of a well-defined Carter adminstration policy on economic cooperation with the region, the activity on North-South issues in other forums like the Group of 77[1] and the Paris meetings, and the flagging of support for the conventions among some of their chief champions, Peru and Mexico (for internal reasons) and Panama (because of the Canal treaties).

Regional debate over the issues covered in the draft conventions will reemerge simply because it is a matter of self-interest to the Latin Americans. Their concern for and general approach to these questions are long standing. Well over a decade ago, a 1965 Special Inter-American Conference provided the following guideline for a committee charged with drafting amendments to the OAS Charter:

> The principles of solidarity that inspire the activities of Inter-American cooperation in the political field and in that of mutual security must, of necessity, be applicable, also, to the economic and social field . . . to attain the greater social justice and more rapid and balanced economic progress essential to the security of the hemisphere.

It is possible to cite similar statements from the Inter-American record reaching back at least to the close of World War II.

To understand the future significance of Latin America's empha-

---

1. The Group of 77 is the ad hoc caucus employed by the less-developed countries to hammer out joint positions for international economic meetings formed during the 1964 UNCTAD meeting in Geneva. The Group now has 110 members but it still has no formal organization or permanent secretariat. High-level Group of 77 conferences are normally held prior to such meetings. The last such preliminary meeting was held in Manila in January 1976.

sis upon economic security and development, it is important to discard the largely rhetorical and always questionable notions about the range of cultural, political, historical, and philosophical similarities that supposedly underlie Inter-American harmony. In the future, we must recognize that the United States and Latin Americans frequently will be on opposite sides in debating the issues on the North-South agenda. A mutuality of interest, hopefully, will exist insofar as both sides will be seeking constructive solutions to continuing problems. However, on matters of substance, disagreements will be frequent and sometimes fundamental.

Latin America is part of the Less Developed Countries (LDC) group, and its leaders will pursue policies that reflect the perspective of the LDCs. In recent years, Latins have figured prominently among LDC leaders in formulating and defending positions to promote what has become known as the New International Economic Order. A Venezuelan was the father of OPEC. A former Mexican president was the driving force behind the United Nations Charter of Economic Rights and Duties of States, and a number of Latin statesmen were effective spokesmen for LDC positions at the Paris CIEC sessions.

Within the LDC context, two points deserve emphasis in an attempt to project Latin America's likely future directions. First, judging by any social-economic criteria one might choose, Latin America is the most advanced of the world's underdeveloped regions. Wealth remains unevenly distributed and enormous problems persist, but economic expansion occurred at the rate of 5.1 percent annually in the 1950s, 5.6 percent in the 1960s, and 6.0 percent in the first half of the 1970s. The level of U.S. involvement is reflected in direct private investment of well over $20 billion, and trade in 1977 amounting to almost $30 billion (with a $3.2 billion deficit for the United States).

With only a few countries ranking among the world's truly impoverished nations, Latin America constitutes something of a global middle class. In fact, one of the problems confronting Latin planners is the fact that they are too wealthy as nations to qualify for preferential aid treatment increasingly being accorded the poorest countries by nations with bilateral assistance programs and by international financial institutions.

Second, within the LDC context, in spite of the tendency to

generalize about Latin America, we are dealing with over twenty separate nations, all of which can be expected to pursue their own particular interests. The gap between a Brazil and a Haiti is large and growing, and their policies naturally mirror that fact. The Latins are capable of joint representations in the councils of the OAS or in the UN, but when it comes to making the hard political and economic choices that all countries will face in the future, the differences among them will be apparent.

As we try to anticipate future developments, Latin America's middle-class status suggests that the goal of many Latin participants in the North-South debate will be pragmatic, mutually beneficial accommodations on such matters as market access, trade controls, multinational corporations, debt relief, and technology transfer. The rhetorically pleasing but ultimately empty ideological victories that appeal to the more radical Third Worlders do not serve the interests of the Latins because they delay rather than promote solutions of which they can take immediate advantage. Agreement on a code of conduct for multinational corporations or internationally accepted rules for the transfer of technology, for instance, are matters that directly affect Brazil's current development, but they may be of no more than political concern to other LDCs not in a position to absorb the benefits of multinational investment and modern technology. The behavior of countries like Venezuela and Brazil, to date, in both bilateral and multilateral contexts has demonstrated their interest in achieving moderate, responsible solutions for global developmental problems.

Because of the variety of specific country interests, it is to the advantage of neither the United States nor the Latins to hammer away at discussions on regional and global developmental issues in a U.S. vs Latin America framework. Countries like Brazil, Mexico, and Venezuela have evolved to the point where they will normally prefer bilateral rather than multilateral contacts with the United States. Their growth has opened up extraregional alternatives and opportunities and provided resources that will enable them to become increasingly independent political and economic actors on the world scene. Others like Argentina, Chile, and Peru may achieve a similar capacity over the next five to ten years, while many of the hemisphere's smaller nations probably will continue to feel most comfortable within the traditional regional context. Their lack of political and economic power narrows their options and dictates that the United States will remain their primary source of financial, trade, and investment opportunities and their security guarantor for the foreseeable future.

Examination of a single issue, like debt relief, is sufficient to illustrate the range of interests in the hemisphere. With respect to commercial, as opposed to governmental debts, smaller and poorer countries like Bolivia and Honduras may see some virtue in Group of 77 support for a formula that would relieve some of the pressures created by oil price hikes and general balance of payments problems. The Brazils and Argentinas and Chiles, however, will resist generalized treatment of the commerical debt problem because their economic strategies depend, in part, upon their maintenance of respectable international credit ratings. They will want no part of a G-77 position that might undermine their credit worthiness and thereby inhibit their access to commercial lenders.

With these brief comments on Latin America's future concerns in mind, some general observations can be offered about possible U.S. responses. Certainly a good starting point would be abandonment of what Professor Abraham Lowenthal has aptly described as the "hegemonic presumption" or the notion that the United States has the unilateral right to intervene in Latin America, either to eliminate perceived threats to its interests, or to promote what it believes is good for Latin America. Lowenthal has already made a convincing case on this point, but it is worth emphasizing, here, that U.S. predominance in Latin America has declined in fact, if not in rhetoric, over the past two decades. Cuba left the U.S. orbit long ago, and the combination of nationalistic sensitivities and growing economic capabilities has enabled the larger Latin countries to assume postures ever more independent of the United States. Many observers have remarked on the established pattern in Latin American countries of developing new trade partners all over the globe and tapping new international sources of financing and technology, investment, and military hardware. In part, this pattern reflects the corresponding evolution of alternate sources to the United States in Western Europe, Japan, and the Soviet bloc. Also involved, however, is a conscious political decision on the part of some countries to decrease their dependence on the United States by going elsewhere.

So long as legitimate U.S. security interests are not endangered (perhaps by the widespread sale of Soviet arms with the attendant political consequences) and U.S. economic interests are not the object of discriminatory treatment, there is little reason to fear this trend. It is inevitable as hemispheric countries mature economically, and there is every reason to believe that the quality and price of U.S. goods, services, and technology will ensure their continuing marketability in Latin America.

It may also be well to discard the idea of a "special relationship" as the basis for policy formulation toward Latin America. There are aspects of inter-American relations that might warrant the "special" designation, but it is a difficult concept to translate into specific policy actions. Furthermore, constant U.S. reference to the phrase has understandably created exaggerated Latin notions about what the United States can and will do, in response to their expressed needs. The rhetorical value of the term is outweighed by its tendency to perpetuate a gap between Latin expectations and U.S. performance.

The regional and multilateral approach to Latin America should give way to an emphasis, albeit not exclusively, on a global and bilateral relationship. As is clear from previous comments, the issues that will dominate the inter-American stage in the future are not unique to this hemisphere. They provide the grist of the North-South mill. It would be wise, therefore, to respond to Latin America's concerns within our global strategy for promoting development, according the area preferential treatment when such actions do not conflict with global objectives. By the same token, U.S. policy makers should avoid initiatives that suggest to the Latins that the United States is insensitive to their developmental imperatives. However mistakenly, many Latins have interpreted the Carter Administration's human rights policy in precisely this light. They perceive human rights sanctions and economic aid cutoffs as evidence that the United States is not really concerned with basic human needs in the underdeveloped world. This is not an argument for abandoning the human rights policy, but rather a reason to consider tactics of implementation more carefully.

Former Secretary of State Kissinger stated in a March 1, 1975, speech that one of the objectives of his "New Dialog" was to promote recognition of the fact that "the global dialogue . . . requires answers that will be difficult to find anywhere if we do not

find them in the Western Hemisphere." Implicit in his remark was
the concept of Latin America as an intermediary in the North-
South debate. Because of the region's middle-class status, argued
some, Latin America shared interests with both the industrialized
countries and the LDCs. It could therefore fulfill the role of a go-
between, encouraging better understanding and moderate positions
by both camps. This remains an interesting and untested concept.
As promising as it may sound, it may prove unfeasible because of
the variety of national interests at play among the Latins and their
reticence about assuming a role that might expose them to a new
dose of paternalism. Latins do not want to be used. Intermediaries
might emerge in the guise of selected nations, but the idea of the
entire region acting in this sense is questionable.

President Carter made the point concerning the advisability of
emphasizing bilateral contacts in his first major policy statement on
Latin America (April 14, 1977, OAS Headquarters, Washington,
D.C.). "A single policy to Latin America and the Caribbean makes
little sense," he noted. "We, the U.S. and Latin America, will
develop policies more suited to each nation's variety and potential."
This is not to imply that the Inter-American System and its
centerpiece, the OAS, is completely outmoded. Such is not the case.
The OAS's record on hemispheric peace-keeping alone would justify
its existence. It also provides a valuable forum for ad hoc treatment
of emergency situations and issues, an institutional basis for the
multilateral pursuit of hemispheric human rights compliance, and a
place simply to let off steam before tensions are released in more
destructive ways. Nonetheless, the OAS is not a promising setting
for discussing the crucial North-South issues. Both the organization's structure and its history suggest that developmental discussion
within its framework would produce the traditional "we-they"
confrontation rather than constructive dialogue. The low profile that
Brazil has maintained in the OAS suggests that some Latin nations
may have reached the same conclusion and that among Latins there
may be a correlation between the level of economic development and
participation in extrahemispheric affairs on one hand, and the
priority assigned to the OAS on the other.

If the basis for fruitful, if not always harmonious, hemispheric
relations exists in our common need to resolve the problems on the
global agenda, the initiative for cooperation must come from the

United States. The Latins must be forthcoming also, but it is the United States that has the most to give. Both sides must recognize their obligations as well as claim their rights if a positive atmosphere is to be established. The United States will have to illustrate that platitudes about cooperation and consultation mean more than informing the Latins collectively after a policy decision has been made. The Latins will have to demonstrate that they perceive cooperation as something more than an opportunity to confront the United States with predetermined demands evolved and defended upon the basis of "regional solidarity."

Short shrift has been given here to questions of hemispheric security in the traditional political-military sense, but a note must be added on an issue of importance—the threat of nuclear weapons proliferation. Energy concerns have prompted deep commitments to nuclear power development in Argentina and Brazil, while others like Mexico, Chile, and Peru have fledgling nuclear programs. Impetus is added by the LDC search for independence and global status. For along with the energy potential of nuclear development comes the status of having achieved a measure of technological parity with the industrial countries and the superpowers. "Near nuclear" status is a key for the "have-nots" to the club of the world's "haves."

While the United States has recognized the right of Latins to pursue the nuclear energy option, the highest priority must be assigned to preventing the spread of nuclear weapons. However, it is unreasonable for the United States to request a traditional friend, Brazil, to develop its nuclear capacity for energy requirements only. It has already strained our relations with this country. Hopefully, wiser leadership will develop with experience.

One last comment as I close this chapter. The United States must avoid human rights initiatives that imply an effort to export our democratic way of life. The United States, for years, has been obsessed with exporting Democracy. Democracy, as we know it, is a way of life rather than a simple political formula. This must be carefully nurtured and developed in accord with conditions that prevail in any given country. We can set a worthy example and encourage democratic tendencies where they emerge, but the United States cannot force its system on others.

—ROBERT C. HILL

CHAPTER 16

What Lies Ahead for U.S.–Japan Relations?

TWO NATIONS AT HISTORY'S CROSSROADS

In this century no relationship among nations has reflected both greater dynamism and greater paradox than that between the United States and Japan. As we examine the varying fortunes of this relationship we find that the mid-1970s may well have been, in the Dickensian phrase, "the best of times." The year 1974 found Japan exulting in a hearty welcome for the first visiting American President. In the following year the American people responded with a cordial welcome to the historic visit of Japan's venerable Emperor. Then 1976 found Japan enthusiastically joining in America's bicentennial celebration. Through it all, shocks and tiffs were notably absent. Understandably these years became known as the "No Problem" era of our relationship.

Then came 1977. The roof seemed to fall in. Suddenly a score of contentious economic and energy issues erupted. Thus, as had happened so often in the past, the Americans and the Japanese once again found themselves immersed in polemical wrangling. Fortunately both nations sought to mute any indigenous animosity. Yet the world was again reminded that these two strong-willed peoples still had much to learn about how to get along with each other.

The checkered pattern of the United States–Japan relationship, past, present, and anticipated, has provided appetizing fodder for many a contemporary appraisal.

While this particular review will focus mainly on the future, we will at times dip into the past and refer to the present as we seek clues to new directions for our evolving relationship.

The Japanese have an illustrious past. So, though our subject is the future, it is to Japan's cultural heritage we shall first turn. Specifically we will retrace the Japanese view of what the future may hold as captured in a few examples from among their rich lode of national proverbs. What we find is that the Japanese neither expect much of the future nor do they believe in wasting much time speculating on it. Repeatedly their proverbs reflect such indifference:

"Tomorrow there will be another wind blowing."[1a] (meaning, the future will take care of itself)

This sentiment is then expanded:

"As to tomorrow's things, worry about them tomorrow."[1b]

Not only indifferent, but derisive is this one:

"Talk of tomorrow and the rats behind the ceiling will laugh at you."[1c]

Having thus scorned idle speculation, they go on to conclude that not only is prognostication silly, it is impossible:

"An inch ahead all is darkness."[1d]

This nation works so hard to achieve a better tomorrow, and yet Japanese proverbs surely show a curious disdain for the future. But, then, the close observer of things Japanese is rarely surprised by instances of cultural paradox. Paradox abounds in Japanese thought

---

1. Okada Rokuo, ed., *Japanese Proverbs* (1955).
   a. "Asu wa mata asuno kase ga fuku."
   b. "Asu no koto wa asu anjiro."
   c. "Asu no koto o iu to jenjoura no nezumi ga warau."
   d. "Issun saki wa yami."

and history.[2] It makes for what is no doubt the ultimate in Oriental mystique.

Perhaps it is this element of mystique that most confounds a Western analyst confronted by the surge and flow of the many undercurrents that mark Japanese society today. Yet the more obscure the path to the future, the more the fascination in pursuing it. Contemporary commentary does not want for trying. Recent superb books about Japan such as those by Harvard's distinguished professor Edwin Reischauer and the Britannica's Frank Gibney both conclude with thoughtful chapters on that nation's future.[3] [4]

On the other side of the Pacific and despite her proverbs, the probing of what lies beyond today for Japan in equally attended. A 1976 Japanese anthology, *The Silent Power,* features three future-focused essays.[5] This is but one of countless contemporary Japanese writings devoted to examining that nation's horizons. The reason the subject now evokes such wide-ranging attention in Japan is to be found in a near consensus that exists there today. The Japanese people are convinced they have arrived at a turning point in their national history. They believe their successful postwar rebuilding effort with its attendant exploding economic progress constitutes an era or phase that has about run its course. New national directions and objectives must now be found and pursued.

Curiously enough, on this side of the Pacific, American thought reflects a similar concern with future national directions. We Americans sense that our three-decade era of superpower hegemony, free world economic domination, and explosive technological advancement is about to give way to a new national flavor and thrust. We too are not yet quite sure just where we want this new awareness to take us. So we indulge in an orgy of critical self-reappraisal.

With our respective nations both caught up in moods of introspection, the time is certainly ripe for a fresh look at what is ahead for our relationship. While we may not be able to see what lies around

2. Ruth Benedict, *The Chrysanthemum and the Sword* (Houghton Mifflin, 1946).
3. Edwin Reischauer, *The Japanese* (Harvard University Press, 1977).
4. Frank Gibney, *Japan: The Fragile Superpower* (Norton, 1975).
5. Japan Center for International Exchange, ed., *The Silent Power: Japan's Identity and World Role* (Simul Press, Tokyo, 1976).

the corner each of our nations may be turning, an examination of possibilities may help us chart a course wise in both self and mutual interest. Such an examination is our purpose here.

COMMONALITIES AND CONTRASTS

In any discussion of the future relationship between Japan and the United States one quick conclusion is warranted. *Nothing about our future relationship can or should be taken for granted.* Our shared diplomatic history is at best a seesaw record. The vast cultural gulf between us almost ensures recurrent misunderstandings. In the world's marketplace the competitive vigor of our respective economies rages almost untamed. The complex role of Japan as a "modernized" Asiatic society and the often uncomfortable mantle of America's superpower status present each of us with unique challenges. Only at intervals, and usually not for long, have our two nations been wholly comfortable with each other.

Yet history and circumstance have a way at times of producing commonalities between unlikely candidates. When such commonality occurs, the fortunate affected nations possess a basis for a congenial embrace that can surmount even the most awesome of differences.

As the second half of this century rolled around, Japan and the United States found themselves in exactly this fortunate circumstance. We shared a wide range of common concerns. These concerns have now brought us together as postwar allies.

Recent years have also found us quietly generating a growing fund of mutual respect and even goodwill that is reflected in many ways. Accordingly we might well next examine the contemporary ingredients that have drawn us into a close alliance.

Through the centuries scholars of foreign affairs have endeavored to sift out the ingredients needed for bringing and holding nations together as allies. Many elements that might at first appear essential and compelling turn out not to be so. The elimination process goes something like this:

Language: A shared tongue indeed aids communication but it cannot be relied on as a guarantor of lasting goodwill.

Culture: A common cultural conditioning obviously promotes mutual understanding, but its effectiveness as a bond often fades when troubles appear.

Race: While racial differences offer the basis for many of the world's animosities, a shared racial heritage provides no assurance of enduring amicability.

Heritage: Shared blood ties provide a sturdy emotional tug, but the tug often weakens when conflict appears on the horizon.

Proximity: Clearly the nearest of neighbors are often the most dubious of friends.

History seems to reflect that such commonalities simply are not sufficiently compelling to avoid conflict.

Usually, however, two bonding elements are cited as being of crowning importance: *common interests* and *common values.*[6] It is here—in similarity of interests and values—that the United States and Japan find both the reason we have come together as allies and the source of hope that we shall continue together for decades to come. As long as our two nations have common interests to promote, as long as we have common values to defend, Japan and the United States have the most sturdy of reasons for continuing to work in harness.

To bear this out we should now examine the roster of interests and values we share. It is quite an imposing list.

Americans are often agreeably surprised when they observe the extent to which today's Japanese embrace so many of the same institutions we value as the most inspiring parts of our American heritage. For instance, the Japanese have gained a remarkable affinity for *democratic processes.* Their version of an *open society* may vary somewhat from ours in style but not much in substance.

Free institutions are not only a part of the Japanese scene, they are fundamental to contemporary Japanese convictions. The news press in Japan is not only free, but omnipresent almost beyond belief. For a people who emphasize group relationships as much as do the Japanese, it is heartening to note that they do not do so at the expense of support for *individual human rights.* And perhaps no

6. George F. Kennan, *The Cloud of Danger: Current Realities of American Foreign Policy* (Little, Brown, 1977).

other nation shares with us a penchant for *creative enterprise* as much as does Japan.

It all adds up to a pattern of parallel support for basic ingredients that distinguish our two free societies from so many others in the world.

We find common cause not only in things we both favor but in things we both oppose. Distaste for totalitarian rule and collectivist ideology rank high among these. Certainly the Japanese share with us a common appreciation of the identity of possible potential aggressors.

Because of our ranking roles as global traders, no other nations have as much of a stake as we two in continuity of the circumstances that have produced our increasingly interdependent economic world. We both seek to preserve conditions that will permit widened international trade, the free flow of investment, open sea lanes, and open access to the world's resources. This also means we each have a major stake in global political stability. This shared desire cannot help but be a continuing powerful force for peace.

During my ambassadorial years in Japan I became intrigued by another shared commonality. In addition to interests and values, I observed that the Japanese and Americans also shared common capabilities. Both our peoples seem to be good at an incredible number of the same things. To an unusual degree we are both good at, in fact we both excel at, such things as business and commerce, modern technology, project management, cohesive organization, and the use of resources. We both have sought and achieved high levels of learning and health. Our literacy and longevity rates both rank among the world's best.[7]

We find, then, that our two nations share not only common interests and values, but also, to an unusual degree, common capabilities. It may be that no two modern nations match these various attributes as closely as do Japan and the United States.

Earlier we spoke of an emerging mutual respect between our peoples. Out of the ashes and antipathies of World War II we have come a long way.

When public opinion polls are now taken in the United States,

7. Tsuneka Yano Memorial Society, Ichiro Yano, ed., *Nippon: A Charted Survey of Japan, 1975–76* (Interculture Association, 1975).

Japan is the only Asian nation that Americans single out as deserving of our support in case of an external security threat.

Throughout their crowded archipelago today, when asked which of the world's countries is the most important to their nation, the Japanese people respond "America" by a three-to-one margin. Travel reflects preference, and of Japan's foreign visitors, nearly half come from the United States. Nearly a million Japanese now cross the Pacific to visit America each year.[8]

American corporations by the hundreds are now joined with Japanese firms as business partners in flourishing joint ventures.

American opinion today reflects a high respect for the impressive Japanese postwar economic recovery, for the civility of their orderly society, and for the creativity and taste reflected in their culture. Thus, a growing undercurrent of goodwill can be found on both sides of the Pacific.

"Why then," we ask, "why, with all these many common interests, values, and capabilities, with this evidence of emerging goodwill, why does an uneasiness continue to exist in our relationship?"

The undeniable fact is, of course, that for all our commonalities, we must also admit to a wide array of contrasts. These contrasts fascinate observers. Unfortunately, it is the difference, not the similarity between us, that is seen as endlessly newsworthy.

The unmet twain of East and West has, of course, been grist for centuries of commentary. But hemispheric separation is only the start of our contrasting national circumstances. Small versus large; island versus continent; an ethnic homogeneity versus a heterogeneous melting pot; a two-thousand versus a two-hundred-year-old history—the list runs on.

Our respective languages ring strangely on the other's ear; our differing mannerisms either startle or puzzle; the verticality of one society seems at odds with the horizontal framework of the other.[9] More fundamental than any of these, however, is the contrast between the United States Judeo-Christian heritage with its emphasis on *individual justice* and Japan's amalgam of Orient-nurtured religious strains that serves to produce a contrasting *group harmony* emphasis in that society. An entire structure of national differences can be traced to these contrasts in heritage.

8. Ibid.
9. Chie Nakane, *Japanese Society* (University of California Press, 1970).

Commentators delight in introducing syntactical inventions into our lexicon to dramatize observed differences between us. Words like "gap" and "lag" are featured. Thus, we are told a "communication gap" exists between our nations and a "perceptual lag" delays needed mutual understanding.[10]

Yet even as we watch the delight of minor pundits in pointing out all that seems alien and curious, each nation to the other, we have found a strange thing happening: our nations have come even closer together. Jointly we have mastered techniques for settling the problems that seem recurrently to arise between us. The difficult Mutual Security Treaty question of the early sixties, the contentious textile negotiations and the Okinawa reversion issue of the early seventies are the examples most often cited.

Perhaps what the postwar history of our relationship has best demonstrated is that our continuing common interests have remained sufficiently compelling throughout to surmount hurdles posed by our many obvious differences. While this record may be far from conclusive, on balance it can be considered a distinct source of hope for an enduring and amicable relationship between us in future years.

As we conclude our review of common interests and shared achievements there exists another contemporary phenomenon which we in the United States particularly should understand more fully as we weigh decisions affecting the future course of our relationship with Japan.

During our first two hundred years as a nation, the United States found itself looking mainly across the Atlantic toward Europe. Our heritage, our culture, our commerce, and our foremost political alliances all served to direct our faces, hearts, and minds eastward.

Each of these ties is now weakening. With every passing generation our European heritage fades further into the distance. We have now created an identifiable culture of our own. Within the past three years even our trade direction has reversed—more now flows across the Pacific than over Atlantic waters.

Today when we look abroad for such prized American attributes as working vigor, expanding opportunity, and creative enterprise, we find these things not so much among the tired nations of the Old World to the east, but rather among the zestful "comers" in the

10. John Condon and Mitsuko Saito, eds., *Intercultural Encounters with Japan* (Simul Press, Tokyo, 1974).

Pacific Basin. This fact provides us with a further reason for seeking to enhance our ties with promising Pacific societies. Of these, of course, Japan is far and away the most advanced.

So the flow of history also dictates that we devote the utmost attention to our relationship with Japan. For if anything is certain about the pundit-proclaimed upcoming "Century of the Pacific," it is that the two leading roles in that theater will be played by Japan and the United States.[11] They are roles that will be best played in harmony.

HAZARDS, HURDLES, AND PROSPECTS

Contemporary Japan may puzzle the analyst but it positively delights phrasemakers. To convey a sense of insecurity they relish pinning on Japan such labels as "fragile," "frail," and "vulnerable." Japan is variously seen as a "fragile blossom" or a "frail nation."[12]

In suitably ominous tones observers bemoan Japan's vulnerability to a variety of internal tensions and external forces. The impression left by all this exotic verbiage is that of a shaky nation adrift on an angry sea without compass, rudder, or tiller, quakingly awaiting overturn by the next episode of history's turbulence.

QUESTION: Is the impression correct?
ANSWER: A partial and hesitant "yes"; a general and resounding "no."

The characterization ignores several things. For one thing, it implies that contemporary insecurity is somehow uniquely Japanese. The world knows it is not. Ferment is everywhere. Change runs rampant in the twentieth century—tumultuous change in ideology and in political structure, in mores and in life-styles, in technological complexity and in exploding knowledge. Japan has no patent on vulnerability to these forces of contemporary change. It is foolish to make it seem so.

Perhaps more important, however, these baleful appraisals ignore Japan's strong points, especially the main source of Japan's profound and enduring strength—*its people.* The Japanese are people

11. Norman McRae, *The Economist,* January 10, 1976.
12. Zbigniew Brzezinski, *The Fragile Blossom* (Harper & Row, 1972).

of exceptional dedication, cohesion, and intelligence. They rank second to none in personal discipline and national pride. They have enduring traditions and magnificently functioning institutions. In sum, the Japanese have clearly succeeded in the formation of a strong national character. No nation can possess a more valued asset. In this sense no modern nation is better buttressed to withstand the errant slings and arrows of future fortune.

Yet while we can conclude that Japan is fortunate in possessing sources of immense internal strength, it is equally appropriate to observe that it will no doubt need all the strength it can muster to cope with testing times ahead. For Japan does indeed face profound problems and difficult decisions.

Certainly one of the more delicate questions for Japan is the most suitable direction to take in its relationship with the United States of America. During the last thirty years many a problem has erupted within that relationship but the relationship itself stayed rock solid. Japan has *needed* the United States: first as a source of food for its war-fatigued people, next as a source of capital and technology to rebuild its shattered industrial machine, and then, later, as a source of markets as its products started flowing abroad.

Politically Japan found it convenient, effective, and inexpensive to tuck itself under the protective wing of American armament. Maintenance of Japan's security and of the political stability of northeast Asia is a U.S. responsibility that Japan has not only welcomed but has come to depend on. To a nation comfortable in viewing relationships in terms of rank order, it has not been a wholly demeaning circumstance for Japan to see itself in a role of something like America's little brother. Japanese psychologist Takeo Doi has pointed out that essentially the relationship has been one of *dependency*.[13]

Meanwhile, as the United States in mid-century found itself thrust onto center stage as free world leader and contending cold war superpower, it had a different set of needs. For one thing the United States needed a reliable Asian ally capable of both self-support and self-discipline. Leaders need followers and Japan followed—followed in resistance to alien ideology, in helping strengthen free world economic performance, and in helpful policy position-

13. Takeo Doi, *Anatomy of Dependence,* trans. John Bester (Kodansha, 1973).

taking at international forums. The tangible advantages of U.S. bases in Japan came into play in American military ventures in Asia, even when those ventures proved less than successful.

Mutual self-interest based on differing but complementary needs—that is what brought us together.

It is now time to examine the forces that may strongly influence the extent and direction of a gradual shift in the roles that mark our relationship. It is a reasonable assumption that some shift can indeed be expected.

With Japan's now solidified economic position, must the United States continue to assume "big brother" responsibilities? With a new generation of leaders there about to take the helm, will Japan seek to burst out from under big brother's benign but shadowing wing? Will the United States fold up its nuclear umbrella and go home? Could our recurrent family spats over economic differences deteriorate into something more fractious than competitive arm wrestling?

Most any informed assessment of these or other possible abrupt shifts in our relationship would reject them as highly unlikely, at least in anything like the near future. The geopolitical glue of common interest will continue to hold fast. Rupture should not be anticipated. Yet we have acknowledged that we are each groping for new paths. It may be that from this point on those paths will turn out to be more parallel than merged, as often they have seemed in the past.

For the United States some new wind directions are already apparent. No longer do we view ourselves as the world's security policeman. When President Gerald Ford announced our post-Vietnam Pacific Doctrine in December 1975, it clearly set forth our continuing Asian interest.[14] Yet is also reflected our national intention of sharing the responsibilities for Pacific Region peace and economic advancement with other nations capable of bearing part of that burden. While the Pacific Doctrine establishes Japan as our number-one Asian ally, by implication it also establishes Japan as our number-one burden-sharing candidate.

An upcoming insular "fortress America" attitude is so unlikely as not to be feared, but economic protectionism is an emerging force at

14. Gerald R. Ford, "The Pacific Doctrine" (speech delivered in Honolulu on Dec. 18, 1975).

home that must be either turned around or accommodated. Japan's understanding and help will be needed in doing either.

As Secretary of State, Henry Kissinger saw the wisdom of placing our ties with Japan on a basis closely akin to partnership.[15] In fact, the term "partnership" increasingly shows up in American diplomatic references to our preferred future relationship with Japan.[16] Clearly our use of that term is intended to spur Japan to a greater assumption of shared Third World economic development costs, to supportive free world economic policies, to greater but complementary international political initiatives, and even to a more equitable sharing of security costs.

The composite flavor of emerging U.S. foreign policy positions seems to reflect an American conclusion that the time has now come for us to ask more of our free world allies, particularly to ask and expect more from our number-one Asian ally, Japan. Kyoto University's Professor M. Kosaka suggests this means that "America has lost its generosity."[17] From a Japanese perspective the professor is probably right.

These emerging American expectations leave us with a key question: "How will Japan respond?" To gain some insight into that probable response we must now turn to an examination of the more evident influences and trends manifest in contemporary Japanese society and to the Japanese outlook on the world.

It is not difficult to decide where to start with such a recitation. When a nation's chosen path and policies have placed it squarely in a position of extraordinary dependence on the world beyond its borders and when its instincts and record reflect a persisting difficulty in achieving a comfortable relationship with that outside world, a confounding paradox exists. Japan today is in exactly that position. It is a position that will present many a hurdle for it in the years ahead.

Modern-day Japan is above all else a huge industrial processing plant. Lacking resources of its own, Japan uses the world's sea lanes

15. Henry Kissinger, "The U.S. and Japan in a Changing World" (speech to the Japan Society, New York City, on June 18, 1975).
16. Mike Mansfield, "Reflections on the U.S.–Japan Partnership" (speech to the Japan Society, New York City, on February 2, 1978).
17. Masataka Kosaka, *Japanese and Americans in Competitive Alliance*, Chapter I of Part III of "The Silent Power" (Simul Press, Tokyo, 1976).

as a converging conduit that each day of the year funnels ashore a huge tonnage of raw materials from the world's four corners. Once ashore, Japan's talented work force, technical expertise, and managerial skills take over. The result is an incredible outpouring of high-quality, competitively priced finished goods.

The process is then reversed as a goodly portion of those goods flows out to distant markets. The Japanese equation here is evident: *external resources plus internal skills equal salable products for the world.* For the equation to work well several things are essential. Look at the list:

• Raw products, available in quantity from elsewhere
• Open sea lanes for transport
• Accessible foreign markets
• Absence of destabilizing political conflict in key regions
• Free (or at least nondiscriminatory) world trade conditions
• Some consensus among nations concerning economic goals

Disturbingly for Japan, most of these things lie outside its direct control. What you cannot control you must try to influence. And it is here, in endeavoring to assert an influence to ensure continuity of these things, that Japan will have trouble. With its dubious "feel" for international sentiment and reaction, frequent frustrations and prickly problems lie ahead.

There are of course those who disagree. They point to Japan's ever growing international economic power of the past thirty years and suggest that worry about its ability to pursue effective foreign relations is misplaced. Perhaps. The record does provide some support for such a view. What Frank Gibney calls Japan's "Kow Tow Diplomacy," whether applied to China, the Arabs, the United States, or elsewhere, seems to have been quite a success.[18]

Yet if we look behind this record we find some special, perhaps even unique circumstances prevailing during most of this period. The world's copious resources were readily available and modestly priced. Modern technology could be cheaply purchased from the United States and elsewhere. Japan's bill for its military machine and cultural diplomacy was only about one-eighth that of the

18. Frank Gibney, *The Fragile Superpower.*
19. Masataka Kosaka, *Japanese and Americans in Competitive Alliance.*

United States—a marked competitive advantage.[19] Japan was in a "catch-up" rather than competitive phase of its rebuilding. In fact, until recently Japan was seen abroad more as a precocious "wunderkind" than as a ferocious competitor.

Will these conditions continue to prevail? Obviously some may not. The oil embargo of 1973 introduced resource diplomacy to the world as a brutal fact of modern times. Technology by purchase from abroad now comes increasingly dear if it comes at all. Japan can no longer exploit a "have-not" posture in international bargaining. The world looks to Japan for stepped-up foreign aid and political contributions. And, as we have noted, the United States' "partnership" concept for Japan carries costs with it. This picture suggests that for Japan some significant adjustments will be required.

Perhaps the most delicate of these adjustments will be in Japan's U.S. relationship. To abandon its past relationship of dependency in order to assume something more like a full partnership role could produce traumatic consequences for at least one of the partners.

One of the reasons for this uncomfortable prospect is to be found in the rather emotional nature of Japan's view of its dependency status. Americans often are unaware of a powerful psychological characteristic of the Japanese people that is involved here. In return for dependency status, Japan expects a quid pro quo from America. It feels it has a right to exact a "price" of us for assuming such a role. A concept of mutual obligation the Japanese call *Amae* is involved. Applied here, *Amae* means that Japan not only expects but insists on the right to preferred and benign treatment from the United States. To Americans this seems shocking; to the Japanese it seems entirely natural.[20]

When the United States shows "indifference" to this obligation great consternation ensues in Japan. The resultant imbroglio is often entirely unexpected on the part of the United States. That is what happened in Japan's unrequited reaction to the so-called "Shokus" (shocks) of the early seventies. The way Japan saw it, we completely ignored its interests and our obligations with our surprise actions: opening relations with Peking, declaring a soybean embargo, and

20. Takeo Doi, *Anatomy of Dependence.*

tacking a 10 percent surcharge on imports in August 1971. Because of these "surprises" the nature of our relationship will probably never be quite the same again.[21]

This circumstance, however, suggests two things. Japan must try to understand that while *Amae* may be a useful concept at home, it isn't understood and can't be readily applied abroad. It also suggests that the United States must show more sensitivity not only to this but to other unique Japanese psychological characteristics. To say the least, both of these things will be hard—very hard—for each of us to do. It just won't come naturally to either of us.

For real communication between Japan and the United States we need to gain a penetrating insight into each other's thought patterns. For instance, the Western world must struggle to understand the Japanese "not-only-but-also" thought concept. Westerners tend to think solely in terms of "either-or." We have only to look into Japanese history to realize that they have long been accustomed to reasoning through "combination." They combine the essentially different and assimilate the dissimilar. Sometimes this is termed "learning to live with ambiguity."

Japan's cultural anthropologist Professor Kunihiro offers the following "tetralemma" to illustrate the difference between the cognitive styles of East and West:

When Zen Buddhism asks . . . "Do we have an afterlife?"
A *four*-fold answer is given:
1. Yes
2. No
3. It can be said there is and at the same time it can be said there is not.
4. It cannot be said there is and it cannot be said there is not.

On the other hand, when Immanuel Kant asks . . . "Does one's ego survive oneself?"
A *two*-fold answer is given:
1. Yes
2. No

21. Martin Weinstein, *The U.S.-Japan Alliance: Is There an Equivalent for Mutual Indispensability?* September, 1975.

The "flexibility" of Japanese thought is apt to befuddle Americans. Being open-ended it does not yield to Western insistence upon a pulling in of all variables and the distillation of two often equally balanced alternative courses: good—bad, go—no go.

In Japan we find not only flexibility of thought but a view that words are often not the best communication. Ancient Chinese concepts influence the Japanese, viz: *"Truth is the discarding of words. It lies outside words."* Similarly, the Chinese say, *"The heart of ink painting is in the blank space, in what is left undrawn."* In other words, what is left unsaid is the more important.

While Americans admire the man who strikes to the heart of the matter with a few well-chosen sentences, we are not well trained in the art of divining that which is left unsaid.

An astute Japanese is also adept at knowing when "yes" really means "no." Such indirection in response strikes an American as lacking in forthrightness. Both Japanese and Americans must come to realize that our respective thought and communication processes are not negatively directed toward the other. Though at times it may be tempting to think otherwise, basically positive motives underlie most behavior on both sides of the Pacific.

Perhaps the biggest single fact recently emerging in the United States–Japan relationship is Japan's now confirmed role as an economic superpower. This role cannot but influence its perspective and its future relationship with the United States.

We can expect Japan, as a now established power, to find ways gradually to ease out from behind its U.S. dependency shield. As it does so, Japan could well find itself using its ties with the United States as the foundation upon which to build the structure of a credible worldwide diplomacy. United States cooperation could be expected.

Let us now go on to examine one domain where it seems in Japan's self-interest to establish a stronger identity in foreign affairs.

Some observers of Japan's successful economic thrust into the outside world have suggested that having "grown out," Japan must now "grow up." This is simply an unkind way of saying that from abroad Japan is often seen as reflecting a distinct distaste for shouldering the responsibilities expected of a ranking world power. As U.S. Ambassador to Japan Mike Mansfield observed, the Japanese have been slow to recognize that their economic power imposes responsibilities.[22]

Nowhere is this reluctance more apparent than in Japan's attitude toward its own security. Article nine of Japan's postwar constitution rigidly prohibits that nation from creating anything like an aggressive military force. Yet Japan does have a defense force of sorts. As former U.S. Defense Secretary James Schlesinger noted, however, this defense force is simply not adequately equipped to fulfill the "defending" role assigned to it.[23]

This deficiency is of special concern because Japan's archipelago lies exposed in a most contentious corner of the world. On the Asian continent, at its backyard, two of the world's superpowers snarl at each other in a decade-long standoff along the world's longest border. Just beyond a narrow sea to its west looms an ideological adversary who boasts the largest naval fleet now in Asian waters. The Soviets would relish nothing more than to share this sea with a complaisant "Finlandized" Nipponese neighbor. At Japan's western extremity it looks across a mere strait at a peninsula that bristles with two armament-laden antagonists who have already had one bloody go at each other in this half century.[24]

So we must ask, "Is this an environment that warrants an indifference to national security?"

Hardly!

Yet, though indifferent Japan seems, it explains its passivity as reflective of a national passion for peace.[25] In this expression Japan is wholly sincere. But while its passion is understandable and its sincerity admirable, its judgment is suspect.

For a nation to reflect a credible desire for peace it should at least be able to demonstrate the ability and will to preserve peace at its own borders. Unprepared as it is, Japan could not do this. Credibility of intent is not matched by credibility of capacity. Until it is, the Japanese will suffer serious international communication and credi-

22. Mike Mansfield, "Reflections on the U.S.–Japan Partnership."

23. James Schlesinger, "Mutual Security Needs" (speech to Japan Press Club, Tokyo, on August 29, 1975).

24. Martin Weinstein, *Japan's Postwar Defense Policy, 1947–1968* (Columbia University Press, 1971).

25. Eisaku Sato, *In Quest of Peace and Freedom* (Japan Times Limited, 1973).

bility problems. Some Japanese internationalists are well aware of this problem. Some—but not yet enough.[26]

With Japan's new role as an economic power, the world looks to it for a more forthcoming stance and a more outward view. For cultural and historic reasons Japan cannot be expected to meet the world's need for a change in stance overnight. The world does expect, however, that Japan will move in this direction.

OVERVIEW FROM THE UNDERSIDE

Perhaps the foremost advance in twentieth-century weather forecasting can be credited to the satellite camera. From its high arc overhead, this space-age sleuth now captures every movement of earthly wind and cloud.

Forecasts in the affairs of men and nations would benefit from a comparable overview device. But here science has failed us. We must continue to scan the horizons of these affairs from an earth-bound stance. From such a stance, only a short distance away the earth curves out of view of eye and mind. So does the future.

A shortened view limits vision. Respecting those limits and with suitable apologies for them, I shall now proceed with a look into the years ahead.

There are three possible patterns for our future two-nation relationship: *accommodation, disputation,* or *drift.* I sense that these are the three most likely possibilities. In preceding sections I have sought to depict some of the underlying circumstances on which I base this judgment. I have rejected the likelihood of an outright rupture in the bonding forces that have brought us into our present alliance. Neither do I think it likely that we two shall be so fortunate as to reach terms of early easy intimacy.

I see it this way: our cultural differences will continue to preclude intimacy; equally, our common interests will continue to preclude rupture. The likely pattern of our future association lies somewhere between these two.

Relationships between nations, of course, need not necessarily

26. Tadao Umesao, *Escape from Cultural Isolation,* Japan Interpreter: A Journal of Social and Political Ideas, Vol. 9, Summer, Autumn 1974.

trend in any one definitive direction. They can and often do just *drift*. When drift occurs it is usually because forces and events outside the relationship are permitted largely to determine its nature. The course of the relationship then reflects an uneven parade of policy improvisations, each based on the then current state of constantly changing circumstances. Little long-term policy content is involved. Drift becomes the end product and it is not a product of high quality.

Though I think drift is not the most likely of the three suggested possibilities, it could nonetheless occur. This likelihood would be enhanced if either Japan continues to avoid a definitive role on the world's political scene, or should the course of events cause U.S. foreign policy attention to be unwisely concentrated elsewhere. In any circumstance that might find either of our nations taking its relationship with the other for granted, the seeds of drift would have been sown. The ensuing harvest would be unfortunate.

In my view, drift, with its attendant deterioration in our relationship, would be a doubly unfortunate eventuation. I have become convinced that not only do our two nations need each other, but that by working in harness in the years ahead the United States and Japan could jointly make a powerful contribution to free world leadership.

Perhaps an even more unhappy alternative to a drifting relationship would find our two nations entering an era of unfriendly disputation. Should this happen, it will simply be because both of us have failed to devote adequate attention to building the kind of constructive relationship that lies well within our grasp. Yet a disputatious relationship is not a wholly improbable possibility.

The Japanese and Americans are both strong-willed people. Strength of will is not always matched by breadth of vision. Insular attitudes have not been absent from either of our national histories. This is specifically true of the history of our relations with each other.

That these insular attitudes might reassert themselves is a troubling thought. Though now few and muted, unfriendly voices admittedly exist within each nation. Unless checked, these voices could become strident, and with the advent of unfortuitous events, possibly even gain undue attention. The possibility of this circumstance occurring would surely be heightened if either Japan or

America should emerge from its current period of introspective reappraisal with a weakened sense of national purpose.

Narrowness of view commonly accompanies shallowness of purpose. So I would suggest that we watch the vigor and thrust with which both our nations emerge from present intervals of self-reexamination. A regenerated sense of purpose would markedly improve the odds that, as the years wear on, we both will prove capable of remaining above petty and internecine wrangling.

The third suggested course for our relationship is one I have called *accommodation.* Accommodation is not an inspiring term. No man will charge from the trenches of his own self-interest to fight for it. Yet in today's world of realpolitik, accommodation is a suitable course for the future relationship between Japan and the United States. Indeed I believe it has conspicuous merit. A pragmatic aspect of that merit is that such a relationship is readily achievable. Most important, it is a course that seems most in tune with contemporary reality.

Let us now examine what we mean by accommodation as applied to a two-nation relationship. To start with, let's contrast accommodation with another course with which it is often confused—compromise. Compromise often has much to recommend it as a way of resolving a specific disputed issue. Yet as an overall policy it produces a less than satisfactory result. Each party grows increasingly dissatisfied with the process. Always ending up with but half a loaf, each questions whether it is continuing to serve well its own self-interest.

Accommodation is an approach more profound in concept and more harmonious in result than compromise. Accommodation calls for an intensive examination by each party of its own and the other's basic needs. Both parties then chart courses that will, insofar as is possible, enable each to achieve its own needs in concert with the needs of the other and with a minimum of overt challenge to the interests of the other. The essential distinction is this: compromise *splits differences;* accommodation *coalesces interests.*

Since Japan and the United States possess so many contemporary interests in common, accommodation is a viable course for us to pursue as we seek to enhance our maturing relationship. Let me suggest something that illustrates a policy of accommodation.

After spending nearly three diplomatically instructive years in

Japan, I came up with something I have called *Hodgson's law for dealing with the Japanese*. To explain the genesis of this "law" I must first discuss two distinctive elements of the Japanese scene.

In Japan *form*—the proper form to be followed in doing or deciding something—is a matter of towering importance. We Americans are so substance-minded, we tend to ignore form. To the Japanese, however, form is so intertwined with substance it often seems to become substance.

A second element that distinguishes the Japanese from the American scene is *pace*. In Japan the rate of speed with which decisions are first made and then implemented is almost the reverse of the American pattern. Because of the time involved in the Japanese consensus process, decisions there normally come slowly. Implementation, however, is startlingly fast. In America we are more inclined to come up with a quick decision followed by a slower implementation process. These two basic national differences underlie Hodgson's law, which perhaps is best stated thus:

> If the United States will accommodate the Japanese on matters of *form* and *pace,* the Japanese will in turn seek to accommodate America on the *substance* of its interest.

An instance that illustrates this law comes readily to mind. In September 1976 a Soviet air force plane swooped down out of the sky and came to ground on a northern Japanese airfield. The surprised Japanese thus found themselves with an asylum-seeking Soviet pilot on their hands, and as an incredible bonus for free world intelligence, they were in possession of a late-vintage Soviet military fighter airplane. While American government officials realized there would be limits to the amount of information on the plane that Japan could release, they were eager for early access to what might be available. As a result the United States immediately started pounding on Japanese ministry doors. The Japanese, of course, handle such matters with punctilious regard for propriety of form. And, of course, the decisions involved also had to be made through their labyrinthine consensus process.

So Japan responded slowly. Washington became impatient. The pressure on the Japanese mounted. Their delay was interpreted by some American officials as noncooperation. It was not. Given time, the Japanese eventually responded in a most satisfactory way.

This incident once again served to demonstrate that American attempts to force the pace or alter the form of Japanese reaction patterns are futile. It equally served to confirm that when allowed to do it *their* way, the Japanese will normally respond positively to the substance of American interest. This pattern of behavior is something we Americans must come to respect if we are to develop a suitable relationship of mutual accommodation with the Japanese.

Mutual accommodation not only depends on mutual restraint, it requires improved mutual understanding. There are many things both Japan and the United States should better understand about each other. A few illustrations are in order.

The United States must come to understand that when the Japanese apply their standard consensus process to economic decisions, the result should not be viewed as a "Business-Government Conspiracy" against American economic interests. The United States must also understand that Japan's attempt to adopt useful Western ways at the same time it seeks to preserve its traditional values often produces behavior strange to Western eyes. We must not interpret Japanese differences in style and habit as a deliberate attempt to create barriers, no matter how much it may have that result.

In seeking to apply a policy of accommodation, the Japanese in turn face a wholly different situation. In the conduct of international affairs statements of abstract principle and other position-taking evasions by the Japanese will never be seen by America and others as credible responses for a powerful nation to make with respect to the world's pressing political problems.

In dealing with America, Japan also needs to gain a better understanding of the Western concept of *fairness*. Many trade and payments imbalance disputes between us in the seventies were evoked by this fairness concept, which in Western thinking includes an ingredient of equity.

In general it can be said that while America must accommodate Japan's still limited ability to see itself as others see it, Japan in turn must seek to gain such comprehension.

Meanwhile, the tugs and tensions engendered by our differing cultures can be expected to continue. But so will our ability to master them.

As we examine the relationship between Japan and the United

States today a few things are strikingly apparent. We see two
peoples with chasmic differences in heritage, culture, race, and
language. We also see a relationship history that reflects a disturbing lack of continuity in attitudes and practices toward each other.
Then, however, we go on to a realization that fortuitous times and
events now find our two nations sharing a remarkable fund of
common interests, values, and capabilities. Out of this commonality
we have fashioned a mutually beneficial alliance. We now seek a
future course that will strengthen and give added maturity to this
alliance. When we ask how best can we do this, I suggest the most
constructive answer is mutual accommodation.

Let us hope we settle for no answer less than the best.

—JAMES DAY HODGSON

CHAPTER 17

────────◦◦◦────────

America and the Defense
of the West

The decade from the mid-sixties to the mid-seventies of this century witnessed an alteration in the world balance of power. Up until then, the strategic superiority of the United States appeared unchallenged and unchallengeable; the world economic system seemed firmly anchored in the Bretton Woods accords and, in any event, proof against a serious recession; unprecedented prosperity and political concord enlivened Western Europe's quest for unity and a place, in partnership with the United States, among the world powers; and, above all, the Western peoples, despite the unresolved issues of the East-West confrontation, looked confidently to the future. It has been the shift of the public mood from the guarded optimism, prevailing until the end of the sixties, to the somber self-interrogation, if not self-doubts, of the 1970s, that has marked a psychological watershed in the evolution of Western politics, domestic and foreign.

Will this mood pass, as the West's previous bouts with its own troubled consciousness—as, for example, the malaise of the 1930s—have passed, or does it reflect the impact upon Western public opinion of real changes in the world's military, political, and economic equilibrium? The question, thus put, is bound to provoke some critical rejoinders: does the historical and cultural pessimism now prevalent in select intellectual circles articulate faithfully the public mood; and, more cogently, is there such a thing as a Western public mood; and, if it were to exist, how can it be measured?

Rather than seeking to answer these questions and, in the attempt, losing our way in epistemological thickets, we can hardly go wrong letting events guide us to insight. If real events have betokened real Western retreats from global positions of power and influence, then, conceivably, the West's public mood has good reason for taking a dim view of the West's prospects—and might be closer to a sober assessment of the international situation than is the soothing rhetoric of the West's political leaders and their respective officialdoms.

The most proximate benchmark of the West's historic retreat is still the American withdrawal from Vietnam together with the divisive commotions, at home and abroad, that preceded it, and the blurring of the American initiatives in other contested regions of the world that followed it.

It is not proposed here to meditate upon the *ifs* of history—what might have happened *if* the Vietnam War had been fought to a military conclusion, or *if* antecedent strategic judgment had prevailed and the United States had abstained from this peripheral engagement. These questions are speculative—and unanswerable. There is nothing speculative about the consequences of the Vietnam disaster insofar as they have affected the standing of the United States in the world. Certainly, the outcome of the Vietnam War has not persuaded the United States' adversaries to lower their sights, or America's friends, whatever the degree of their affection, to repose undiminished trust in the effectiveness of American power and the constancy of American purpose. This raises the question of what is appearance and what is reality? The United States might still have been as capable and as willing as it has ever been to deter its enemies from attacking it and its friends. But both enemies and friends have perceived the war in Vietnam as having inflicted upon the United States a military stalemate in the field and a political trauma at home. The United States might have been heading anyway—Vietnam or no Vietnam—for a domestic economic recession and a payments crisis abroad. But friends and foes alike have viewed the economic reversal as having been triggered by the drain upon American resources by foreign commitments, notably that of Vietnam. In brief, the United States has been seen as faltering under the weight of its global burdens—as being overcommitted. This view might have been a gross oversimplification of the causes underlying the Vietnam fiasco as well as the concurrent domestic tensions that have strained the fabric of American society. Yet this view has been widely held abroad while the Vietnam War was still making news. This perception of the American image, although it might no longer focus on the Vietnam experience and its immediate consequences, still continues to inform world opinion, for the evidence that might erase it, to wit events, is still lacking. Beneath the surface of American society, visible abroad to the common view, regenerative forces might well be at work. But here and now, those who profess to doubt that American society is cohesive enough to stand up under the pressure of world politics—that America is made of the stuff of a Great Power—are assured of a large and increasingly receptive audience.

While it is, as yet, a moot question as to whether the run of events is pointing toward a future renaissance of American power and influence, some statistics of past performance appear to record a decline in America's status as the leading world power. Although the sum total of American military power might be as formidable as it has ever been, it is, relative to Soviet military power, not as formidable as it has once been. The Soviet Union's achievement, during the late 1960s, of strategic (nuclear) parity cannot be construed, even by conceding the rationality of the Mutual Assured Destruction doctrine, as having redounded to American military strength. Conceivably, this massive—and generally unanticipated—event has stabilized, as some strategic thinkers have claimed, the global strategic equation and thus diminished the danger of intercontinental nuclear exchanges. But the present situation, stable as it might be strategically, does foreclose those military and political options that, once upon a time, strategic superiority placed at the discretion of American diplomacy. A large deficit in foreign trade need not, by itself, presage an irreversible decline of American competitiveness in world markets. Together with a sharp depreciation of the dollar in relation to other major world currencies, it has tended to erode international confidence in the stability, if not the soundness of the American economic system.

It is possible to interpret these indices of national power, military and economic, in various ways and, in any event, as reflecting short-term trends rather than the secular thrust of what is still the world's greatest economic power and, potentially, the greatest military power as well. Indeed, it is possible, by toting up the statistics of American wealth, to arrive at growth projections that could belie those prophecies of irreversible decline that gained currency in the wake of America's recent embarrassments.

The Soviet leadership must be assumed to be conversant with these statistics, all of them publicly available. The conclusions that it has drawn from its readings have differed markedly from the habitual optimism that has enlivened the messages of confidence and hope issuing from successive American administrations. Chairman Brezhnev, addressing in April 1975 the 24th Congress of the Communist Party, declared that the "correlation of forces" now favored communism. All the communist media of information have made this diagnosis their own and have been dwelling routinely on the Soviet Union's uncontestable military might and the defeat of American imperialism in Southeast Asia. No one knows whether or not the Soviet leadership really believes in the validity of this assessment. It has, however, invested the notion of the Vietnam debacle as marking a watershed in American-Soviet power relationships with the full weight of its doctrinal authority. It would be rash to assume that the views propounded by the Kremlin, mistaken as they may seem in light of the available information about the Soviet Union's glaring shortcomings, have failed to impress public opinion throughout the world, including public opinion in the lands of America's allies. Undeniably, the balance of power *has* changed— and American foreign policy has explicitly acknowledged, at least, a reduction in the freedom of choice with which American power can now—as compared with the 1950s—be applied to the resolution of international issues.

Among the consequences of the Vietnam War and the subsequent disturbances of American politics not the least unfortunate one has been a blurring, both in America and throughout the West, of historical perspectives. The shocks to public confidence from these events having been severe, it is understandable that, in the popular view, they are perceived as signifying a sudden and unpredictable turn in America's fortunes: it is as if, during the first two decades of the post-World War II era, nothing had happened that could have portended the development of the 1970s, and whatever has happened, happened because of a unique configuration of circumstances confronting the United States and the United States alone. This view, widely held abroad and in the United States itself, bespeaks the notoriously short memory span of the Western democracies as well as their ethnocentricity, unredeemed by their statesmen's understanding, avowed in public forums, of how fatefully each depends on the other. In fact, the drift of international politics in the 1970s is incomprehensible if it is not seen as an extension of what has gone before—the long retreat of the West as a whole from those positions of power and influence that it seemed to hold so securely at the end of World War II.

What has happened, during these thirty-odd years, to the West as a whole has been so obvious that, so it would seem, the West's educated public, not to speak of its statesmen, could not have missed its significance. Yet, albeit obvious, it has apparently failed to arouse the West's attention.

All throughout the West's geopolitical retreat the West has continued to perform prodigies of scientific-technological productivity. Its peoples have grown richer, and its respective welfare states have succeeded, beyond the boldest expectations of the previous generation, in redistributing their nations' riches. Although all Western governments' domestic budgets have exacted ever larger levies on the respective national economies, the contributions of the West to the economic development of non-Western nations have flowed ever more abundantly. It is these manifestations of Western intellectual and economic prowess that have lulled Western publics and not a few Western statesmen into a sense of complacency about those obdurate symptoms that point to the decay of the West's global positions and, by way of feedback, the erosion of the political and economic base supporting Western society. As illustrations of this contention a few examples will suffice: at the end of World War II, (1) the West's primary influence in the Middle East, military and political, was unchallengeable; (2) Western influence in Africa, from Tangiers to Capetown, was paramount; (3) the Indian Ocean was, strategically, a Western lake; and (4) the idea that a commodity cartel, composed mostly of states that owed their very existence to the exertions of Western military power and diplomacy, could cast with impunity the West into economic turmoil would have been laughed out of court. The global balance of power *has* changed— and it does not seem to have changed in the West's favor.

At the end of World War II, Europe's colonial empires in Asia

and Africa, with the exception of that of Italy, appeared to have
survived the tribulations of their motherlands. Yet their days were
counted, for both domestic sentiment and political expediency
impelled the colonial powers to divest themselves of their dominions
overseas and to accede to the colonial peoples' demands for national
independence. Some did so more gracefully than others; some had
anticipated more wisely than others the inevitable demise of a
system that the very spirit and practice of Western democracy had
rendered both odious and anachronistic. Although, in the process,
the former colonial powers stood to lose strategic bases, preferential
outlets for their goods, and secure access to sources of valuable
commodities, the Western peoples expected that long-standing common cultural and economic interests would reassert themselves, and
that the newly independent nations, now full members of a peaceful
world order, would embrace the fulfilling tasks of developing, in
cooperation with the Western democracies, their economic resources. No people counted upon the flowering of this mutuality in
endeavor, eased by the benign transition from colonial subservience
to national freedom, more confidently than the Americans. And this
might well have been the happy outcome, if the postwar order had
not been riven by political and ideological antagonisms of unprecedented dimensions—or if the Western and the ex-colonial peoples
had been the sole occupants of this globe.

In history the breakup of empires has never been a smooth and
orderly process. It has always been paced by violence; it has always
issued in wars, civil or foreign or both. In some instances, the
benefits to mankind that have been wrested from the dissolution of
empire have been so great and so palpable as to offset amply the
heavy costs of the transaction; in other instances, the results have
been more ambiguous or altogether deleterious to individual well-
being and the progress of civilization. It is still too early for drawing
up the balance sheet of the gains and the losses that have accrued
from decolonization to the one-time colonial powers and the peoples
emancipated from their rule. On the face of it, the former, with the
exception of Portugal, have advanced economically as rapidly as
those other West European countries that, on the eve of World War
II, had not held overseas possessions: the "loss" of their colonies, far
from impairing their economic productivity, seems to have relieved
them of unrewarding military and administrative commitments as

well as the increasingly repugnant moral burden of empire. Most, though not all, of the ex-colonial nations—emergent or resurgent—have shared in the expansion, during the last twenty years, of the world economy and have made long strides on the road toward the modernization of their material productivity. Indeed, the increase in the wealth of some now beggars the imagination. Despite the shadows that the lingering penury of a few ex-colonial peoples and the lag, in most developing countries, between economic performance and rising popular expectations have cast upon the morrow of decolonization, the debris from the breakup of Western empire should, by now, have been cleared away. Should not the patent mutuality of interest that links the ex-colonial peoples and the Western democracies have helped to heal old wounds and ensured the peaceable cooperation of all parties in mutually profitable undertakings? So it should have been. In fact, this has *not* been the outcome of decolonization. If the breakup, after World War II, of Western empire has spawned wars between nations almost as destructive of human lives and property as the World War—long and bloody civil wars, cruel tribal and sectarian warfare, ubiquitous political terrorism, and most everywhere, in the "developed" Western lands as well as the "developing" lands, a growing sense of insecurity—if this has been the real rather than the expected outcome, then it behooves us to ascertain the force that intervened to thwart Western expectations.

A good many of the blithe hopes for the world's future, pinned by Western public opinion upon the results of World War II and, notably, upon the founding of the United Nations, have been killed by the icy blasts of power politics. The hope that the process of decolonization could be sheltered from the global contest between the democratic West and the totalitarian East proved even more short-lived than that reposed in the United Nations as the guardian of world peace. Right from its start, the new order created by the dissolution of Western empire suffered the rending onslaught of extraneous forces, to wit, the intervention of communist power.

There are many approaches to an understanding of the Soviet Union's behavior at home and abroad. We can view the Soviet Union as a military power—as strong as the military power of the United States, or weaker, or even stronger than the sum total of the military forces arrayed against it. We can view the Soviet Union as the bearer of an ideological message, proclaiming the transformation of human society in accord with Marxist-Leninist doctrine. We can view the Soviet Union as a Great Power, heir to the pan-Slavist and imperialist aspirations of Czarist Russia. Each of these perceptions affords an insight into the conduct of the Soviet Union. Yet none suffices for an understanding of the Soviet Union's global strategy.

Ever since the first years of the communist dictatorship, Soviet Russia, while consolidating its rule over both its European possessions and the Asian conquests of the czars, has sought to rouse the non-Western peoples against the West and to exploit those conflicts between the West and the non-West that it has not managed to spark. If any Soviet foreign policy has been consistent, it has been the support of revolutionary movements throughout that part of the world which is now called the Third. What is remarkable about the Soviet Union's pursuit of this particular policy is that, in contrast with other policies, it has remained unaffected by the fluctuations of Soviet power and the twists and turns of Soviet policy toward individual Western nations. So constant and unremitting has been the Soviet drive against the West's residual holdings and influence in the non-Western world, as to warrant the conclusion that all other policies of the Soviet Union—military, political, ideological, and cultural—converge on this, the overriding purpose of the Soviet Union in world politics.

Lenin's dicta on imperialism have informed and still inform the Soviet view of international politics. They are now being amplified not only by the drumbeat of Soviet official declarations acclaiming any and all "wars of liberation," but also by the abundant flow of Soviet arms to the "freedom fighters." Thus, the bone-dry formulations of Leninist doctrine have come to life, invigorated by the resources of a world power. As Britain's Foreign Secretary David Owen has put it: "The basic premise from which we must start is that the Soviet Union is a world power with national interests and ambitions to match which inevitably will bring it into competition, and sometimes confrontation, with the West. To this we must add that communist ideology invests the national rivalry between East and West with a dynamic of increasing struggle."

In history, there is no precedent for a world power renouncing voluntarily its "interests and ambitions." Certainly, no world power on the rise, professing an ideology of increasing "struggle," has ever yielded to any restraints other than those imposed by the opposition of a force greater than its own. Of all the world powers, past and present, the Soviet Union is the least likely to be an exception to this rule.

Both doctrine and expediency determine the uses of Soviet power. Sixty-odd years of exposure to the theoretical pronouncements and the strategic praxis of successive Soviet leaders should have sufficed to familiarize the West with the Soviet philosophy of war and peace.

The Soviet Union has never intended and does not intend to fight an aggressive nuclear war. Indeed, it does not intend to fight any kind of war—as long as it can attain its end by the use of other means. For the Soviet leaders, steeped in von Clausewitz's thoughts on war, military power that cannot be put to political use has been, quite rightly, an abuse of power. In their scheme of things, the purpose of military power, as well as of any other kind of power, has been to support the strategy of protracted political-psychological conflict. This conflict strategy has always relied on the indirect approach, i.e. the gradual encirclement of the West by reducing its strongholds, strategic and economic, outside the territorial limits of the Western states. This strategy, now shielded by the Soviet Union's nuclear capabilities, employs a wide range of devices effective below the threshold of a fighting war between the Western powers and the Soviet Union itself. Among these devices the most effective have been the fomenting and feeding of proxy—"surrogate"—wars, such as the wars in Southeast Asia, West Africa, and the African Horn; the arming of select Arab and African states aligned against the West and its regional friends; and the employment of external proxies, such as the Cuban expeditionary force, in local proxy wars.

The continued communist struggle for the isolation of the Western "city" from the non-Western "countryside"—as Mao Tse-tung's metaphor has put it—is not incompatible with East-West détente. To the contrary, this struggle is the rationale for détente, for détente provides the optimal condition for waging it.

The economic and technological benefits to the Soviet Union of détente with the West have been considerable and would, by themselves, amply warrant Soviet détente policies—if the Soviet

Union were a status quo power as is the United States. The Soviet
Union's expansionist-ideological dynamism, noted by David Owen,
does not bespeak any attachment to the status quo. Rather, its
thrust has aimed at upsetting that stable equilibrium which the
West deems the ideal condition of international society. It is the
principal objective of the Soviet Union to reduce the world's areas
under the Western writ, to raise the non-Western peoples against
the West, and thus to deprive the West of the non-Western peoples'
material resources and goodwill. As long as the Soviet Union
persists in this quest, the world order will be as perilously unstable
as it has been during the lifetime of this generation. It is the
irreconcilable contradiction between the West's idea of a stable
world order and Soviet designs for upsetting it that threatens world
peace—and *not* the arms competition which is a mere consequence
thereof.

The idea of stability—or rather, gradual change within a stable
system—underlies the West's philosophy of détente with the Soviet
Union. The purpose of the détente, so Western statesmen have told
their peoples, has been to develop "webs of vested interests" that
will join the West and the Soviet Union ever more closely together
in common undertakings such as the quest for mutual security
through arms control and reduction, the fight against some of the
world's great ills, and mutually profitable trade. In this view,
increased commercial and personal intercourse will foster social
change and draw the Soviet Union closer to the West. Implicit in
the West's conception of détente has been the expectation—a
perfectly reasonable one in the light of *Western* experience—that
the Soviet Union will develop an urban society bent upon ease and
consumption, like the West's own; take its place, content with the
blessings of material abundance, among the status quo powers—
and, thus, grow more Western not only by acquiring the West's
material accessories but also by entering, slowly but surely, the
West's political and social way of life.

The history of Russia, czarist and communist, does little to
substantiate the West's assumptions about the mutability of Soviet
society, exposed to the benign emanations of détente. For one, the
Russian people, including some of their greatest writers, have
always regarded the West with indifference, if not with disdain and
distrust. It is highly probable that Soviet man aspires to a great

many things that men elsewhere think worth having. Yet, if there is any evidence showing his desire to be Western, that is, a citizen of an open society, then it is well hidden. The recent history of dissidence in Soviet Russia, far from revealing a change in traditional popular attitudes, shows that the demand of the Soviet masses for Western political-moral values is as feeble and, in any case, as inarticulate as it has ever been

Russia is heir to the same Judeo-Christian and Greco-Roman traditions that have shaped, to this day, the culture and beliefs of the Western peoples. Thus, both Soviet Russia and the Western democracies share some ingredients of their respective value systems. Yet in the Soviet Russian ethos something seems to be lacking that Western society deems essential to the elevation of the human condition: the freedom to exercise individual responsibilities and rights; the freedom to express, within the broadest limits of public toleration, whatever views that come to mind; the freedom to travel; the freedom to work at a job freely chosen—or not to work at all. Most of us will agree that, in practice, these freedoms are not unalloyed. But throughout the West—and this might be the fundamental difference between Western and Soviet man—these freedoms are clearly identified as the lodestars of political progress. For Western man, the right to these freedoms is self-evident. For Soviet man, it is not. Therefore, it is not surprising that he lacks empathy for Western democracy. It is even less surprising that his rulers have not enlightened him about the real nature of democracy, rather than its real and alleged warts. Quite to the contrary, they have employed every instrument of their formidable apparatus for thought control to distort and blacken the image of Western democracy, in general, and that of American democracy, in particular. This is why the dialogue between the Western and the Soviet peoples cannot rise above an almost inaudible whisper.

The essential features of the Soviet regime—a rule imposed from above; an omnipotent bureaucracy; tight censorship; monolithic control of public opinion, education, and cultural life; the state's stony indifference to human rights; and the Russian peoples' unprotesting acceptance of all these things—are kin to czarist autocracy and all the despotisms known to history. Soviet man, far from demurring, takes pride in what Soviet absolutism has wrought, notably the might of the Red Army, which not even the boldest dissidents have cared to deride. In sum, Soviet Russian popular sentiment reinforces the anti-Western thrust of Leninist dogma.

Even if it were not for the doctrinal ambiguities of "peaceful coexistence" familiar to every Komsomol and Red Army private, the Soviet people could not help perceive an East-West détente in a context quite different from that of the Western peoples. For them, as for the West, détente signifies security against total war. Unlike the Western peoples, the Soviet masses ascribe this condition to the weakening of the West, brought about by the internal decay—the "contradictions"—of "capitalism," i.e. Western society. This weakening, so they are being told by the myriad voices of public indoctrination, is, though historically foreordained, now hastened by the pressure of superior communist power. In brief, Soviet domestic propaganda hails détente as another battle won on the long road to communist victory: the Western "capitalists"—now chastened, though as malevolent as ever—have no choice other than to settle for "peaceful coexistence." Now it only remains, as Lenin has put it, "to push what is falling." This push can now be applied, with renewed force and without incurring unacceptable political-military risks, to the soft underbelly of the West, i.e. the regions overseas on which the Western countries depend as markets for their produce and sources of supplies, notably oil and minerals.

It would be a grievous misunderstanding of the Soviet global strategy to view its probes and incursions in the Third World as ends in themselves. The Soviet Union, endowed more richly with natural resources than any other country in the world and possessed of a great colonial empire extending from Central Asia to the Pacific Ocean, does not intend to incorporate—nineteenth-century colonial style—the rimlands of Asia and the African continent. Its abiding goal remains what it has always been: to crush "capitalism," "capitalism" being synonymous with the West. What, so far, has stood between Soviet strategy and its goal has been the Western Alliance and its organized defense, to wit, the North Atlantic Treaty Organization.

For a long time, Soviet strategy, checked by NATO along the perimeter from the North Cape to Erzerum, has probed the West's vulnerable flanks, left uncovered by the treaty guarantees of NATO. Of late, these probes have reached more deeply into this gray area of Western defense, sometimes with devastating effect upon the prosperity and tranquility of the allied Western lands and their friends overseas.

These inroads and their political-economic consequences have inflicted heavy damage upon the West as a whole; but they have not affected all Western nations in the same way and to the same degree. Thus far, the West seems unaware of its community in fate and, in any event, has not yet developed that collective sense of urgency that would seem appropriate to the magnitude of its collective predicament. In fact, the West's global retreat, far from persuading the Western peoples to close ranks, has tended to drive them apart. Not all of them perceive the implications of that retreat quite the same way: some feel themselves more immune against its deleterious consequences than do others—and some are inclined to ignore them altogether. Consequently, the erosion of the West's global position threatens to erode the bulwark of Western solidarity, namely, the North Atlantic Alliance.

For more than a century, industrial Europe, poorly endowed with domestic natural resources per capita of its dense population, has depended critically on free access to raw materials produced abroad and, hence, upon trade. Far more than the United States, Europe depends on foreign commerce. Europe's prosperity derives from processing commodities imported from abroad and balancing its international accounts by the export of processed goods. A break in this cycle imperils European prosperity.

For Europe, the progressive enfeeblement of its historical trading position intimates fatality. So far, this fearsome contingency has been masked by Europe's accumulated reserves, "the fat of centuries"; by the technical skills of the great international financial institutions, backed by the immense wealth of the United States; and, all throughout the West, by that sense of fatalistic indifference that, so we are told, living by the side of a volcano induces in the local population.

The worldwide economic recession, triggered by the steep and sudden increase in the price of oil, revealed Europe's prosperity as resting upon foundations more brittle than the extrapolation from twenty years' uninterrupted growth had made them to appear. Rising unemployment and the public's diminished confidence in the stability of national economic systems that, only a generation ago, had risen from the wreckage of World War II and the shambles of inflation, set off political tremors that have shaken all European governments. During the last few years, all European governments have been weak, kept in office by miniscule parliamentary majorities or the grudging abstention of the opposition. It stands to the credit of European democracy that the political balance has nowhere tipped too far to one side or the other and that extremist factions have not succeeded in thwarting representative government.

The United States, too, has suffered the debilitating effects of the world economic crisis. The United States, too, depends on the supply from abroad of essential raw materials. Yet, in the United States, the domestic market accounts for more than nine-tenths of the nation's business, and large domestic resources of strategic raw materials are still available for exploitation. Conceivably, the United States can live, albeit austerely, at home. Western Europe cannot. Even the presence of oil and natural gas in the North Sea, helpful as it has been in buffering the economies of the United Kingdom, Norway, and the Netherlands against the shocks of the energy crisis, cannot free all of Western Europe of its crucial needs for imports of raw materials. Indeed, the good fortune of the oil-rich European states has not relieved the anxieties of those European countries that do not share in it.

If Europe's anxieties were centered only on the state of her economy, a general upturn of the world economy might well still them: in the past, has not such a cyclic event always cleared the economic sky and heralded another era of confidence and hope? This might well happen—if Western Europe's economic worries were not compounded by gnawing doubts about those arrangements that, for almost thirty years, have secured Europe against communist aggression. Public confidence in the military security of Europe has fostered public confidence in Europe's economic future. The remarkable progress Europe has made in so short a time toward economic prosperity and integration would have been impossible without the security guarantees of the North Atlantic Alliance. The centerpiece of these security guarantees has been American commitment to the defense of Europe.

It has shocked most Americans that not all of Europe is as firm in its faith in the worth and permanence of the American pledge to Europe as they themselves have been in redeeming it. Yet this discrepancy in perceptions has always been inherent in the fact that the respective geographies of America and Europe differ fundamentally. Obvious as this fact might be to the Americans, it does not cause them any deep anxieties. It is not only equally obvious to the Europeans, but it is also the root cause of their anxieties about the American-European connection.

The United States is beyond the reach of Soviet power, strategically and ideologically; Western Europe is not. As long as the standoff between the two nuclear strategic forces obtains, the United States is secure against a Soviet military attack; Western Europe is not. The United States, as long as it does not suffer an internal social-economic crisis of as yet unimaginable severity, is proof against political subversion; Western Europe, despite, or because of its fabulous economic recovery sparked by American investment, is not.

The defense of Continental Western Europe, as well as the United Kingdom and the Mediterranean allied states, rests upon the validity of a strategic doctrine, namely that of Flexible Response. The central idea underlying this doctrine is to deny the Soviet Union the advantages of superior numbers in manpower and material and of geographical proximity by (1) the deployment of conventional forces sufficient to bar an attack by the Warsaw Pact's conventional forces that could speedily overrun a large part of Europe allied with the United States and hold it hostage against Alliance retaliation; and (2) the availability of sufficient tactical nuclear forces to deter the Soviets from the use of *their* tactical nuclear forces and, if deterrence fails, right the balance upset by the superiority of the conventional forces of the Warsaw Pact. The centerpiece of this Western strategy is the presence in Europe of substantial American conventional forces, backed by American tactical nuclear weapons, and, in the last resort, the U.S. nuclear umbrella over Europe, expected to deter the Soviet Union from the use of its strategic weaponry and to confront it with the terrible uncertainties of nuclear escalation.

This is not all there is to Flexible Response. Here, a rough outline must suffice, though some military experts might well cavil at the above summation of an immensely complex strategic scenario, evolved during the last twenty-five years from the workings of the best strategic minds. There is much to be said for the strategy of Flexible Response, especially its psychological premises, and, be-

Robert Strausz-Hupé

cause of the many political and economic restraints upon Allied governments, very little against it. But one thing cannot be said for it, namely, that it guarantees the United States' European allies that same degree of invulnerability which geography and strategic missilry bestow upon America itself.

It is this issue—the disjunction of Western security—that impinges on virtually all the other major issues on the agenda of American-European relationships—be it the trade in nuclear technology and arms; the "special relationship" of France to NATO; Allied consultations on SALT; MBFR; and, above all, the search for a common perception of, and position on, Soviet policy toward the West.

It stands to reason that, if the strategy of Flexible Response could be shown to be ineffective in the "hour of truth" or based upon a misreading of the Soviet Union's true and altogether peaceful intention, then its heavy costs to the European allies, hard pressed by domestic economic needs and claims, would represent a gigantic waste of scarce resources. This is exactly what the Soviet Union has been telling the Europeans. Since the United States is the acknowledged leader of the Western Alliance and has inspired, if not authored, the doctrine of Flexible Response, the brunt of the Soviet message falls upon the United States: it is the United States that holds Europe in thrall, compels its European allies to divert their resources to costly armaments rather than domestic improvement and international economic competition, and perpetuates its protectorate of Europe under the pretense of defending it against a threat that does not exist.

The Soviet Union has been highly successful in spreading this message to every corner of Europe. Indeed, in this endeavor, the Soviet Union can count on a receptive hearing quite independent of the political affiliation of the hearers, and on a publicly licensed system of communication in Europe, organized, at least at its inception, for no other purpose than the transmission of messages from the Kremlin.

Whatever might be the divergencies between the "nonruling" Communist parties of Europe and the ruling ones, the issue of European security is not among them: all agree upon the proximate dissolution of the Western Alliance and, hence, upon the removal of the American security guarantee from Europe. In brief, they all agree to labor for the expulsion of American influence from Europe—and to make that part of the Continent now covered by the American-European alliance as "Euro" as the rest of it.

As can be seen, the West's global retreat has been paced by the aggravation of strategic and economic issues that threaten to set the Western allies against one another and to break up the Alliance. We need not embrace the Spenglerian theory of Western gloom-and-doom to view the West's future with apprehension. Manifestly, the West has been drifting from its historic moorings. Can this drift be halted? Can the West restore its global position?

The answer to these questions is, of course, affirmative—provided the right answers will be given to the following questions: Do strategic arrangements that, so far, have safeguarded the Allies against aggression from the East now suffice to protect its extended flanks and global lifelines? Has the time not come to reexamine the strategic premises of Allied defense, dating back to the Age of Linear Containment? Does not the change of the strategic environment—a change placing the West increasingly at risk not only militarily but also politically and economically—point the Western Alliance toward novel institutional forms, more cohesive and authoritative than those devised twenty-eight years ago? Does not the North Atlantic Alliance need to achieve that closer political union that corresponds to the already existing community of strategic, economic, and cultural interests—and to the West's community in mounting danger?

In the last resort, the answers to these questions can be given only by the American people, for each calls for initiatives that only the leader of the Western Alliance can launch. The Western Alliance cannot be expected to stand more resolute than its strongest member. Perhaps, in no time in the history of Western democracy has the task of leadership been more exacting than it is now: coolly to steer the ship of state between the extremes of apathy and panic. Only the steadiness of the American judgment and purpose can sustain the will of the Western peoples to face common dangers and to do great things together.

Is the United States strong enough to right the balance of world power? Will the American people resolve to bear the costs and the risks that, in these times of mounting dangers, the leadership of the West entails?

Is it true that we lack the resources—manpower and tools—

needed for keeping the place in the world which we so incontestably occupied from the 1940s to the 1960s? Statistically, this is not true.

Present U.S. productive capacity is a multiple of that of World War II and of that of every other single nation, including the Soviet Union and Japan. As a matter of fact, it is one of the principal arguments of the advocates of full employment policies that part of our productive capacity is not used. Notwithstanding the hundreds of billions which, since 1941, the United States spent on defense and foreign assistance, the standard of living of the average American has been rising and, despite inflation, is rising still. The real wages of the American worker, too, have been increasing, and so has individual productivity. The immense increase in the mass production of goods that bring comfort and joy to the average American bent on leisure and play bespeaks the plenitude of a hedonistic society without precedent in history and parallel in the present.

In the Soviet Union, about one-seventh of the gross national product, which is only one-half the size of ours, goes into the making of the tools of state power, mostly weapons. It has been argued that the Soviet people are unhappy about the war tax levied upon them without consultation, and that the Soviet civilian economy, starved of investment, will, sooner or later, cut in on the military budget, lest it become even less competitive in world markets than it already is. This may well happen in that future which is now so dimly perceived. For the time being, the Soviet economy seems to be holding its course, and that course seems to lead to global military, hence, political supremacy.

Here, we come to the heart of the matter—to the answer to *why* America, despite its fabulous riches, chafes and stumbles under its global commitments? The American giant is stumbling because he is hobbled. He is hobbled because he has hobbled himself.

The opinion is widely held, especially in the Western democracies, that autocratic governments can conduct foreign policy more effectively and make war more ruthlessly than democracies can. This view is not borne out by history, notably the prehistory and history of the last two world wars. It is necessary here to point out its fallacy, for it compounds the confusion about the causes that underlie the decline of the United States as a world power. These causes must be sought in our attitude to the society in which we live, and hence, in our individual life-style. Throughout history, the life-style of the great mass of men and women has oscillated between the two extremes of asceticism and hedonism. It is the predominance of one or the other of these metaphysical conceptions of our purpose upon this earth which determines the conduct of a people at home and abroad. No social structure is a seamless whole, and only a very few men and women have ever attained the absolute. The absolute ascetic is a saint; the absolute hedonist is a monster. In any real society, not all people hold to the dominant norm. No doubt, in Sparta, the Roman republic, and Frederickian Prussia some preferred the soft life to the wholesomeness of austerity and the sweetness of death for one's country. No doubt, in the third century after Christ, a few Romans still clung to the stern values of their ancestors; but most Romans looked to the state to sustain them in their pleasurable indolence and preferred to expose their bodies to the gentle ministrations of bath attendants rather than the rigors of Parthian wars.

No civilization has fostered hedonism as sedulously as has that of contemporary America. Its symbolic figure is the consumer, enlivened by unlimited appetites and passionately determined to prolong life. American sales promotion is but an endless litany on how good life upon this earth can be—as long as it is lived pleasurably and free of any restrictions except those placed upon it by the limits of one's pocketbook. Paradoxically, our society, which prides itself so much on planning grandly for the future—the exploration of the universe and the building of cities without smog and ghettos—is doing its utmost to center our minds on the here and now—*and upon ourselves.*

Thus, the question arises as to whether a hedonistic society can endow its government with the means, material and moral, needed for the making of foreign policy and, thus, for assuring its own survival. A philosophy of individual survival is the philosophy least apt to ensure collective survival. Yet survival ethics has been leaching out those traditional ethical systems which, only a generation ago, governed civic behavior, honored as their rules may have been by frequent and shocking breach.

In order to ensure the defense of any society, there must be enough individuals willing to do and die for it, and the society as a whole must honor their purpose. If there are not enough of these individuals, and if the society as a whole does not share or even mocks their patriotic purpose, then even those who still aspire to the conduct of rational policies—rational because they embrace the interests of the collectivity, rather than of any of its parts—must ultimately yield to frustration and, at best, settle for a compromise between the calculus of international risk and the calculus of electoral probability.

The ability to solve foreign problems and the ability to solve domestic problems are the two sides of the same coin. A nation sure of itself and moving confidently forward derives strength for doing the one from doing the other. A people that seeks to cut its effort abroad in order to save enough for efforts at home will be meagerly rewarded at home and exposed to mounting risk abroad as well as division at home. Power needs to be evenly deployed across the whole spectrum of a Great Power's concern. The one sin that history will not forgive the possessor of great power is not to use it while he has it.

It seems that the United States has entered a valley of dismal shadows similar to that traversed by Britain at the time of the Boer War—a war which, militarily and politically, very closely resembles the Vietnam War. English society, its traditional devotions not quite eroded, managed to overcome the deep malaise into which this ill-prepared, costly, and increasingly unpopular venture had plunged it, and, later, to fight victoriously two wars for national survival. But British power is now a mere shadow of its former self, Victorian and Edwardian. Fortunately for Britain, there has been the "special relationship" with the United States, and now there is the promising gleam of a place in a united Europe. But where is there for the United States a "special relationship" and a new association which could give it shelter against the ambitions of rising powers? If there is now any nation in this world which cannot entrust its security to others and must rely upon its own strength to secure its possessions and to put muscle into what is left of that lawful international order which it led in creating, it is the United States.

To be sure, despite much fumbling, the United States still has friends throughout the globe. But their strength cannot make up for the strength it loses. They will be the stronger, the stronger the United States makes itself. This is the first condition of a wider union in which the members equitably share the burden of common defense in war and economic-social progress in peaceful international competition. The United States can travel this road if it wishes. But it must wish it with its whole heart.

The burden of the above discussion is this: the United States has the means to blunt the strategies of its adversaries and thus to halt the erosion of the West's global position. The "decline of the West" is anything but inevitable—as long as the United States does not abdicate its role as the West's leading power. Since America possesses the means to outbid any and all of its adversaries in the competition for who will shape the future world order, the one—perhaps, the one and only—issue of world politics is this: will the American people marshal their resources in the defense of the West? The American people, once they agree on the Western priority, will bear the costs and risks of Western leadership. Indeed, the logic of the international situation leaves them no other choice: the United States must stand by the Western community, lest it fall with it.

Americans are a practical people—and proud of it. Adapting themselves to the profound changes in the international environment, discussed in this essay, will mightily tax their practicality. By their past performance under stress, they can be expected to heed the sturdy pragmatism of their own tradition. The very challenge of the tasks ahead, all of them feasible though difficult, will stir the innate optimism and zest of the American people, brushing away the philosophical cobwebs of "decline" and "fall." Absence of any choice but one does clear the mind wonderfully.

In sum, if the American people are to brace themselves for the unavoidable tests to come, their leaders need to disclose with candor their understanding of the Western priority so that average men and women, too, can understand its import and the burdens it places upon them. America's leaders need to do so in order to be understood by the West at large *and* by its enemies. It would be the bitterest irony of history if the world let itself be pushed over the brink because of a misunderstanding.

The United States is Western democracy's link between the precarious present and a more stable future. If this link holds, Western democracy has a fair chance to outlast the misbegotten offsprings of totalitarianism, for the false promises of the latter cannot fool all the people all the time. Some non-Western people might cavil at the priority assigned here to the preservation of the

West. But what hope is there for all of humankind, if Western civilization were to perish under the onslaught of totalitarian power? Another dark age would be global, and it might last forever.

Transitoriness is the one assured condition of all things wrought by man. In history, no state, no people has remained on top of the heap forever. But some peoples have left behind traditions and insights that have lived on in the memory of mankind, enriching succeeding civilizations. Incontrovertible as is the axiom of the rise and, then, the decline of all states it tells us nothing about the relative vitality and longevity of individual states. Some states have been pathetically short-lived; others have managed against all odds to stretch out their "decadence" over several centuries—as did the Byzantine empire; and some succeeded in rising from the depth of despondence and starting a new life, more vigorous than ever before.

Toward the close of the eighteenth century, some of England's wisest statesmen and thinkers had convinced themselves that the loss of the American Colonies and the collapse of the European order under the blows of revolutionary France spelled the end of Britain as a Great Power. Upon the defeat, a few years later, of the would-be world conqueror Napoleon, Britain stood as Europe's leading Great Power, unchallenged ruler of the Ocean Seas, Europe's industrial powerhouse and banker of the world. True, within another hundred years, the descent of Britain's power had begun—irreversibly, so it now seems. But during these hundred years, the sagacity of British statesmanship, assisted by British naval superiority, had given mankind a longer stretch of stability, local wars notwithstanding, than it had ever known. Without it, a lot of beneficial things could not have happened, notably, the flowering of Western democracy and its implantation in some non-Western lands.

Perhaps, within another hundred years, history will judge America by how much better or how much worse it has done the work of keeping would-be world conquerors at bay and democracy thriving than, in its day, Britain managed to do. Conceivably, no matter how well the United States will have accomplished this task, the power of America, as a sovereign state, might, by then, have "declined" relative to that of other sovereign states. This will matter little if, as the result of America's labors, the Western community will have found strength in unity. The West as a whole will be greater than the sum of its parts. In such a wider and stronger union, the traditions and insights of America will live on in the memory of the Western peoples. Power has never been a rewarding end in itself. If America will have used its power to transform today's archaic system of sovereign states into a Western federation and, thus, secure the home base of human freedom, it will have played the role allotted to it by history as it will be written by free men.

—ROBERT STRAUSZ-HUPÉ

Index